DEBUSSY: HIS

VOLUME

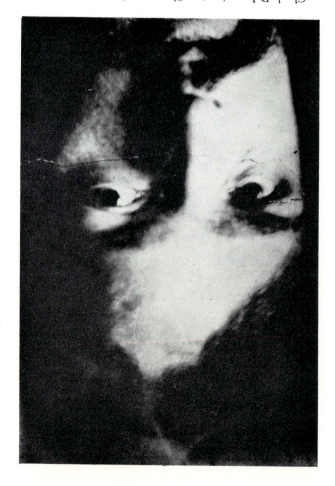

Claude Debussy in 1894. Photo, mutilated by Debussy, taken by Pierre Louÿs

DEBUSSY: HIS LIFE AND MIND

VOLUME I
1862–1902

EDWARD LOCKSPEISER

CAMBRIDGE UNIVERSITY PRESS

CAMBRIDGE
LONDON · NEW YORK · MELBOURNE

Published by the Syndics of the Cambridge University Press
The Pitt Building, Trumpington Street, Cambridge CB2 IRP
Bentley House, 200 Euston Road, London NW1 2DB
32 East 57th Street, New York, NY 10022, USA
296 Beaconsfield Parade, Middle Park, Melbourne 3206, Australia

First published 1962 by Cassell and Co. Ltd, London
Second edition 1966
Reprinted with corrections 1978 by the Cambridge University Press

First printed in Great Britain
by Jarrold and Sons Ltd, Norwich
Reprinted in Great Britain
at the Alden Press, Oxford

Library of Congress Cataloguing in Publication Data:
Lockspeiser, Edward, 1905–1973.
Debussy, his life and mind.
Reprint of the ed. published by Cassell, London.
Bibliography: v. 1, p. ; v. 2, p.
Includes indexes.
1. Debussy, Claude, 1862–1918. 2. Composers – France – Biography.
[ML410. D28L85   1978]   780'. 92'4 [B]   78-6795

hard covers:
ISBN 0 521 22053 X volume I
ISBN 0 521 22054 8 volume II
paperback:
ISBN 0 521 29341 3 volume I
ISBN 0 521 29342 I volume II

Tel qu'en Lui-même enfin l'éternité le change,
Le Poëte suscite avec un glaive nu
Son siècle épouvanté de n'avoir pas connu
Que la Mort triomphait dans cette voix étrange!

Mallarmé

Contents

Illustrations

[ix]

It has not proved possible to trace the sources of all illustrations. If there are any still in copyright the necessary acknowledgement will be included in all future editions.

Acknowledgements

Methods of research in a work of this kind, the signposts along the way, and even the distant goal can only be discovered as one plods forward, but it is certain that without help from many generous people I should hardly have been able to embark on this venture. Something more than acknowledgements is therefore due. At least I hope that the friends I have made will think that the advice and guidance they have given has been heeded. Not only guidance has been generously offered, but documents of many kinds, manuscripts, obscure publications, letters, photographs, and family records. These have been the bricks and mortar of my work.

Unknown manuscripts of Debussy's works have kindly been made available to me by Monsieur Alfred Cortot, Monsieur André Meyer, Monsieur Marc Pincherle, Professor Vallery-Radot, Monsieur G. van Parys, and Dr. Martin Bodmer. In Paris the Bibliothèque Nationale and the Bibliothèque du Conservatoire have provided me with photostats of their rich collections and, among the American libraries, I am also grateful for the use of manuscripts from the Library of Congress, Yale University Library, Stanford Memorial Library, the Eastman School of Music at Rochester, and the New England Conservatory of Music at Boston.

I have been able to consult many unpublished letters both from Debussy and from his correspondents. I offer my thanks to Madame Fauré-Frémiet (for Debussy's letters to Gabriel Fauré); to Miss Winifred Myers (letters of Pierre Louÿs); Mr. Michael Mann (letters to Pierre Louÿs, Gustave Charpentier, and Walter Rummel); Mr. Lucien Goldschmidt and Monsieur G. Morssen (letters to Arthur Hartmann); Madame Varèse (letters to Edgard Varèse); the Library of Congress (correspondence with Jean Marnold, Jenö Hubay, René Peter, and Serge Koussevitzky); Mr. Merle Armitage (letter to Manuel de Falla); and Mr. John Lade (letter to M. D. Calvocoressi).

Debussy's letters frequently appear in sales catalogues and friends associated with sales in many countries have kindly advised me of the appearance of letters which I have often been able to consult. I am grateful for information given to me over several years to Dr. and Mrs. Hellmut Feisenberger of Sotheby's; to Mr. J. Pashby of Sotheby's; Monsieur François Lesure of the Bibliothèque Nationale; Monsieur Marc Loliée; Miss Emily Anderson; and Monsieur A. Rosenthal. Mr. Heinrich Eisemann has gone to endless trouble on my behalf, seeking out references to Debussy's autographs throughout Europe and the United States and enabling me to consult, among others, the important series of letters to Gabriel Mourey and René Peter. I do not claim, of course, to have consulted all Debussy's unpublished letters in private collections. But I think I can claim that there emerges from this new material a view of Debussy's life and work that further correspondence can only endorse.

Other documents have kindly been supplied to me from the diaries of Richard Strauss by Dr. Willi Schuh; on Erik Satie by Monsieur V. Fédorov; on Debussy's relationship with Robert Godet, by Monsieur Aloys Mooser; on the French connexions of Mahler by Dr. Hans Redlich; and on personal recollections of Debussy by Monsieur Ernest Ansermet. I had earlier had the opportunity of consulting, during their lifetime, several friends of Debussy, among them Robert Godet, Louis Laloy, Gabriel Pierné, and Paul Dukas, and also his sister Adèle Debussy and his stepson Raoul Bardac. Information they gave me has often been corroborated by new evidence.

I have been fortunate in being able to expand on my earlier studies on Debussy in Russia. Here I have been greatly helped by the grandchildren of Debussy's patroness, Nadezhda von Meck, Count George Bennigsen, Madame Galina von Meck, and Mr. Georgy Korsakov. Their painstaking investigation of family records, the letters of relatives they kindly placed at my disposal, and the rich collection of photographs they were able to procure have clarified many obscure points. With Monsieur Pierre Souvtchinsky and Monsieur Vladimir Jankélévitch, authorities on Russian music, I have had many valuable conversations. Mrs. April Fitzlyon has kindly translated Sonia von Meck's memoirs and other Russian sources.

Debussy belongs to the history of the ideas of his time as well as to the history of music specifically, and no study can ignore contemporary developments in literature and painting. On the connexions with Oscar Wilde I have been supplied with indispensable material by Monsier Guillot de Saix, Dr. J. Montgomery Hyde, and Mr. Rupert Hart-Davis. Dr. Ada Polak has given me the benefit of her special knowledge of the Art Nouveau, and Professor Meyer Schapiro has greatly stimulated me by his penetrating analyses of Impressionist painting. Mrs. B. Lasenby has given me much help on art publications. Mr. John Royde-Smith and Professor Cecil Y. Lang have enlightened me on the French connexions of Swinburne, and Dr. Eileen Souffrin-Le Breton has provided me with valuable sources from her own and other studies on Swinburne, Banville, Verlaine, and Mallarmé. Mr. W. D. Halls has presented me with material relating to Maeterlinck, and Professor John Cocking has piloted me through the more obscure lanes and by-paths of the Symbolist world. With Mr. George Painter I have had revealing discussions on André Gide and Marcel Proust.

Unpublished photographs of Debussy, members of his family, his daughter, and his friends have been kindly supplied to me by Madame D. G. de Tinan, Mr. Alex de Bussy, Monsieur André Meyer, Monsieur Aloys Mooser, Madame Jane Bathori, Madame Jean Lerolle, Madame Henri Morin, the Baroness Cerise, Mr. Georgy Korsakov, Monsieur Georges de Meck, and the Tchaikovsky Museum at Klin.

Monsieur Oswald d'Estrade Guerra kindly helped me to procure the photographs of Debussy's family and of Gabrielle Dupont, and has also supplied me with obscure publications. Information from Madame Yvonne Tiénot allowed me to trace Debussy's English relatives. Monsieur Henri Borgeaud has allowed me to consult his private collection and has helped me to interpret doubtful references. Madame Roosevelt-Arosa has informed me of the connexions between the Debussy family and Monsieur Achille Arosa, and I have had many profitable discussions with Monsieur François Lesure of the Bibliothèque Nationale and, on psychological aspects of Debussy's character, with Dr. Max Goldblatt.

Grateful acknowledgements are made to Dodd, Mead & Co., New York, for permission to publish Oscar Thompson's translations of two letters to Henri Lerolle; to Maurice Goudeket for the description of Debussy by Colette in *Les Oeuvres Complètes de Colette*, subsequently published in *En Pays connu*; to W. H. Allen & Co. for an extract from *Paris-Album 1900–1914* by Jean Cocteau, translated by Margaret Crossland; to the Editions Gallimard for the letter of Paul Valéry in his *Lettres à quelques-uns* (© Editions Gallimard, 1952); and to Madame A. M. Emmanuel for the conversations between Debussy and Ernest Guiraud.

Two scholars who have been working in the same field have generously offered their co-operation over several years. Monsieur Marcel Dietschy's documentation, which he placed at my disposal, has been of the greatest value in establishing for the first time the facts and circumstances of Debussy's early life. I had the honour of translating a part of Monsieur Dietschy's work in 1960, and his entire work is now due to appear. From Monsieur André Schaeffner, president of the Société Française de Musicologie and the foremost French authority on Debussy, I have received constant advice and support, often on matters that were enigmatic or disheartening. If I have been able to illuminate at any rate part of Debussy's character it has been largely due to his steadfast encouragement.

London, 1962   E. L.

Introduction

Nearly all the literature on Debussy has so far been based on Léon Vallas's *Claude Debussy et son temps* which first appeared in 1932. This was a biographical and aesthetic study, revised in 1958, which had several admirable qualities in its day and still has. Vallas was alone in having established a vast documentation relating to the dates and origins of Debussy's known works, contemporary criticisms, and the main landmarks in his career. With this knowledge he set Debussy's achievements against the French musical scene as he saw it at that time. Vallas seldom looked beyond the surface, however, and he was concerned primarily to establish Debussy as a national composer, the saviour from foreign and particularly German domination. We can no longer accept this view. The national attributes of Debussy's work, which are plain enough, were over-emphasized by an earlier generation partly from a desire to revolt against the unalterable fact of a German musical hegemony, but also because a closer study of Debussy's mind would have demanded the investigation of certain aesthetic and moral problems which had not hitherto come into the province of writers on music and which have even embarrassed literary critics. Though he was a devoted scholar there were many aspects of Debussy's life and work by which Vallas was shocked. Accordingly, he prudishly closed his readers' eyes to what he judged were the less acceptable features of his personality. It was perhaps only natural that this poker-faced attitude should have aroused curiosity, and it must be said that although Vallas's reserve was well intentioned, his refusal to come to terms with any of the inner motives in Debussy's character has done considerable harm. Certain later studies have as a result been appallingly tasteless, an ironic fate to befall the work of a composer who reintroduced taste as an aesthetic value.

Vallas was also indifferent to contemporary movements in literature and painting. I do not believe that one can approach the art of Debussy as an isolated musical phenomenon. It belongs as much to the history of literature and the visual arts as, specifically, to the history of music, and it plays a part, too, in contemporary psychological thought. In my view it is the hinterland of Debussy's world that is most likely to illuminate his mind. As with other figures of this period, Verlaine, Gauguin, and Wilde, we cannot be concerned, in any view of their contribution, with moral judgements for the reason that these were artists who claimed moral values of their own. Inevitably, hostility was aroused by actions in the personal lives of such figures, providing a curious contrast to the esteem in which they were so widely held. It is admittedly difficult to establish the interpenetration of an artist's life and work, and there are many writers, particularly on music, who believe that it can serve no purpose. This is partly because the biographer of a musician must deal with a form of creation that is nebulous and unyielding by comparison with the revelatory prose or poetry at the core of biographies of literary figures. Yet I think the effort should be made. If the style is the man so is the achievement.

Research over many years has convinced me that the art of Debussy is not merely a reflection of one aspect or another of his period. It is the period. Music was at that time regarded as the quintessential, privileged art, and I see no other composer who so closely realized the musical ideals to which the writers and painters of his time openly aspired. I would concede that this was not only the strength of Debussy but his weakness. Inspiration drawn from so many sources can easily lead to disintegration. Whatever the reason, a disintegrating element did take root as a result of Debussy's explorations, and it is my belief that we can only come to terms with later developments in music to the extent that the moral and aesthetic crisis faced by Debussy is seen for what it was.

This first volume extends from Debussy's childhood and early formative years, revealing important facts not hitherto disclosed, to *Pelléas et Mélisande*, marking the triumph of opera as a form of poetry. Concepts of the dream preoccupied Debussy during this period, as they preoccupied Freud in his contemporary early works, and the roots may be seen here of a new sensibility that has persisted to our day. The subsequent volume, covering the period from *La Mer* to Debussy's death at the end of the first World War, will branch out to the world of Proust and the early works of Stravinsky in the hope of illuminating further problems which every musical person must have at heart.

E. L.

PART I

Youth
1862–1887

I

The Debussy Family

'En vérité, on n'y peut rien, on a l'âme que vous ont léguée
un tas de gens parfaitement inconnus. . . .'

Letter to André Caplet

Until recently we knew singularly little, beyond the names and
occupations contained in a few public records, of Debussy's ancestors; and we were even less well informed on the essential facts of
his early family life, his early education, and the general emotional
and artistic factors by which he was affected during the first ten
years of his life. The reason for this unfortunate state of our knowledge was curious. The available records had only been superficially
investigated by Debussy's first biographers, chief among them Léon
Vallas. But in regard to his immediate family it was maintained that
Debussy deliberately obscured or withheld during his lifetime the
vital biographical data we need for any kind of assessment of his
childhood years, and that more than this, there were certain secrets
of the Debussy family which he was anxious should never be disclosed. It turns out that this mystery was entirely the creation of the
composer's biographers, possibly motivated by a desire to idealize
their subject. In his correspondence Debussy frequently refers to his
family, his mother particularly, to whom he was greatly devoted,
also to his father and the younger of his two brothers, and there is
never a suggestion that he was anxious to conceal their activities,
still less that he was in any way ashamed of them. As for his remoter
ancestry, this, not surprisingly, was unknown to him, though he was
certainly moved from time to time by the mysteries of heredity.
'The soul we possess,' he comments in a letter to André Caplet of

1911, 'has been inherited from a vast number of completely unknown people and compels us to act in one way or another without,
as a rule, leaving us much choice.'

The genealogical facts of Debussy's family can be briefly stated.
Our authority here is Marcel Dietschy, whose painstaking researches
into public records have yielded the first reliable view of Debussy's
ancestors. On both sides of his family Debussy was of Burgundian
stock. Early paternal ancestors were Bridot de Bussy, a farm-
labourer, born *c.* 1615; Edme de Bussy, a vine-grower, born at
Benoisey, 1639; and later Valentin de Bussi, born 1682, registered
as a farm-labourer from Courcelles-sous-Brignon in the Côte d'Or,
and who married Marie Carré at Seigny in 1724. The name can
probably be traced to the neighbouring town of Bussy-le-Grand,
near Dijon, seat of the Counts de Bussy. One of these noblemen was
Bussy-Rabutin, or Roger de Rabutin, the cousin of Madame de
Sévigné, a libertine well known in French literature as the author of
the scandalous *Histoire Amoureuse des Gaules*. Though he lived at
Bussy-le-Grand during the second half of the seventeenth century
we have no evidence that an ancestor of Debussy was related to him.
Nor have we any knowledge of a possible connexion with one
N. de Bussy, the mid-sixteenth century composer of chansons
published by the famous Attaignant.

Valentin de Bussi's son, Pierre, was a farrier and his son, also
named Pierre, was originally a farmer. According to Monsieur
Dietschy this ancestor, Debussy's great-grandfather, was in Paris or
near by at the time of the Revolution. The first to leave the soil, he
became a locksmith at the end of the eighteenth century at the
revolutionary centre of Bellevue and later lived in Paris and
Montrouge. From then on we see the paternal line of small French
tradesmen with large families, bearing their full share of misfortune.
Pierre de Bussy had four children: Suzanne who married a carpenter;
Pierre-Louis who became a locksmith and who died mysteriously
during the Commune;[1] Achille-Claude, a locksmith too who died
at Montrouge at the age of twenty-five; and Claude-Alexandre de
Bussy, grandfather of the composer, born much later when his
father was forty-four. He was a carpenter who for a time was also

---

[1] Monsieur Dietschy quotes a graphic description of him in the census returns
(1823), *Archives de la Seine, Paris*, indicating a figure of striking facial characteristics:
'Black hair and eyebrows, grey eyes, low forehead, long nose, large mouth, protruding
chin, oval face, thick lips'.

a publican. He married an illiterate seamstress, Marie-Anne-Françoise Blondeau, by whom he had nine children of whom the two eldest were Clémentine, Debussy's godmother and benefactress, and Manuel-Achille, his father. The seven remaining children of Claude-Alexandre, Debussy's paternal aunts and uncles, were: Louise-Adèle, a milliner who apparently went into a decline; Rosalie who lived only eighteen months; Emile-Henri who became a coach-builder; the twins, Achille-Clément and Jules-Alexandre, the latter probably having died in infancy; a second Jules-Alexandre; and the youngest, Albert-Henri.

The surviving Jules-Alexandre (1848–1907) fought in the Franco-Prussian War and was a prisoner-of-war in Germany. On his release he emigrated to England on account, according to his grandson Mr. Alex de Bussy, of a conflict with the French military authorities. About 1872 he settled in Manchester, where he taught French at the Central High School, Whitworth Street, and gave private lessons in music, in all probability the piano. This paternal uncle of Debussy who spent the greater part of his life in England was thus the only member of the family who is known to have had a connexion with music. Married on 27 December 1877 at Chorlton, Manchester, to Mary Ann Saddington, aged eighteen, daughter of a butcher, he is described on his marriage certificate as an 'artist musician'. Of his three children born at Chorlton, Alexandre Frederick, Emile Alfred, and Lucy Madeline, Debussy's cousins, the second, Emile Alfred, was appointed organist in 1904 at Upper Brook Street Free Church in Manchester, and until his marriage in 1913 taught the piano and singing. According to Mr. Alex de Bussy, Debussy was never to meet any of his English cousins.

Manuel-Achille Debussy, the composer's father, was born at Montrouge (Seine) on 10 May 1836. At sixteen he had left his parents and was living in Paris alone, at 18 Boulevard Montmartre. Two years later he embarked on a military career, enlisting for seven years in the Second Regiment of the Marine Light Infantry, spending some time 'in a remote island'. The suggestion put forward by Monsieur Dietschy is that the island was Martinique or, more likely, Guadeloupe or New Caledonia, where he may have been at the end of 1856. On 11 July 1861 he was discharged and lived at Levallois, 15 rue des Frères Herbert, with Victorine-Joséphine-Sophie Manoury, his mistress, born in Paris on 28 October 1836, whom he had known when garrisoned in Paris and whom he married at Levallois on 30 November of the same year.

Victorine Manoury's mother, Debussy's maternal grandmother, was Eulalie-Sophie Delinotte, a cook from Tonnerre in Burgundy,[1] married to Louis-Amable Manoury, a wheelwright in the rue Saint-Lazare in Paris, who died on 28 May 1859, three years before Debussy's birth, of general paralysis at a home for the insane at Clermont-de-l'Oise. Not the slightest hint of this significant fact, ascertained by Monsieur Dietschy, had ever been disclosed.

In December 1861, immediately after their marriage, Manuel Debussy and his wife took over, at 38 rue au Pain, Saint-Germain-en-Laye, an old three-floor house with a modest china shop downstairs. There at 4.30 a.m. on 22 August 1862 the first of their five children was born. He was named Achille-Claude, in memory, according to Monsieur Dietschy's plausible theory, of his great-uncle, the locksmith who had died at Montrouge in the prime of life. Thus his name appears on his birth certificate. In his infancy, however, he was apparently called Claude. The census list (1864–5) for Saint-Germain-en-Laye reads, under 38 rue au Pain: 'Debussy (Manuel-Achille); son fils Claude'; and he is described as Claude-Achille Debussy on his baptismal certificate of 31 July 1864. During his adolescence and youth he was invariably known as Achille, reverting to Claude about 1892.

The child's appearance was remarkable for the bony protuberances on his forehead, referred to as *un double front*. These protuberances appear to have been a form of benign bone tumours known as 'ivory osteomata'. As described by Dr. C. E. Corrigan in *The Clinical Diagnosis of Swellings* (London, 1939), these hard bone tumours, shaped like a dropped mass of baker's dough, are

---

[1] The unusual name Delinotte has some prominence in the records of Tonnerre during the Revolution, and it is likely that a maternal ancestor of Debussy was involved at this time in illegal financial transactions. Writing of the period 1793–4, G. Moreau in *Tonnerre pendant la Révolution* (Paris, 1890) states: 'Mme More de Quingery, femme du Directeur de la Poste à Tonnerre, était en relation avec des émigrés. Elle se servait d'un nommé Edme Delinotte, soldat réfractaire, pour leur faire venir de l'argent, en particulier au chevalier de Chamberlain et à un officier des hussards de Lauzun, qui avait été en garnison à Tonnerre.' Delinotte was denounced by the vigilance committee of the Revolution in Tonnerre and interrogated by the police, the records of his activities forming the 'Affaire Edme Delinotte'. As a result of this enquiry Madame de Quingery was condemned to death, her sentence having been commuted only on account of pregnancy.

commonly found on the outer table of the vault of the skull, in Debussy's case on the forehead, and are normally liable to no complications. There can be no connexion between Debussy's abnormal bony protuberances and the fact that his maternal grandfather died of general paralysis at a home for the insane, clearly an indication of syphilis. Nor has the abnormal formation of Debussy's forehead any connexion with the fact that his youngest brother, Eugène-Octave, born in 1873, died in infancy, in 1877, of meningitis. There is a type of meningitis of syphilitic origin and it is possible that this was the disease of Eugène-Octave.

In adolescence and in later life Debussy became self-conscious of the protuberances on his forehead. At about the age of twenty, in order to conceal them, he trained his wavy hair down over his forehead in imitation of the fashion of a girlish fringe, set by his friend, the painter Georges Rochegrosse. Later these protuberances were only partly covered by his head-dress, and his appearance then created an altogether unusual impression. Fernand Gregh, in his memoirs, L'Age d'or (1947), states that at the Taverne Pousset, which Debussy frequented from about 1887 onwards, he was commonly known, on account of his 'enormous cranium', as 'Le Christ hydrocéphale'. He apparently gave the impression of a hydrocephalic, but of course hydrocephalus was not the cause of the shape of his forehead. A striking view of his forehead is provided in a close-up photograph taken of him by Pierre Louÿs in 1894 which appears as the frontispiece. Significantly, Debussy ruthlessly crumpled this photograph up, signs of its destruction being still evident in the form restored years later by his second wife, Madame Bardac-Debussy.

Our information regarding the activities of Debussy's parents during the years of his infancy presents a picture of extreme poverty and anxiety. By the end of 1864, only three years after they had taken over the china shop, they restored the property to its former owner, Mallet, and left Saint-Germain-en-Laye. No trace of their whereabouts or activities is found until the middle of 1867 when they were living at 11 rue de Vintimille in Paris. Manuel was at this time a travelling salesman in household goods while his wife was obliged to take in work as a seamstress. The following year the family were living at 68 rue Saint-Honoré, and Manuel had found employment in the lithographic printing works of Paul-François

Dupont. This post, too, was held only for a short time. The Franco-Prussian War broke out on 15 July 1870, and four months later Manuel was engaged in a clerical capacity at the Commissariat of the First Arrondissement in Paris. In 1870 he is recorded as having changed his address once again: he was then living with his father at 3 Impasse de l'Ecole. From all of which it is clear that the child Debussy's life at this time was extremely insecure. His parents were constantly changing their address, moving home no less than four times in five years.

Manuel was obviously an adventurous though an unstable character, short in stature (about 5 ft. 4 in. according to the military records), unambitious, but good-looking and attractive to women. As is often the case with weak-willed people—his records in the *Archives Nationales* state unequivocally that he is 'of weak character' —he was impulsive. Intellectually of a primitive, uncultivated standing, he had no profession beyond that of soldiering, first in the Marines and later in the National Guard and in the revolutionary forces of the Commune. He was manifestly unable to provide for his growing family. He had, however, a definite view of the career of his eldest son. He was to be a sailor, following his own career in the Marines. The imagination of many writers has boggled at the idea of the sensitive, indeterminate figure of Debussy as a coarse, adventurous sailor. But the idea of this career was not lightly entertained. In 1889, asked in a questionnaire which life he would have chosen had he not been a musician, he stated unequivocally, 'A sailor'. The idea remained with him, and perhaps even haunted him. In 1903, when writing *La Mer*, he wrote to André Messager: 'You perhaps do not know that I was destined for the fine life of a sailor from which I was led away only by the hazards of life.' Much of the sailor's restlessness, rooted perhaps in the character of Manuel, was to drive him on, the restlessness of the traveller in life, and, as in the poem of Baudelaire, the traveller compelled to leave life:

> Mais les vrais voyageurs sont ceux-là seuls qui partent
> Pour partir; coeurs légers, semblables aux ballons,
> De leur fatalité jamais ils ne s'écartent,
> Et, sans savoir pourquoi, disent toujours: Allons!

Whatever he may have had of his son's adventurousness, Manuel was soon to be left far behind. We see him, after the first eight years of his married life, playing cards in cafés, giving himself airs as a connoisseur of plays, pushing a pen as a subordinate clerk in a job which he eventually secures but from which, after fourteen years' steady employment, he is abruptly dismissed. The post was that of assistant book-keeper at the metallurgical works of the Compagnie de Fives-Lille, rue Caumartin. Appointed in January 1873, he was dismissed in April 1887. We have no knowledge of his activities from this time on, until eight years later when, on 1 January 1895, he is reinstated in the same post. He appears to have had little sense of family responsibility, not only towards his children but towards his aged father, whose death at a home for old people at Issy he failed to notify to the civil authorities.

In conversation with me in Paris in 1934, Debussy's life-long friend, Robert Godet, stated that Debussy incriminatingly described his father as *le vieux galvaudeux*. Two allied meanings are associated with this expression: *un galvaudeux* is a loose-liver; *se galvauder* is to sully one's name in shady business or to go to the bad. According to a statement of Henry Prunières, received from a friend or associate of Debussy, Manuel played a sinister role in regard to the appropriation of money at the time of the attempted suicide of Debussy's wife in 1904. From all of which it is clear that Manuel was a paternal figure of some suspicion. Moved by his death in 1910, Debussy nevertheless felt bound to confess in a letter to André Caplet of that year that 'we hardly ever saw eye to eye'. Caplet had recently achieved great success with a performance of Debussy's early prize-winning cantata, *L'Enfant prodigue*, in Chicago. The artistic gulf between Manuel and his son may be judged by the fact that this conventional cantata seems to have been Manuel's favourite work. 'The Chicago success would certainly have delighted him beyond words,' he regretfully adds. 'It is a pity he was denied this simple pleasure.'

The figure of Debussy's mother is hazy. An amazing fact is that she brought up none of her five children. This may have been due to material reasons, but it also appears that she had little maternal instinct. In his biography published in 1930 and based on material supplied by Debussy's sister Adèle, Jean Lépine baldly states that 'Madame Debussy did not like children'. A letter to Monsieur Dietschy from Madame Sirret, an intimate friend of Adèle Debussy, supports this. 'Very independent, Madame Debussy found that children were a responsibility that interfered with her activities', this writer almost incredibly states, 'and she did her utmost to part with them.' Whatever lay behind all of this, it was Manuel's sister Clémentine de Bussy, later Madame Roustan, who became chiefly responsible for the upbringing and welfare of her sister-in-law's children. As a result the child Debussy had no regular education. Following exhaustive investigations it has been established that he went to no school. In one respect the composer whose development was to be affected almost as much by literature as by music never overcame his lack of schooling. His spelling remained faulty until the end of his life, particularly his compulsion to spell past participles as infinitives.

There is evidence that despite Victorine Debussy's apparent ruthlessness in these early years and her desire, like that of her husband, to egg her favourite son on to popular success, Debussy remained closely attached to her. His letter written to Edgard Varèse at the time of her death in 1915 in the first World War shows that signs of his grief could not be withheld even from the notepaper on which he was writing: 'The loss of my mother affects me more painfully than I can say for I know that at this time there are tears for everyone.' During his early student years, and even later, he remained a devoted son, anxious to offer his parents the small pleasures or comforts his unconventional career could produce. For the joy it would give his old parents, as he told Paul Valéry, he accepted the Légion d'Honneur, and in a period of relative material ease, when he was first associated with Madame Bardac, he made it one of his first duties to see that they were established in a reasonably comfortable home.

Manuel was a ne'er-do-well with no clearly defined profession, and so in the main were each of his younger children. The eldest of a family of five, Debussy happened to be a genius thrown up in this offspring with no suggestion of comparable qualities among his antecedents or relatives, unless we may discern a link between his civilized refinement and the features of disintegration or near-disintegration that marked the personalities of his brothers and sister. Very little has hitherto been brought to light concerning these younger members of his family, it having been assumed that in later life he maintained little contact with them. Even if this had been true we should be wrong not to take their personalities into account for whatever light they might throw on Debussy's hereditary features and the environment of his childhood years.

Adèle Debussy (1863–1952), the eldest of the four younger children, is said to have had a difficult nature. In her youth she was employed at millinery establishments in Stuttgart and Paris, and later at an outfitter's. Having suffered a disappointment in love at the age of twenty-nine, she remained a spinster. No mention of her occurs in Debussy's published correspondence, and indeed when I met her in 1934 at her modest apartment on the top floor of a building in the Avenue des Champs-Elysées, originally servants' quarters, she affirmed her distant relationship with her brother during his lifetime. Alfred Debussy (born 1870 at Cannes), brought up with Adèle by their aunt and godmother, Clémentine de Bussy, was the most successful of the younger children in later life, though he appears to have followed no single career. He apparently had some knowledge of English, having been apprenticed in an unknown capacity to an English lawyer in Paris. Later he spent some time at Cardiff as a buyer for a French railway company.[1] He was also employed by Dufayel, a French department store. He married first a dressmaker of unbalanced mind, by whom he had a daughter who died a spinster in 1949, and married again in 1931. He is mentioned once or twice in affectionate terms in Debussy's letters, notably in one to Roger-Ducasse who was asked to help find him some work. In 1910 Jean-Aubry invited him to a concert of his brother's works at Le Havre. Debussy commented: 'You must have upset him rather. He is a very pleasant fellow, but a frequenter of music halls for which I have no desire to blame him.' Another brother, Eugène-Octave, the youngest, was born in 1873 and died of meningitis at the age of four. There remains the curious figure of Emmanuel (1867–1937) who caused trouble from an early age. His mother, according to Emmanuel's surviving granddaughter Claudine Debussy, had frequently to fetch him from the police station. At school he was reported to be dull-witted and slow. At eighteen he joined the colonial troops and later this unmanageable brother of the composer of *Pelléas* wandered throughout France as a journeyman, even taking a job as a scavenger of cesspools, finding himself prosecuted and

---

[1] In *La Revue Indépendante*, November 1887, a translation of Rossetti's poem, *The Staff and Scrip* (*Le Bourdon et la Besace*) was published under the name Alfred Debussy. Though he was only seventeen at the time this may well have been Debussy's brother.

eventually ending up as a farmhand in the department of Gers. There, in 1894, he married, and had four children, the youngest of whom founded a family near Bordeaux. Emmanuel is the grandfather of the last male member of the Debussy family, who was born in 1934.

2
Childhood

RODERICK USHER: Connaissez-vous des êtres qui peuvent
se rappeler leur enfance sans terreur?
Debussy after E. A. Poe

Nearly all the writers on Debussy have hinted at some mystery
surrounding the part played in his childhood years by his aunt.

In 1932 Léon Vallas looked up Debussy's baptismal certificate at
Saint-Germain-en-Laye, and published his findings. A clue to this
supposed mystery was then suggested. It transpired from this certificate, dating from almost two years after his birth, that his god-
parents were his paternal aunt, Mademoiselle de Bussy, who had
assumed the pretentious name of Octavie de la Ferronière, reminiscent of La Belle Ferronière, the notorious mistress of François Ier,
and her lover, Achille Arosa, a wealthy financier and art-collector
known in the history of the period as the brother of Gustave Arosa,
the guardian of Gauguin. To Vallas is due the merit of having
uncovered the bare fact of a connexion between the Arosa and the
Debussy families, though apparently from a prudish desire not to
dwell on anything in the nature of a scandal he felt himself obliged
to withhold the nature of this connexion. Not unnaturally Vallas's
forbidding attitude towards a matter on which, more than anyone
at that time, he was entitled to comment, merely aroused curiosity,
and with it the wildest of speculations on the legitimacy of
Debussy's birth.

Apart from the fact that he drew conclusions which have since
been shown to be inaccurate, Vallas's role in this controversy was
unimpeachable. Reams of fanciful literature have since been written
on the subject of whether Debussy was the son of Manuel Debussy

or of Achille Arosa, and it is necessary to state emphatically that there is not the slightest reason for any kind of investigation on these lines. The question, raised by Henry Prunières in *La Revue Musicale* (May–September 1934) following the publication of Vallas's work, through what he later confessed to be a misunderstanding of Vallas's vague references to Achille Arosa, was immediately settled by an explicit statement from Vallas to the effect that no such idea was ever in his mind. 'The mountain has given birth to a mouse', Prunières declared with some embarrassment at having misconstrued his colleague. The idea was of course ludicrous, he admitted: 'Nous sommes en plein vaudeville.' And there one would have expected this insignificant matter, conclusively dealt with at that time, to have remained. If it is unearthed again now it is from the necessity of indicating this readily available source to writers who, right up to the present day, have preferred to pander to elements of sensationalism.

At this point it will be useful to produce the evidence of a letter, dated 7 June 1936, sent to me by the later Paul Arosa, son of Debussy's godfather, in reply to enquiries I had made regarding what then appeared to be the confused matter of the relationship between Debussy, his parents, his aunt, and Achille Arosa. In the light of our present knowledge it appears that Monsieur Arosa was himself influenced by current myths: he maintains that the child's name, Achille, derived from that of his godfather and that in later life Debussy was ashamed of his family and their activities. Nevertheless Monsieur Arosa's letter is a first-hand document establishing valuable facts. He writes:

> It is quite true that my father knew the Debussy family intimately and had the honour of holding Achille, for he had not then any other Christian name but that of his godfather, over the baptismal font. He owed this honour to the relationship he maintained with one who called herself Octavie de la Ferronière and who was the sister of Debussy's father. My father, then a bachelor and rather well-to-do, appeared to be the ideal godfather for this child who had come from an almost wretched family, and he undertook what was expected of him in good part, providing, over the years, for the musical education of a child whose gifts were brilliant. Fortunately, for Claude and for us, my father was not a philistine.

I know of nothing mysterious in this, and my father never said a word which might have cast an aspersion on the perfectly normal circumstances of his birth. If things had been otherwise you may be sure he would have known for the aunt, who was the benefactress of the family, knew everything.

This idea of a mystery derives, in my opinion, from the fact that Debussy persistently hid everything connected with his descent. Indeed, when he was famous he never wished to acknowledge my father who, moreover, outside the family, never disclosed the spiritual ties which bound him to one whose glory was continuously reaching new heights.

The truth is that the family of our great Claude was not respectable, and he was ashamed of this fact all his life. His own life was hardly more so, but from another viewpoint. However this may be, my father was always grateful that by luck he had been able to encourage a little the blossoming of one of the greatest geniuses of music.

Thanks to Monsieur Dietschy's investigations we are able to amplify some of the statements in this letter. Debussy's aunt, Clémentine de Bussy, was born in 1835 and was listed in 1860 as a seamstress. At this time she ran a business under the name 'Maison Debussy, Couture' at the home of her parents, 13 Boulevard des Capucines. About 1864 she became the mistress of the thirty-five-year-old broker, Achille-Antoine Arosa, of part Spanish descent, assuming the fictitious name Octavie de la Ferronière when, together with Arosa, she signed Debussy's baptismal certificate. It is likely that she adopted this fantastic name for the occasion to mask her relationship with Arosa among susceptible circles at Saint-Germain-en-Laye. She settled at Cannes, probably about 1866, where she let rooms during the winter season, and at the age of thirty-six married the twenty-five-year-old *maître d'hôtel* Alfred Roustan. The significant point here is that Clémentine de Bussy's humble marriage took place on 12 June 1871, five months before that of her former lover, Achille Arosa, celebrated in the presence of the Spanish Ambassador in Paris on 8 November. The relationship between Clémentine de Bussy and Achille Arosa could not have lasted long since Debussy's benevolent aunt had early settled at Cannes where, contrary to all previous statements, she lived alone and not with Arosa.[1] It was at Cannes that the child Debussy's musical gifts were awakened by piano lessons from a local Italian teacher. Clearly, therefore, this was due to the intuition of his aunt to whom, at Cannes, he was entrusted for one or more periods.[2]

Despite the claims made by Paul Arosa in his letter quoted above, the influence of Achille Arosa and of Clémentine de Bussy, jointly or singly, on their ward remains mysterious. We cannot say how long the child Debussy was entrusted to the one or the other, nor even, apart from the visits to Cannes, where he resided during these early years. Léon Vallas maintains, without giving his sources, that under Arosa's influence Achille Debussy began to paint. In support of this there is the fact that a palette of his childhood years remained with him until his first marriage and was kept for many years by his first wife, Lilly Texier-Debussy. This being so, it is a significant fact that Arosa, a cultivated man and patron of the arts, had many important connexions with the painters of his time.

On his discharge from the Navy in 1871 Gauguin was entrusted by his mother to the guardianship of Achille Arosa's brother, Gustave. It is possible that the period of Achille Debussy's association with his godfather may have extended to the period of the guardianship of Gauguin by Gustave Arosa. The Arosas had a luxurious mansion at Saint-Cloud which housed a collection of paintings by Delacroix, Courbet, Daumier, and others. Gustave Arosa's collection, sold in 1878, included seventeen Delacroix, four

---

[1] This was confirmed to me by Madame Hilda Arosa-Roosevelt, widow of Paul Arosa. Achille Arosa never lived at Cannes. Another Debussy family appears in the census list at Cannes at this period, a widower with two young boys, which may have been the reason, Monsieur Dietschy plausibly suggests, for Clémentine having settled there.

[2] The early biography of Louis Laloy, unreliable in regard to dates and facts on many important matters though published in 1909 with Debussy's approval, states: 'En 1871 il se trouvait, avec ses parents, à Cannes, chez une soeur de sa mère [sic] qui eut la fantaisie de lui apprendre le piano; un vieux professeur italien, nommé Cerutti, lui enseigna le premier rudiment, et ne remarqua rien.' Monsieur Dietschy has been able to identify this first, obscure teacher of Debussy. A violinist as well as a piano teacher, he had at this time reached no great age. He was Jean Cerutti, born in 1830 and married to a German, Elisabeth Neuweiller, living in 1872 at Cannes on the Boulevard Pihoret. Recollections of the visit to Cannes are described in a letter from Debussy to Jacques Durand of 24 March 1908: 'My memories go back to the time when I was six. I remember the railway passing in front of the house and the sea stretching out to the horizon. You sometimes had the impression that the railway came out of the sea or went into it—whichever you like. Then there was the route d'Antibes, where there were so many roses. I never saw so many altogether in my life. I hope the railway is still there, so that you will be able to come back, and also the roses, because there is no better way of decorating streets. With a Norwegian carpenter who used to sing— Grieg, perhaps—from morning to night I close my memoirs.'

Daumiers, seven Courbets, and three Pissarros. Achille Arosa's collection, sold in 1891, included works by Sisley and also by Pissarro, who was commissioned in 1872 to paint the four door-panels, *Les Quatre Saisons* (now at the Municipal Museum, The Hague), for the Arosas' house at Saint-Cloud, rebuilt after the Franco-Prussian War.

The Arosas' mansion, La Maison, Saint-Cloud, was painted by Gauguin in 1885, and a reproduction of it appears in *Gauguin* by Maurice Malingue (Paris, 1948). Here another relevant fact was discovered by André Schaeffner: it was Achille Arosa who encouraged Gauguin to go to Tahiti, having made the journey there himself in 1873 or before. It is conceivable that the composer who was always instinctively drawn to the Orient had heard in his early youth of the adventures of Arosa in Tahiti or of Gauguin in Peru and Brazil. In any case he must have heard of the exotic adventures of his father when serving in the Marines.

The choice of a musical career for the child was the decision of a person from an entirely different milieu, Madame Mauté, the mother-in-law of Verlaine. Our evidence here is a statement in the biography of Louis Laloy, corroborated as we shall presently see by other sources. This statement reads: 'He had known by chance Charles de Sivry, the whimsical brother-in-law of Paul Verlaine, and later his mother who became Madame Mautet [*sic*], a former pupil of Chopin. It was this charming woman who, having heard the young boy strum on the piano, predicted what everyone, including himself, had failed to see. "He must become a musician," she said. She looked after him like a grandmother and was so sucesssful that in 1873 [*sic*] he entered the Conservatoire.'

To see the circumstances that led to this sudden and, as it appears from Laloy's account, dramatic decision we must branch out into the life of Verlaine at this period and also to that of Manuel Debussy and his adventures during the stormy months of the Commune. The Franco-Prussian War broke out on 15 July 1870. Four months later Manuel, having lost his job through lack of work at Dupont's printing works, was employed at the Commissariat of the Mairie of the First Arrondissement (the Louvre) in Paris. This was known as one of the Paris centres of revolt, and the records show that Manuel was engaged there until 15 March 1871, when as a former soldier he joined the National Guard. On 18 March the rebellion broke out, and by 3 May he had joined the revolutionary troops as captain in command of the second company of the 13th Federal Battalion. The records of the *Bureau Historique de l'Armée* at the Château de Vincennes, consulted by Monsieur Dietschy, provide a precise account (published in *The Musical Quarterly*, July 1960) of the part played by the headstrong young captain in the defeat at Issy which was one of the turning-points in the battles of the Commune:

On 8 May 1871, at two in the morning, Captain de Bussy, at the head of his company, was sent to Issy with his battalion. At three the commanding officer, Corcelle, kicked by a horse, had to withdraw. He entrusted the battalion to Captain de Bussy with orders to occupy the fort of Issy. Verlaine was in the vicinity on the same side of the barricade. The former shop-owner at Saint-Germain-en-Laye led the attack. But no sooner did the Versailles riflemen open fire than his men deserted him and he gave himself up to the staff-officer at Issy, who had him arrested forthwith. Set free on 10 May, he returned to Paris. On 22 May the Commune was defeated and Captain de Bussy was imprisoned at the Bastion de la Muette. He was then incarcerated at Satory, interrogated, court-martialled, and at his trial on 11 December 1871 was sent to prison for four years. . . . After a year of incarceration his sentence was reduced to four years' suspension of civil and family rights.[1]

[1] The dossier of Captain de Bussy at the *Bureau Historique de l'Armée* contains the following details: 17 August 1871, first interrogation at Satory; 11 September, second interrogation; 11 December, trial and judgement; 11 May 1872, ruling on petition for reprieve; 12 June 1872, notification. The petition for reprieve was in the form of a letter to the military authorities, dated 8 June 1871, from Madame de Bussy, offering a clear enough view of the turbulent background of the child Debussy's life during these months:

Monsieur le Commandant,
    Je vous envoie ci-joint les pièces que je pense pouvoir être utiles à M. Achille de Bussy, mon mari, ex-capitaine au 13ème bataillon de la garde nationale, fait prisonnier au bastion de la Muette le 22 mai dernier. J'y ajouterai quelques mots pouvant lui servir d'excuses à sa participation aux derniers événements. Ayant perdu sa place par le manque de travaux, le 15 novembre dernier, comme le marque dans la lettre que je vous envoie M. Paul Dupont, il fut employé du 15 décembre au 15 février [should be 15 March] à la Mairie du Ier arrond. dont ci-joint aussi un certificat. (Le chef des services des vivres certifie que M. Debussy a été employé du 15 décembre au 15 mars et n'a qu'à se louer de son travail, probité et activité.) Depuis cette époque, mon mari fut sans occupation ainsi que moi depuis le commencement de la guerre. Nous avons quatre enfants, la gêne était grande dans notre intérieur. Pour l'amoindrir il se décida dans le courant d'avril à accepter le poste de capitaine dans la garde nationale afin que sa femme et ses enfants puissent vivre.

It was during the Commune, at the Mairie of the Louvre, or at the prison at Satory, that the ambitious captain met Charles de Sivry, son by her first marriage of Antoinette-Flore Mauté, Debussy's piano teacher and half-brother of Mathilde Mauté, the unfortunate child-wife of Verlaine and the inspiratrice of his famous *La Bonne Chanson*. Our sources here are the memoirs of Mathilde Verlaine and the letters of contemporary musicians. During the siege of Paris and the dramatic months of the Commune the worst and the best elements were thrown up in annihilating conflicts. Bizet and Chabrier describe the sickening looting and vandalism that daily threatened the life of everyone, the poorer folk, conscious of their sudden power, proclaiming magnificent schemes, but others among them huddling for safety from shelter to shelter. The windows of Mathilde's home on the heights of Montmartre commanded a view of the devastating fires lighting up the whole of the agonized city. The dramatic scene was not lost on the imagination of Verlaine and his friend Edmond Lepelletier. 'Faites-nous donc servir le café ici,' Lepelletier sardonically ordered, 'au coin du feu.' We can guess the anxieties of the child Debussy at this time, his father imprisoned, his mother struggling in one way or another for a bare existence.

Describing the adventures of Sivry and Verlaine during the Commune, Mathilde Verlaine states: 'It was during this time that Charles made the acquaintance of the father of Claude Debussy. He and my mother were the first to discover the astonishing gifts of the child and to persuade his family to encourage him in this direction. We kept in touch with him in the course of his life and were happy to see him become one of our greatest composers.'

Who were these figures, Charles de Sivry and his mother Madame Mauté, who in one way or another appear to have decided the child's musical destiny? Since we are concerned here with matters of obvious artistic and psychological importance, namely the

C'est la seule considération qui a dicté sa conduite. J'ose espérer, M. le Cdt., que votre grand coeur admettra ces circonstances atténuantes et que vous voudrez bientôt rendre mon mari à l'amour de ses enfants dont il est le seul soutien. Veuillez agréer, M. le Cdt., l'assurance de mon profond respect.
Votre très humble servante
V. de Bussy.

The official report challenges her case: 'Debussy en acceptant le grade de capitaine, se mettait plus que jamais en relief. ... Pour l'occupation du fort d'Issy ... il avait donc l'intention formelle d'accomplir sa mission et il l'aurait fait ... si ses hommes ne l'avaient abandonné.' All the memoirs and histories of the period are agreed on the conditions of great cruelty that obtained at the prison of Satory.

possibility that Debussy as a child may have studied with a pupil of Chopin, and that during this impressionable period he may have been a witness of the debaucheries of Verlaine, the brutal treatment by Verlaine of his child-wife Mathilde, and his seduction by Rimbaud, the available evidence deserves close scrutiny. Charles de Sivry was a bohemian musician of versatile though very modest attainments. He was associated with the *décadents*, his conversation running to painting, poetry, occultism, archaeology, medicine, chemistry, and alchemy. A friend of Chabrier, with whom he played duets, and of Villiers de l'Isle Adam and Verlaine, whose verses he set, he was a composer of ballets and light music and was principally known as the pianist at the bohemian cabaret, the Chat Noir. We need not be greatly concerned with Verlaine's description of him as 'le bon musicien de génie plus encore que de talent'. He was Verlaine's intimate friend whom he introduced to his sixteen-year-old half-sister, Mathilde Mauté. In the awkward courtship between Verlaine and his young sister Sivry played the role of intermediary, delivering to her, as they were written, Verlaine's desperately lyrical poems, *La Bonne Chanson*, inspired by his idealization of the simple-hearted girl. Verlaine and Mathilde were married in 1870. Sivry died in 1900, having lived to hear the settings of *La Bonne Chanson* by Fauré as well as the early Verlaine songs of Debussy.

The figure of Madame Mauté, who clearly played a benevolent role in Debussy's childhood, must similarly be sketched out. Here the memoirs of Mathilde must be read with caution. In her later years Mathilde became an incorrigible snob and her memoirs contain many references to relatives with aristocratic names who turn out, according to the investigations of Monsieur Dietschy, to be 'a set of harmless cranks connected with hustling, speculation, freakish activities of one kind or another, some of them inflamed by absinthe, all of them impecunious'. Madame Mauté, born Antoinette-Flore Chariat, is described in her youth as a 'maîtresse de musique'. Her first husband, the 'Marquis de Sivry', was the son of Sivry, a hat-maker. Her second husband, who assumed the high-sounding name of Mauté de Fleurville, was the son of Mauté, a grocer. It may be that Madame Mauté was associated with some of the notable figures mentioned by Mathilde, among them George Sand, Alfred de Musset, Balzac, and Wagner. She may also have known Chopin and have heard him play. But we have no evidence that she was Chopin's pupil. Her name is nowhere listed among the pupils of Chopin nor is there any record of her public activities as a musician. [1] She must certainly have been a woman of an affectionate and generous nature. We gather as much from the rose-coloured recollections of Madame Mauté by both Verlaine and Debussy. She was remembered at vital turning-points in each of their lives for her tolerance and wisdom. In 1894, a year after her death, Verlaine, recalling his mother-in-law's sympathy at the time of his stormy scenes with Rimbaud and Mathilde, wrote in his *Confessions*:

Vous fûtes bonne et douce en nos tristes tempêtes.
—L'Esprit et la Raison parmi nos fureurs bêtes,—
Et si l'on vous eût crue au temps qu'il le fallait
On se fût épargné que de chagrin plus laid,
Encor que douloureux! . . .
                                        Soyez aimée
Et vénérée, ô morte inopportunément!
Qui sait, vous là, précise et sûre au vrai moment,
Votre volonté, toute indulgence et sagesse,
Eût prévalu sans doute et nous eût fait largesse
D'un pardon mutuel obtenu par son soin; . . .

            Dormez, ô vous, sous votre pierre grise,
Qui fîtes le devoir et ne cédâtes pas,
Dormez par ce novembre où ne peuvent mes pas
Malades vous aller porter quelque couronne.
Mais voici ma pensée, ô vous, douce, ô vous, bonne!

'She was a charming soul,' Verlaine adds in the same moving terms, 'an artist of instinct and of talent, an excellent musician of exquisite taste, intelligent and devoted to anyone she loved.'

Could Verlaine have been thinking of her devotion to the young Debussy? In 1915, near the end of his life, Debussy similarly speaks

[1] Despite Debussy's own recollections of Chopin from his association with Madame Mauté, François Porché, the editor of Mathilde Verlaine's memoirs, is suspicious of the assertion that Debussy's first teacher was a pupil of Chopin: 'Mademoiselle Chariat était bonne musicienne. Mais pour l'admettre, est-il nécessaire de croire, qu'elle fut, comme le dit Mathilde, l'élève de Chopin . . . Hum.' He is referring to the following passage in Mathilde's memoirs: 'My mother showed a decided calling for music and at fifteen was a very fine pianist. My grandmother had her take lessons from Chopin who perfected her talent. It was from the master himself that she learnt to play so admirably his Polonaises and his Impromptus.'

[21]

of her with gratitude. He mentions her twice in his correspondence of this year and it is interesting to note that on both occasions his memory of her is aroused by her connexion with Chopin. On 27 January, when working on an edition of the works of Chopin, he wrote to his publisher, Jacques Durand: 'It is a pity that Madame Mauté de Fleurville, to whom I owe the little I know about the piano, is dead. She knew many things about Chopin. We must nevertheless try and do the best for his interests.' And on 1 September of the same year: 'With all respect to his great age, what Saint-Saëns says about the pedal in Chopin is not quite right, for I remember very well what Madame Mauté de Fleurville told me. Chopin wanted his pupils to study without using the pedal and only to use it sparingly when performing. It was this use of the pedal as a kind of breathing that I noticed in Liszt when I heard him in Rome.' We note that Debussy does not specifically state in these letters that he studied with Madame Mauté. We must assume that he did, though it is curious that no mention is made of the lessons he took with Madame Mauté where we should expect to find them mentioned, namely in the pretentious memoirs of Mathilde, designed to reflect glory on herself by her connexion with notable personalities.

However this may be, the period of Achille's studies with Madame Mauté could only have been very short. A mere seventeen months extend from the defeat of the Commune on 28 May 1871 to his admission to the Conservatoire on 22 October 1872. From our knowledge of the activities during this period of the various figures with whom he was associated several facts emerge. One assumes that, having met Sivry during the Commune, Manuel must have taken some pride in introducing his promising son to this bohemian musician who in turn recommended him to his talented mother. Thereafter, until his admission to the Conservatoire, Achille was associated with Madame Mauté who 'looked after him like a grandmother'.

During this time his father was in prison and his mother penniless. I do not think there can be any doubt that the child was in some way made aware during these months of the agonizing strife between Verlaine, Rimbaud, and Mathilde. The fact that, despite exhaustive research, no mention can be traced of a meeting in later years between Debussy and Verlaine is a mystery, but it may also be significant. One would expect there to have at least been some correspondence on the matter of the rights of setting Verlaine's poems, similar to the published correspondence between Fauré and Verlaine. Had something occurred which caused them to avoid each other? Since they had many mutual friends they could hardly have done so successfully. At Verlaine's funeral in 1896 Charles de Sivry was the chief mourner. We know that after the Commune Achille was living with his mother, 'Dame de Bussy', at 59bis rue Pigalle, not many streets away from 41 rue Nicolet, the home of Madame Mauté and also the temporary home of Paul and Mathilde Verlaine, married a few months before the Commune. It is extremely likely that the nine-year-old Achille Debussy was often there. In September 1871 Rimbaud arrived at the rue Nicolet and Mathilde's marriage was doomed. Mathilde had in the meantime given birth to a son, to which event Verlaine responded with unbelievable scenes of drunkenness and brutality. In July of the following year the long-suffering Madame Mauté accompanied Mathilde to Brussels in the hope of redeeming her son-in-law from the seductive Rimbaud. Verlaine at first agreed to a reunion with Mathilde, but suddenly reversed his decision and at the frontier town of Quiévrin was seen by Mathilde and her mother for the last time grimly pulling his hat down over his eyes in a weak-willed gesture of defiance.

In September, Verlaine and Rimbaud arrived in London, and before long the two great poets were fighting with knives. In October, three months after Madame Mauté's return from Brussels, Achille Debussy was one of the few successful candidates admitted to the Conservatoire. Throughout this period Madame Mauté was desperately striving to control a triangular situation of which her daughter was the victim. We cannot escape the conclusion that it was under these conditions that the child Debussy, no doubt naturally gifted, was successfully taught by Madame Mauté, resulting in his passing the highly competitive entrance examination to the Conservatoire.

Such is the hinterland of Debussy's childhood years. We cannot possibly know all the lanes and by-paths of this entangled territory. It is perhaps not even necessary that we should. But we know enough to see that his memories of these dark and troubled years of childhood were to appear forgotten and buried only to the outside world. 'Ah! je n'oublie rien,' he wrote to his wife on one of his ceaseless journeys towards the end of his life. The son of an undignified father, of a mother who contrived to rid herself of her children, driven from pillar to post and finding only temporary refuge in a good-natured aunt, a wealthy godfather or a generous stranger, he was uprooted from the start and remained so. In later years he was to build no home of his own. There emerges, too, a picture of divided allegiances. 'Sauvage', with the double meaning of fierce and shy, is the description agreed upon in the early recorded impressions, and so he must have appeared with his square, box-like head, the great forehead bulging forwards, his swarthy complexion and the concentrated, violent expression in the eyes. At some time, during these early years, the pattern must have been established that drove him to gratify the senses in ecstatic pleasure and that also reduced him to abject poverty. Spendthrift—for what else can money gratify but the senses?—Baudelaire was similarly such an instinctive spirit, ready to pawn even his lyre for the intoxication of the moment.

> Buvez-vous des bouillons d'ambroisie?
> Mangez-vous des côtelettes de Paros?
> Combien prête-t-on sur une lyre au Mont de Piété?

3
Early Conservatoire Years

Le Conservatoire est toujours cet endroit sombre et sale que
nous avons connu où la poussière des mauvaises traditions
reste encore aux doigts.

Letter to André Caplet

Ever since the foundation of the Paris Conservatoire in 1795
entrance has been by state scholarship awarded as the result of a
competitive examination. Something of a sensation was caused by
Debussy's admission to the Paris Conservatoire. Among the thirty-
eight applicants who competed to enter the piano classes in October
1872, eight male students only were successful. Achille Debussy,
just turned ten, was one of the youngest. On 25 October he was
inscribed in the class of Antoine Marmontel.

The sixty-year-old Marmontel, one of the pillars of the Conservatoire, was held in great affection by his pupils and contemporaries.
He developed a whole generation of French musicians, among them
Bizet who declared that in his class 'one learns something besides the
piano; one becomes a musician'. Marmontel had heard Chopin and
Liszt and wrote an interesting book on the styles of the virtuosos of
his time. But he appears to have been conservative in outlook and,
to judge by his theoretical works on the piano and his pedantic
studies, he remained rooted in the methods of the forgotten
Zimmermann. He comes to life for us in a portrait by a fellow-
student, Camille Bellaigue, later a brilliant writer and critic of *La
Revue des Deux Mondes*:

Marmontel was a bald-headed little man with a grey, pointed
beard, with grey fingers too, stunted as if they had been worn
down in the practice of his art. . . . He was the patriarch of the

piano. Perhaps he had at one time been a virtuoso; he was now not even a pianist. At any rate none of us had ever heard him play. The most he would sometimes do, and even this was difficult for him, was to play a run, illustrate a fingering, or the value or accent of a note, but it was done so clumsily that he himself was the first to smile. But how he made up for this shortcoming in his lessons! In everything he did he showed impeccable style. He loved music, and he loved us too for what we meant in music for him, this old master surrounded by his apprentices. Sometimes he would grasp his long beard with his two hands, pulling at it as if to lengthen it still more. His eyes half closed, he would utter deep sighs, muttering to himself, 'Oh mon Dieu! Oh mon Dieu!' It seemed as if he were calling on the heavens to witness our blunders and the suffering we were causing him, though he tried his best to conceal it. With the slightest sign of intelligence on our part, on the other hand, his face would invariably light up.

From the first, Marmontel perceived something unusual in the young Debussy. 'A charming child,' he stated in his report after the first year's study. 'A true artistic temperament; much can be expected of him.' At the yearly examination Achille had played a Rondo and Fugue of Mozart, and six months later, in July 1874, he won a second certificate of merit with his performance of the Second Piano Concerto of Chopin.

To have reached this standard in so short a time obviously denoted a natural vocation for the piano, and Manuel Debussy must surely have been justified in looking forward to his son's career as a pianist. The following year brought still more encouraging results. The examiners were enthusiastic in their reports of the way in which the precocious student played the Chromatic Fantasy of Bach and the Rondo, Op. 16, of Chopin. Later, in July 1875, he won a first certificate with the Second Ballade of Chopin. Among the press notices of the annual Conservatoire awards Achille Debussy was described as nothing less than 'a twelve-year-old prodigy who promises to be a virtuoso of the first order'. The same impression was created at his first appearance in public six months later. At a local concert organized at the small manufacturing town of Chauny, near Saint-Quentin, Achille accompanied the singer, Léontine Mendès, and played in a trio by Haydn. 'A delightful temperament,' the local newspaper stated of his début on the concert platform, 'this budding Mozart is a regular devil.'

It was not, however, to be roses all the way. Another view of Debussy's early student years with Marmontel emerges from the fascinating reminiscences of his fellow-student, Maurice Emmanuel. Here a parenthesis must be opened to present this devoted friend of Achille at the Conservatoire who was to become a humanist among the musicians of the period, a remarkable scholar and a penetrating critic. The author of research works on Greek music, polyphony, and rhythm, he later held the chair of the history of music at the Conservatoire. His compositions include two symphonies and a set of six sonatinas for piano in which he used Oriental modes, one of them dedicated to Busoni, with whom Emmanuel has sometimes been compared. In his youth Emmanuel was so impressed by the ideas of the young Debussy that he went to the trouble of recording verbatim his conversations with his composition teacher, Ernest Guiraud, which he set out in the form of questions and answers. The notebook in which these conversations were recorded was preserved by Emmanuel and is a moving tribute from a fellow-student. Earlier, Emmanuel recorded his impressions of Debussy as a piano student and also set down his altercations with his teachers of theory and harmony. One would be tempted to think of all this as a case of adolescent hero-worship on Emmanuel's part were it not for the fact that his records are by no means biased; they are carefully drawn accounts of the young Debussy's musical character, subtle, amusing, and human, illuminating in many different ways the hard, stormy passages of his student years.

The personal friendship between Debussy and Emmanuel did not outlive their student days. 'He had a conception of life that I could hardly share; I kept my distance from him,' we read in a letter written shortly after Debussy's death, in 1920. Emmanuel was writing to Saint-Saëns who, alarmed by the æsthetic and also the moral values which the art of Debussy represented, delivered the most vitriolic of his numerous attacks on his eminent rival. 'What is so amazing in the matter of Debussy's reputation,' Saint-Saëns wrote to Emmanuel, 'is the hypocritical, naïve way in which the public has allowed itself to be taken in. He publishes a piece under the attractive title *Jardins sous la pluie*, recalling *La Forêt mouillée* of

Victor Hugo, and he gives us an interminable series of arpeggios on *Do, do l'enfant do* and *Nous n'irons plus au bois*. He writes a *Dialogue du vent et de la mer* [Saint-Saëns says *de la vague et de la brise*] and we hear a trumpet playing *Voilà l'plaisir, Mesdames*. *L'Après-midi d'un faune* has a pretty sound but there is not the least truly musical idea in it; it is no more a piece of music than the palette on which a painter has been working is a picture. . . . Debussy created no style; he cultivated the absence of style as well as the absence of logic and common sense.' Devoured by envy, Saint-Saëns reserved his most bitter diatribe for the end: 'But he had a name that has an harmonious sound. If his name had been Martin no one would ever have spoken of him, though it is true that in this case he would have adopted a pseudonym.'

Though Emmanuel appears to have been similarly alarmed by the implications of Debussy's aesthetic, he steadfastly defended his artistic integrity, and in terms of exquisite courtesy replied to Saint-Saëns: 'My dear master, you are committing an error on the matter of this musician which will be held to be an injustice if you do not retract. . . . No question of friendship with Debussy can affect my judgement, but I am profoundly convinced that his artistic conscience was both the highest and the freest. . . . I do not believe that there was ever an artist who was more sincere.'

In a shrewd account of the relationship between Achille and his piano teacher, Marmontel is described by Emmanuel as an admirable master, but exceedingly meticulous and exacting. Strange as it may seem to us today, the supremacy of vocal music was such that words had to be fitted even to instrumental works. In later years Debussy recalled his horror at the sound of Marmontel chanting the Rondo of Beethoven's Pathétique Sonata to the sentimental words 'O mère, douleur amère'. There were often clashes between the elderly master, who enjoyed at the Conservatoire an almost priestly authority, and his young pupil, who was not always inclined to submit to the discipline of a severe technical training. The brilliant pupil, we are told, pursued his studies in fits and starts, preferring to indulge his gifts as a sight-reader by playing arrangements of the quartets of Mozart and Haydn. Before opening a piece he was required to play he would arouse his master's curiosity by improvising sequences of unusual arpeggios and chords. And there is an intriguing account of a 'highly original' performance he gave of the F minor Prelude from the second book of Bach's 'Forty-Eight'. Presumably he played it in a spontaneous, romantic manner. This had greatly impressed Marmontel but turned out to be completely unacceptable to the aged director of the Conservatoire, Ambroise Thomas—not surprisingly since Thomas, composer of the opera *Hamlet*, belonged to a generation of French composers that considered the keyboard works of Bach to be mere exercises. The vision is indeed choice of the future composer of the *Préludes* and the marvellous *Etudes*, a swarthy, uncouth, fourteen-year-old lad, astonishing these established masters with a novel view of Bach, the bald-headed Marmontel, with long pointed beard, looking on approvingly while the remote Ambroise Thomas, with deep-set eyes and flowing hair, his overcoat slung over his shoulders, had the appearance of a ghostly, extinct Verdi.

Sometimes lessons were given at Marmontel's home, particularly when examinations were approaching. This was a strange old house in the rue Saint-Lazare, believed by Bellaigue to have been haunted by a bedraggled old woman looking like the mother of Max, he says, in *Der Freischütz*. And he goes on: 'One had to go through several rooms before arriving at the master's music room. The light shining through stained-glass window-panes cast a mottled effect all over the pictures on the walls. Bronze and marble figures, brass and china covered the tables or stood on brackets. Music was scattered over the piano and over the carpet. In the midst of this disorder, something of a museum or a curiosity shop, the figure of Marmontel, in his dressing-gown, seemed stranger than ever—a character from a tale of Hoffmann or a novel of Balzac.'

Eventually Marmontel was left in two minds about the young Debussy's prospects. 'He doesn't care much for the piano', was his final verdict, 'but he does love music.' Shortly after his early triumphs as a pianist, Debussy may have begun to feel that despite these triumphs he was not primarily destined for the career of a pianist. He had begun to compose, and the year 1876, the date of his first public appearance at Chauny, is also the date he ascribed to the earliest of his published compositions, the song *Nuit d'étoiles* on a poem by Théodore de Banville. However this may be, he was to suffer a severe set-back in his piano studies about this time. At an examination in 1876 the performances by the fourteen-year-old student of a Rondo by Weber and Beethoven's Sonata, Op. 3, were put down by Marmontel as 'irresponsible and muddle-headed'. Though he was later to live down this set-back the verdict on these two performances had been severe and his promise as a prodigy was at any rate jeopardized.

What sort of a figure did Debussy cut as a pianist in his adolescent student years? He did not always show the fine temperament observed at this first appearance. It is curious to read in the memoirs of Emmanuel that the composer who was to turn the piano into an instrument of make-believe and illusion played Beethoven in his youth 'heavily'. The impressions of other fellow-students corroborate this. Gabriel Pierné, who was to become one of the most distinguished of French conductors, recalls a streak of violence in his playing. 'Whether it was from clumsiness or shyness,' Pierné writes, 'he literally charged at the keyboard and overdid every effect. He appeared to be in a rage with the instrument, ill-treating it with impulsive gestures and puffing noisily during the difficult passages.' Pierné did not, however, consider this nervous brutality at the piano to represent the whole picture of his friend at this time. He also observed an inner refinement. The harsh pianist was extremely fastidious in other matters—in his choice of food, for instance, and his taste for pictures.

Other impressions suggest that Achille both magnetized his friends and estranged them from him. Camille Bellaigue gives us the earliest glimpse of his physical appearance. The students of Marmontel's class had assembled in a spirit of eager co-operation. 'We saw a puny little fellow come in, often late. Dressed in a sailor-suit with a belt, he held in his hand a kind of beret edged with braid and with a red tassel in the middle, as on a sailor's cap. Nothing about him, his appearance, his conversation or his playing, suggested anything of the artist. The only remarkable thing about him was his forehead. He was one of the youngest pianists but not one of the best. I particularly remember his mannerism of marking the strong beat in the bar by a kind of hiccup or harsh puff. . . . Uncommunicative, not to say surly, he was not attractive to his friends.' In 1877 the fourteen-year-old Debussy won the second prize with a performance of the first movement of the Sonata in G minor by Schumann. It was the highest distinction as a piano student that he was to secure. At the annual examinations of the following two years he received no further award, and the prospect of a career as a virtuoso, which we gather had been so fondly imagined for him by Manuel Debussy, had eventually to be abandoned.

During Achille's first three years at the Conservatoire he also attended classes in theory. The master was Albert Lavignac, an erudite young musician of wide interests who later became well-known as the editor of the finest of the French musical works of reference, the great *Encyclopédie de la Musique et Dictionnaire du Conservatoire*. He also produced a work on musical aesthetics, remarkable at the time for its insight into music of the Near East and the Far East; and a book describing the pilgrimages of French musicians to Bayreuth. Achille became his pupil at the very time when Lavignac was embarking on his teaching career. In 1871 Ambroise Thomas had entrusted Lavignac with planning a new course at the Conservatoire in sight-reading and musical dictation. This course, for which the Paris Conservatoire subsequently became famous, was calculated to develop among composition students an exceptionally high standard of aural perception. Lavignac's exercises, used at the Conservatoire to this day, require the pupil not only to read at sight in the four C clefs, the two F clefs and the G clef, enunciating the *solfège* syllables while singing in rapid tempos and complex rhythms, but to transpose the exercises with the same facility. One cannot fail to acquire in this course a command of the rudiments of the musical language which students often lacked when plunged without preparation into the study of harmony and counterpoint. It is interesting to note, in regard to Debussy's later use of the pentatonic scales, that among the exercises provided by the erudite Lavignac were examples of exotic modes.[1]

Achille enjoyed with the youthful Lavignac a much more fruitful relationship than with the forbidding Marmontel. They were able to discuss new music on a friendly basis in the musty old Conservatoire building on the corner of the rue Bergère—all accounts agree on its dilapidated state. There Lavignac introduced Debussy to the music of Wagner. We read in the memoirs of Maurice Emmanuel that one winter evening after class time the score was set out on the piano of the Overture to *Tannhäuser*, the work which had recently created a notorious scandal at the Paris Opéra. One is almost reminded of an episode in Marcel Proust in reading the description

---

[1] No. 39 of Lavignac's *Cinquante Leçons de Solfège* is described as an exercise on 'the five-note modern Scottish scale: D, E, F sharp, A, B'.

of Achille, presumably still clad in sailor-suit and cap, confronted for the first time with the work of the composer who was soon to exert the most powerful influence on his creative life. The experience must have been overwhelming. The young professor and his eager pupil became so absorbed in the novel Wagnerian harmonies that they forgot all sense of time. When they eventually decided to leave they found themselves locked in and were obliged to grope their way out, arm in arm, down the rickety stairs and the dark corridors of the crumbling scholastic building.

An enquiring turn of mind marked Achille's approach to his theory lessons. On rhythm and on metre he had already ideas of his own. 'On étouffe dans vos rhythmes', he provocatively declared; and he would often twit Lavignac on the rhythmic poverty of his sight-reading exercises. He also complained of the dearth of melodic ideas in these scholastic exercises and was puzzled by the use of certain stereotyped theoretical terms—'compound time' for instance, used for bars in which a unit is in triple time, and which is indeed a meaningless term. It is said that Achille in all innocence left his teacher nonplussed by asking what there was to compound in such a bar. Yet Lavignac was an enlightened as well as a methodical musician, and the three years, from 1873 to 1876, which Achille spent in his class laid splendid foundations: he gained successively the third, second, and finally the first *solfège* medal.

Less fortunate in their outcome were Achille's studies in the harmony class of Emile Durand. Again the rebellious youth attempted to assert his independence but there is little to suggest that Durand, the composer of two insignificant operettas, *L'Elixir de Cornelius* (1868) and *L'Astronome du Pont Neuf* (1869), glimpsed anything of his pupil's gifts. Emmanuel dismisses this obscure musician as an acrimonious figure who had no love either for music, his work, or his pupils. A student who was found improvising at the piano after class while the master would be fumbling his way into the sleeves of his overcoat was likely to find the piano lid slammed down on his fingers with the admonition: 'You'd do better to work on your progressions!' Durand's harmony treatise, which won the approval of Saint-Saëns, is, however, admirably clear and meticulous in its classification of chords, and though in later years Debussy took a malicious pride in confessing that he was never able to harmonize a melody in the accepted manner, a friendly bond seems to have been

Manuel-Achille Debussy as a private
in the Marine Light Infantry

Victorine Debussy

Debussy. Photo taken in Rome,
circa 1886

Alfred Debussy

Adèle Debussy

Clémentine de Bussy in her youth

Emile Alfred de Bussy, the composer's English cousin

established between Achille and this rather dry pedagogue. The manuscript of an unpublished Trio in G, his earliest chamber work (written during his stay, to be presently described, with Madame von Meck) is dedicated to Durand with the inscription: 'Beaucoup de notes accompagnées de beaucoup d'amitiés.'

No prizes or awards were received as a result of the three years (1877–80) spent under Emile Durand. At some time during this period, we cannot exactly say when, Debussy was a member of the organ class of César Franck. He was, however, not officially enrolled as a pupil of Franck and he appears not to have made any serious study of the organ. It is certain that the music of Franck could not have left him indifferent. He admired the *Béatitudes*, though not uncritically, and Vallas rightly maintains that he could hardly have remained unaffected by Franck's Quintet which appeared in 1879. We know little, however, about this short association with César Franck. According to one account Debussy fell out with Franck as a result of the great organ composer's incessant exhortations to modulate. 'Mais pourquoi voulez-vous que je module,' he asked in exasperation, 'puisque je me trouve très bien dans ce ton-là.'

We have finally to consider Debussy's studies with a fifth teacher during these early years, Auguste-Ernest Bazille. An organist too, but also an opera coach and an expert arranger of orchestral scores, Bazille held classes at the Conservatoire in advanced practical harmony and score-reading. His students were required to show proficiency at the keyboard in all practical aspects of composition: to sight-read a wide variety of orchestral scores, to improvise a poly-phonic chorale on a given chant, and to provide a complex accompaniment, embodying modulations, on a bass. Debussy excelled in these purely practical exercises and in 1880, after only a year's study, he received the first prize in this department of practical harmony.

At this point it will be convenient to break off our account of Debussy's studies at the Conservatoire to consider aspects of his life during the long summer vacations. At the age of eighteen he had been at the Conservatoire eight years. The record of his achievements over these years shows a gratifying list of academic awards: 1874, third medal in *solfège* and second mention in piano; 1875, second medal in *solfège* and first mention in piano; 1876, first medal in *solfège*; 1877, second prize in piano; 1880, first prize in practical harmony. With this last award the way was open to him to follow his studies in composition. He does so at the very time when vital changes occur in his material and also his emotional life. Disappointed at Achille's failure to fulfil his promise to become an infant prodigy, Manuel Debussy had nevertheless held down his job as assistant book-keeper at the Compagnie de Fives-Lille, rue Caumartin, but had changed his address once again: at an unspecified time the family had settled in a humble fourth-floor apartment in the rue Clapeyron. Financial difficulties must still have been acute for, apart from seizing the first opportunity to appear in public, Achille had been obliged to eke out the family's meagre budget by giving lessons to aspiring children, among them one Georges Guignache. With the knowledge of these circumstances, Marmontel was doubtless pleased to be able to put in his pupil's way, during the summer months, engagements as pianist and accompanist to wealthy amateurs. They happened to live in palatial surroundings, and for four years, during the summer months from 1879 to 1882, Achille found new worlds open to him and travelled widely throughout Europe. From the misery of his parents' Montmartre home he moved to the Château de Chenonceaux and, among the residences of the Russian millionairess Nadezhda von Meck, the Villa Oppenheim at Fiesole and Plesh-cheyvo near Moscow.

4
Chenonceaux

Rising like Venus from the bosom of the waves. . . .
Larousse

Among the unconventional young pupil's friends at the Conservatoire was a coloured student from Trinidad, José-Manuel Imenez, who had been engaged as a pianist, along with other chamber musicians, at the Château de Chenonceaux. In the days when music-making was mainly the preserve of the wealthy it was common for students to find such employment during the long summer vacation, though not often in such a princely establishment. In the summer of 1879 Marmontel, obviously from a desire to put this agreeable post in the way of another of his less fortunate pupils, recommended Achille Debussy to replace Imenez. The few months that the seventeen-year-old student spent at the historic château in the Touraine has hardly been mentioned in any of the biographies; at most it has been dismissed in a line or two as an episode of no significance. I do not think we can over-rate this early experience. Responsive to the luxury of physical surroundings, the impecunious youth, insecure in his family environment in the rue Clapeyron, must have been overwhelmed by the magnificence of the former residence of Diane de Poitiers and Catherine de' Medici. Responsive, too, to the interplay of personalities, he could not have been unimpressed by his extraordinary hostess, Madame Marguerite Wilson-Pelouze, a woman of strong character who played a strange part, not hitherto disclosed, in the social and artistic life of her time.

The daughter of Daniel Wilson, a Scottish engineer settled in

France who made a fortune by introducing gas-lighting in Paris, Mademoiselle Wilson married in 1857 Eugène Pelouze, an official of the newly formed gas company, and received from her father the Château de Chenonceaux, which his enterprise and wealth had enabled him to purchase. Her dominating personality emerges from the memoirs of Léonce Dupont dealing with the period of the Franco–Prussian War:

> Without perhaps being quite so seductive as Madame Récamier, Madame P. had the art of attracting to Tours some very important personalities and of retaining them there. When their courage failed them she was there to revive them; to the disillusioned she gave new hope. Madame P. was really most pre-possessing, fair, an Englishwoman through and through and a splendid patriot. She was especially attracted to politics and had a warm spot for all who shone in this field. She had a brother, Monsieur Wilson, who, so she decided in 1869, was to become a deputy. She went about this mission in the English manner, making bounteous gifts, and eventually she achieved her aim. One thing she had in her favour, indeed it was one of her great attractions, was the Château de Chenonceaux of which she was the owner. She had bought [sic] this marvellous residence which, before her time, the kings of France had coveted and possessed. Forsaking her lighter activities, she spent the whole of the winter of 1870 in society at Tours, at the Hôtel de Bordeaux, which she dreamt for a moment of turning into another Hôtel Rambouillet. She was a most admirable hostess, anxious to bring together the finest minds that the war and the Republic had driven to this county town.

Elsewhere, in the memoirs of Robert de Bonnières, Madame Pelouze, wearing a diamond tiara, is described as a woman of breath-taking beauty, 'as sensuous and as intoxicating as a magnolia'. Her interests extended to the arts, but it was in politics and social affairs that she shone. During Debussy's stay at Chenonceaux she was known to be the mistress of Jules Grévy, President of the Republic. This fact is of more than passing interest since in 1881 the President's daughter, Alice Grévy, was to marry Madame Pelouze's brother, the notorious Daniel Wilson junior whose unscrupulous activities were disclosed in the *Affaire Wilson*, the first of the nation-wide scandals of the Third Republic, resulting, in 1887, in the President's resignation.

As we shall presently see, Debussy long remembered this picturesque adventurer, but before outlining his activities in so far as they have a bearing on Debussy's stay at Chenonceaux, we must see the part played by Wilson's irresistible sister in the musical life of her time. She was apparently a fanatical Wagnerian. In 1876, together with a small group of French musicians, she was among the first French visitors to Bayreuth. *The Ring* was first given there in this year, and the visitors from Paris included Augusta Holmès, the mysterious friend of César Franck and Mallarmé, Vincent d'Indy, Ernest Guiraud, later Debussy's teacher of composition, and Saint-Saëns. Between 1884 and 1891 Madame Pelouze returned to Bayreuth no less than five times, being listed with Debussy as having heard the performances there, in 1888, of *Parsifal* and *Meistersinger*. Earlier, in 1885, she was one of the founders, with Houston Stewart Chamberlain, Baron Emmanuel de Graffenried and others, of *La Revue Wagnérienne*, organ of the French section of the United Richard Wagner Society, her influence on this important publication extending over the first two years of its appearance.[1]

It was probably due to concern with her brother's activities that she is recorded, in 1879, the year of Debussy's stay at Chenonceaux, as suffering from severe insomnia. 'To fill out her sleepless nights in an agreeable manner,' we read in the memoirs of Robert Burnand, 'her husband went to the length of engaging a young musician whose duty was to play the piano until the good lady's eyelids began to drop. His name was Claude Debussy.' The young piano student, who was already feeling his way as a composer—his earliest songs, *Ballade à la lune*, *Nuit d'étoiles*, and *Beau soir*, on poems of Alfred de Musset, Théodore de Banville, and Paul Bourget, date from about 1876—was to be the last, in fact, of a distinguished line of visitors to Chenonceaux, among them Buffon, Marivaux, Fontenelle, George Sand, and Flaubert. Earlier another musician had been enchanted by Chenonceaux, Jean-Jacques Rousseau. Of his visit there in 1747 Rousseau writes: 'On s'amuse beaucoup dans ce beau lieu: on y

---

[1] In 1886 the Earl of Dysart, president of the London branch of the United Richard Wagner Society, joined the board with Madame Pelouze of *La Revue Wagnérienne*. In the same year and in January of the following year lectures on *The Ring* were given under the auspices of the London branch, illustrated by Tobias Matthay and others at the Surrey Conservatoire of Music at Clapham.

faisait très-bonne chère, j'y devins gras comme un moine. On y fit beaucoup de musique; j'y composai plusieurs trios à chanter d'une assez forte harmonie.' Built almost completely on piles across the river Cher, Chenonceaux, displaying to this day important architectural restorations ordered by Madame Pelouze, is unique among the châteaux of the Touraine. One can only imagine the impressions retained by the composer of *Reflets dans l'eau* and *Ondine* of these early months spent in this palace rising from the waters.

What was the soothing music demanded from the young Debussy up to the small hours of the morning by his harassed châtelaine? We should dearly love to know. Possibly some of his earliest compositions or, less appropriate to the residence of Diane de Poitiers, Wagner, whose *Ring* Madame Pelouze had heard only three years earlier. Harassed and distraught she certainly must have been, and it is difficult to imagine that she could have been successfully charmed even by the youthful Debussy's valiant efforts. Her brother, Daniel Wilson, an enormous square-bearded man of ruddy complexion, had fast been running through the family fortune, courting the favour of the peasants of his constituency, the Indre-et-Loire, by offering them handsome repasts at Chenonceaux, paying for their journeys by balloon, and spending no less than a million francs on launching the celebrated *cocodette* Caroline Hasse. In 1887 the scandals of his public career were brought to light. As Under-Secretary of State and son-in-law of the President, he was accused of appropriating the President's signature, of bribery in the public services and of a scheme for the award of official titles to anyone who happened to be in his favour. Indignation broke out in the satirical popular songs, *Ah! quel malheur d'avoir un gendre, Monsieur Gendre* and others less delicate, and Jules Grévy was forced to resign. The following year Madame Pelouze was bankrupt, her possessions were seized by the bailiffs,[1] and the Château de Chenonceaux temporarily became national property.

Though the *Affaire Wilson* came to a head eight years after Debussy's visit to Chenonceaux, he was surely aware of Daniel

[1] According to the memoirs of Robert Sherard, Ferdinand de Lesseps reports in 1888: 'There is to be a sale in the Château where Diane de Poitiers lived and loved. What would Catherine de' Medici have said to find bailiffs in her bedroom? We are wondering why neither Grévy nor Wilson who both have sacks of money don't help her out of her difficulties for the credit of her name. Surely there have been enough Wilson scandals. The debts amount to over a million and a half francs and include such miserable amounts as 100 francs owing to the village baker.'

Wilson's activities at the time for many years later he had occasion to recall this picturesque scoundrel. In 1902, after the success of *Pelléas et Mélisande*, Debussy was asked to nominate an official figure in support of the proposed award to him of the Légion d'Honneur. Debussy had no opinion of official titles. 'Every artist is able at some time,' he told Paul Valéry, 'to decorate the government.' On 4 December 1902 he sardonically wrote to his friend Louis Laloy on the matter of a sponsor: 'I have only known one political figure in my life; this was M. Wilson. He was a charming man who hated music wholeheartedly.'[1]

[1] Quoting this letter Laloy blunders appallingly in his descriptions of Madame Pelouze and her brother: 'Debussy . . . avait passé un été au Château de Chenonceaux chez Madame Pelouze, fille de Wilson et petite fille du Président Grévy.'

5
Russia

O Claude-Achille Debussy,
En quel endroit de notre sphère
Criez-vous: Vive la Russy!
Comme tout bon Français doit faire?
Pierre Louÿs

Everyone knows of Debussy's association with Nadezhda von Meck and of the journeys he made to Russia at her invitation in his youth. This is of course an important episode in his aesthetic development; it also leads to an interesting sociological question. But because of obvious picturesque and sentimental elements in the association of a Russian millionairess with a great composer in his adolescent years this episode has been shamefully embroidered upon and distorted, notably by certain writers in America. The result has been that the true features of this episode have become almost unrecognizable, and we are bound, therefore, to approach the whole subject afresh. Debussy's Russian connexions, moreover, cannot be dealt with in isolation; they belong to the long history of Russian music in France, itself a complex subject not yet fully investigated. We must thus abandon anything like a strict chronological sequence of Debussy's activities in this chapter and glance over the whole matter of his Russian associations in later years, rooted to some extent in his early journeys to Russia.

Having recommended his pupil to Madame Wilson-Pelouze in 1879, Marmontel did a further good turn the following year by suggesting him for employment in a similar capacity by Nadezhda Filaretovna von Meck, the patroness of Tchaikovsky. The external facts of her relationship with Tchaikovsky are well known. Born in 1831, the daughter of a land-owner, Fralovsky, she married at seventeen a poor government engineer, Karl von Meck, who, largely through her own initiative and ambition, amassed a vast fortune as contractor for the Russian railways. In 1872, at the age of forty-one, she was the mother of eleven children. The memoirs of her grand-daughter, Galina von Meck, describe the circumstances of the sudden death of her husband Karl von Meck in 1876. He died of a heart attack on learning of Nadezhda's infidelity. In the same year she developed a sublimated passion for the music of Tchaikovsky, and also for the man as she fondly imagined him. Idolized by her in long, rambling letters, Tchaikovsky, whom she was never to meet, was maintained with a handsome allowance. Indeed, the fantasies inherent in this attraction compelled on the part of both Tchaikovsky and Madame von Meck an entirely sublimated relationship which would have been disturbed by even the physical sight of one or the other of them. Though stormy at times and guilt-ridden, it was on the whole a beneficial and a beautiful relationship, of great moral as well as material support to Tchaikovsky, harassed by his homosexual nature, of great satisfaction also to Nadezhda, an agitated and restless recluse, constantly moving from one to another of her costly mansions. To the eighteen-year-old Debussy there must have been a slightly humorous aspect of this relationship. He must have wondered why the object of Nadezhda's passionate admiration was kept so completely invisible.

On her ceaseless journeys across Europe and in Russia Madame von Meck was usually attended by several of her children, together with their train of tutors and servants. During three summers from 1880 to 1882 Achille Debussy formed part of this entourage.[1] Madame von Meck's published correspondence with Tchaikovsky allows us to reconstruct the itinerary of his travels. They took him, between the ages of eighteen and twenty, far across Europe and, in the two latter years, to Russia. In July 1880 he joined the von Meck family at Interlaken. By the end of the month they had embarked on a grand tour. Achille journeyed with them across France to Arcachon

[1] It will be useful to set out the sources for our view of Debussy's experiences at this time. Those hitherto available are the two volumes of correspondence between Tchaikovsky and Madame von Meck (Moscow, 1935–6); and the manuscript memoir by Nicholas von Meck in the Tchaikovsky Museum at Klin (U.S.S.R.) published in my Debussy ('Master Musicians', 1951). Further sources used now for the first time are the recollections of Debussy's stay in Russia by Maximilian von Meck, Madame von Meck's ninth child, given to me verbally in 1935; letters from various descendants of the von Meck family placed at my disposal by the grand-children of Madame von Meck, Madame Galina von Meck and Count George Bennigsen; and a letter from Madame von Meck to Debussy of 1881 in the possession of Monsieur Marcel Dietschy.

where they stayed at the Villa Marguerite. Later they went on to Paris, Rome, and Naples. At the beginning of September they arrived at the Villa Oppenheim at Fiesole; he stayed there for several weeks, returning to Paris at the end of October.

At the beginning of July of the following year, 1881, Debussy made his first journey to Russia, meeting Madame von Meck possibly at her estate at Braïlov in the Ukraine, but more probably in Moscow. His hostess was in Moscow from the middle of July until the end of September and at least part of this time was spent with her there. During this period he also visited the estate of her daughter, the Countess Alexandra Bennigsen, living at Gourievo, near the village of Laptevo, south of Moscow. The longest journeys were, however, made in 1882. Debussy travelled to Moscow in August and joined Madame von Meck at her country house at Pleshcheyvo, near Podolsk, about thirty miles from Moscow, on 27 August. They spent the month of September in Moscow. At the beginning of October they were in Vienna, by the middle of the month they were in Paris, and again in Vienna at the beginning of November. This three-months vacation in Russia, Austria, and France, partly taken during term time, extended until the end of November. Debussy left Vienna for Paris some days before 24 November.

His relationship during these three years with Madame von Meck's large family may be approached by setting out their names and ages. In 1880 Madame von Meck's eldest children, Elisabeth and Alexandra, were respectively thirty-two and thirty. Valdemar, twenty-eight, was the eldest son. Then came Julia, twenty-seven, and Lydia, twenty-five. The two boys, Nicholas and Alexander, were nineteen and sixteen, Sonia was thirteen, Maximilian, eleven, Michael, ten, and Ludmilla, eight. Debussy's duties were extensive. He was expected to play piano duets with Nadezhda von Meck, to accompany Julia, who was an amateur singer, to give piano lessons to Sonia, theory lessons to Alexander, and to play in a trio with the violinist Ladislas Pachulsky and the cellist Peter Danilchenko.

The descriptions of the many family entanglements in Madame von Meck's letters, including difficulties of aunts and uncles, adolescent courtships and anxious business matters, belong to the Tolstoyan world of *War and Peace*. It was far from any milieu Debussy had earlier frequented. Many nineteenth-century French musicians visited Russia, among them Berlioz, Saint-Saëns, Fauré,

and d'Indy, but not in their early formative years.[1] Debussy was
there at an impressionable age, at the very time when he first
seriously devoted himself to composition. By contrast with the
heavy pessimism and ennui of a Russian household, he appeared to
the von Mecks to embody some Gallic wit. From her country house
at Pleshcheyvo Madame von Meck wrote to Tchaikovsky on
28 August 1882: 'Yesterday my favourite Achille Debussy arrived to
my great joy. Now I shall have plenty of music; and he enlivens the
whole house. He is a Parisian from tip to toe, a *gamin*, very witty and
a wonderful mimic who takes off Gounod, Ambroise Thomas, and
others most amusingly. He is so good-humoured, also satisfied with
everything and entertains all our people tremendously; a charming
nature.' In Sonia's memoirs we read: 'He was a fidgety, gay, thin
little Frenchman who greatly enlivened our solemn household.'
Nicholas records similar impressions: 'The little Frenchman arrived,
dark, thin, sarcastic and gave everyone amusing nicknames. He
called our plump tutor "petit hippopotame en vacances" and we in
turn nicknamed him "le bouillant Achille".' Other names by which
he was affectionately called were Bussik, Bussikov, and, most
endearingly, Petrouchka.

The memoirs of the von Mecks are, however, not always so well
disposed. Their fortune had only recently been acquired and sometimes an offensive, snobbish note creeps in. 'Il était comme un petit

---

[1] 'If you have nothing better to do I advise you to go to Moscow,' Debussy wrote
to Stravinsky in 1913 before leaving for Russia in that year at the invitation of Serge
Koussevitsky. 'It is a marvellous city which you probably don't know very well.' No
letters of Debussy from the time of his earlier visit to Moscow have so far been
discovered, but it is doubtful if they would contain any literary descriptions of the
places he visited. Such descriptions of his frequent journeys are never to be found in
Debussy's correspondence. He was aware that this was a talent he did not possess.
'Pour Fiumicino,' he wrote from Rome in 1886, 'je n'ai pas un assez grand talent de
description pour vous en parler savamment.' It is impossible, however, to believe that
he did not bring away strong visual impressions of Russia, and particularly of Moscow
as it must at that time have impressed a western European. In 1882, in the same year
that Debussy was at Gourievo, Eugène Ysaÿe was at the nearby town of Tula of which
he gives a wonderfully vivid account: 'Such a coming and going of dirty moujiks,
such a smell of sweat and leather. There is a buffet of attractive but most deceptive
exterior in which various dishes of suspicious composition are on show; there are
mothers anxiously guarding their daughters from the over-polite attentions of commercial travellers; there are merchants, sharp-eyed and close-fisted, in search of buyers
of stolen goods. Quite apart, as it were, a young girl with fair hair and the profile of an
angel gnaws at a sausage in a corner by the door.' On a visit to Moscow in 1904
Vincent d'Indy was impressed by 'cette ville étrangement séduisante en son vêtement
d'architectures multicolores.' The colours of the aristocratic mansions and churches
'vous plonge dans les pays de rêve que racontent certains tableaux primitifs ou certaines
tapisseries du XVe siècle où l'on voit évoluer les personnages autour de palais roses,
d'églises bleues et d'hôtelleries jaunes et vertes'.

coiffeur parisien,' notes Maximilian, who also records a flirtation with his sister Sonia, aged thirteen, in the course of which the eighteen-year-old student childishly asked her to marry him. In a romanticized and unreliable account of the Tchaikovsky–von Meck relationship, published in 1938 under the title *Beloved Friend* by Catherine Drinker Bowen and Barbara von Meck (née Karpov, widow of Valdemar von Meck's son Vladimir), this passing, adolescent flirtation was magnified into a wholly fictitious drama precipitating Achille's dismissal from the service of Madame von Meck. Apart from the fact that Sonia von Meck and Debussy were hardly more than children at this time, it was impossible for Barbara von Meck to have heard anything of this minor incident, related to me by Maximilian, since she entered the von Meck family by marriage only very much later. Absurdly distorted and sensational- ized from my casual mention of this matter in my work on Debussy which had first appeared in 1936, the account in the best-seller *Beloved Friend* has unfortunately been reproduced in many later studies, including those by Debussy's friends D. E. Inghelbrecht and René Peter, and also by Léon Vallas in the revised edition of his *Debussy et son temps.*[1]

The memoirs of Sonia von Meck describe the months they spent together in 1880 at Fiesole at the Villa Oppenheim, an enormous, forbidding mansion which had earlier been a residence of the Empress Eugénie. The family with their tutors and servants lived in complete isolation. In a room 'decorated in an Arabian style' Achille played the music of Glinka and Tchaikovsky, accompanied Julia, and gave piano and theory lessons to Alexander, to whom in 1882 he dedicated his song *Rondeau* on a poem by Alfred de Musset and with whom he long remained in correspondence.[2]

[1] 'Est-ce ce séjour de 1882', Vallas asks, 'qui se termina brusquement lorsque le fils de l'ancien boutiquier de Saint-German-en-Laye, du petit employé parisien, eut l'audace de demander à son hôtesse la main de sa charmante élève Sonia de Meck? Dans une famille russe de la noblesse [*sic*] on n'envisageait guère une alliance avec un très jeune étranger du peuple. Le petit pianiste salarié fut gentiment rappelé à la réalité sociale et l'on hâta son retour en France, au Conservatoire.' If further evidence were required to quash this fabrication it is available in a letter sent to me by Sonia von Meck's son, Georgy Korsakov, from Petropavlovsk on 28 August 1958: 'You are right to distrust the legend of a romance between Sonia von Meck and Debussy. . . . There was nothing of the kind in her relations with the French composer.' It is hardly necessary to say that there is no reference to this matter in Sonia von Meck's memoirs.

[2] Debussy's particular friend among the von Meck children, Alexander, later became a prominent figure in the Russian Alpine Society and wrote numerous accounts of

In 1881 Debussy sent Madame von Meck at her estate at Braïlov a composition for four hands ambitiously entitled 'Symphonie en si'. Later discovered in a Moscow market, bound with a number of arrangements of symphonies for four hands, it was published in Russia in 1933. It is a melodious piece in one movement opening in B minor and ending in B major, but otherwise imitative of the style of Guiraud or Delibes. The title page, however, lists three movements, *Andante*, *Air de Ballet*, and *Final*, and the plausible suggestion is made by the editor of this juvenile work, N. Gilaïev, that further sections of it remain unknown. Madame von Meck acknowledges its receipt in a letter to Debussy from Bratislav, near Braïlov, of 8/20 February 1881, the only known correspondence between them, in which Madame von Meck, an epistolary addict, surprisingly declares that letter-writing has become a forbidden pleasure. She writes:

Dear Monsieur Debussy,

Although nervous troubles have caused me to look upon the delight of writing to one's friends as a forbidden fruit, I cannot in the present case forego the pleasure of writing you these few words to tell you how much I was touched by the happy surprise you gave me by sending me your charming symphony. I am very sorry not to have you here so that you could play it for us. It would make me doubly happy, but alas, one is always a slave of someone or something and I can only place my hopes in the future, thanking you now, dear Monsieur Debussy, most cordially and wishing you all good things, particularly great progress in your fine career. Please take my most affectionate thoughts.

Nadine de Meck.

P.S. Remember me also most kindly to your dear parents. Monsieur Anfray[1] will bring you a little souvenir which I want you to use *always*, so as to remember me. It is a piece made in Moscow illustrating a Russian subject: the picture is of Vanya, the contralto part in Glinka's opera *A Life for the Tsar*. Would you believe that I have almost entirely abandoned music, partly because I am very busy here, but also because my partner

explorations in the Caucasus in the society's journal. Despite widespread efforts Debussy's correspondence with him, kept until Alexander's death in 1911 and clearly remembered by both his brother Nicholas and his son Georges, has not been traced.

[1] Possibly a tutor or an official of the railway company.

(Petrouchka) is so lacking in any appeal as a pianist that he has taken my taste for music away. My young ladies present their compliments to you.

Three months later, on 12 May 1881, Madame von Meck wrote to Tchaikovsky from Braïlov: 'My little Frenchman is very anxious to come here. I shan't have the heart to refuse him although I have a pianist, the older Pachulsky.' It is interesting to see how, in the course of her correspondence with Tchaikovsky, Madame von Meck's opinion of Debussy's character gradually softens. She is at first rather suspicious of him. 'He says he is twenty,' she says in her letter of 10 July 1880, from Interlaken, 'but looks sixteen. . . . His technique is brilliant but he lacks sensibility.' In August of the same year he is praised for his sight-reading, 'his only quality, though he has another which is that he is enchanted with your music'. Debussy and his single-minded hostess had just played together Tchaikovsky's Fourth Symphony and his orchestral Suite No. 1 with an introductory Fugue of which Debussy is reported to have said: 'Dans les fugues modernes je n'ai jamais rien vu de si beau. M. Massenet ne pourrait jamais rien faire de pareil.' On 31 October she tells Tchaikovsky that 'he wept bitterly when he left me, and I was most moved; he has a big heart and he would not have left had his masters at the Conservatoire allowed an extension of his stay'. On 24 November of the same year: 'I miss him terribly; he played me so much of your music.' Debussy had taken back with him, according to this letter, the scores of Tchaikovsky's *Maid of Orleans* and *Romeo and Juliet*.

Earlier, in September 1880, Madame von Meck had attempted to secure Tchaikovsky's approval for two early compositions of Debussy, the *Danse bohémienne* for piano, contemptuously brushed aside ('It's a very nice thing but really too short; nothing is developed and the form is bungled.'), and a Trio which has remained unpublished. The following month she sent Tchaikovsky Debussy's arrangement for piano duet of the Spanish, Italian, and Russian dances from Act III of the *Swan Lake*, requesting their publication by Jurgenson but without, as she stipulated, 'mention of the name of M. de Bussy for if Massenet got to hear of it my young man would get into trouble'. A note in the original Russian correspondence states that these arrangements were in fact published, though a copy of them has not yet been identified. We may note in the meantime the illuminating fact that Debussy's first publication consisted of an arrangement of a work of Tchaikovsky, published in Russia.

Other compositions of this early Russian period include the song *Zéphyr* on a poem by Théodore de Banville,[1] and a number of other works which have disappeared. A letter of 5 February 1936 from Anna, wife of Nicholas von Meck, in the possession of Count Bennigsen, states: 'I had many of Debussy's youthful compositions but they all perished when our house at Voskrosensky [near Moscow] was burnt.' Whatever was the nature of these pieces, it is essential to note that Debussy was already inspired by the poetry of Verlaine during his stay with Madame von Meck. The manuscript of the first version of *En Sourdine*, from the first series of the *Fêtes galantes* of 1892, bears the inscription 'Vienna, September 16, 1882'. The nervous, exacerbated sensibility of Verlaine, *à fleur de peau*, has a certain affinity with that of Tchaikovsky which would not have been lost on the young Debussy.

What was the music he played with Madame von Meck during these years and which works did he hear in the course of these long journeys? In her letter to Tchaikovsky of 29 September 1880, from Florence, Madame von Meck writes apropos of her pianist's facility in sight-reading: 'I am always playing something new or at any rate everything I play is new for him.' This, apart from numerous, specific references to works of Tchaikovsky, is about all of which we can be reasonably certain. From a desire to see the awakening of an interest on the part of Debussy at this early age in the works of 'The Five', whose reputation was later to be triumphantly established in Paris in the form of a Franco–Russian musical alliance, earlier writers eagerly ferreted in this correspondence for support of Debussy's knowledge at this time of the works of Rimsky-Korsakov, Balakirev, Borodin, César Cui, and Moussorgsky. There are none. This does not mean, of course, that the works of these composers were unknown to Debussy at this time. Two of Debussy's friends, Raymond Bonheur and Paul Vidal, mentioned his knowledge of

---

[1] This, together with the *Danse bohémienne* and the song *Rondeau*, formed part of the collection of Alexander von Meck, sold to Schott by Georges de Meck. Two other songs in this collection, *Chanson d'un fou* and *Ici-bas tous les lilas meurent*, originally published under Debussy's name, are respectively by Emile Pessard and the brothers Paul and Lucien Hillemacher.

Borodin following his journeys to Russia, and Bonheur states that he brought back 'an old opera of Rimsky-Korsakov', which could only have been *The Maid of Pskov, May Night*, or *Snow Maiden*. But the controversial subject of Debussy's knowledge of the music of 'The Five' at this period and of its influence on his style which, clearly enough, had not yet evolved, is supported, apart from the memoirs of these friends, by no first-hand evidence and it is safest to leave this matter completely open.

In his masterly study, *Debussy et ses Rapports avec la Musique Russe*, André Schaeffner, in an attempt to reconstruct Debussy's Russian background, has minutely investigated the whole history of Russian music in France from Debussy's earliest years up to the time of the completion of *Pelléas*. It was hitherto held that Debussy first became acquainted with *Boris Godounov* in 1889, a score of the work, belonging originally to Saint-Saëns, having been lent to him in this year by his friends Robert Godet and Jules de Brayer.[1] At this time, according to Godet, he appeared to be not greatly taken by it, characteristically declaring that without understanding the Russian text he was hardly inclined to make a thorough study of the score. It was thus not until 1896, according to this version, that, following the lecture-recitals in Paris of Pierre d'Alheim and Marie Olénine, Debussy became aware of Moussorgsky's genius.

We must branch out here to set out the main facts of Moussorgsky's early reputation in France. Many of Moussorgsky's songs were first heard in Paris, in French. The first Moussorgsky recital, given by Pierre d'Alheim and Marie Olénine, took place at the Théâtre d'Application, known as La Bodinière, on 10 February 1896, and consisted of a group of songs including *The Orphan* and *Darling Savishna*, both on Moussorgsky's words, and arias from *Sorotchinsky Fair*. The following week, on 27 February, the first performance was given in Paris of Moussorgsky's cycle *The Nursery*. Writing in the *Magazine International* of 1896, Francis Viélé-Griffin, who was later to publish poems by Debussy, stated: 'Moussorgsky's works,

---

[1] Organist at Chartres, composer of an opera entitled *Merlin* and a forward-looking spirit in the arts, Jules de Brayer played a small but significant role in the history of the 1890s. He introduced Renoir to Wagner at Palermo, resulting in series of drawings and portraits made of him by Renoir; and he was among the first French musicians to uphold Moussorgsky. Monsieur Schaeffner discovered that the first performance of a work of Moussorgsky in France consisted of a fragment of *Boris* played on the organ of the Trocadéro in Paris by Jules de Brayer on 7 November 1878. The first French book on Moussorgsky, by Pierre d'Alheim and published in 1896, was dedicated to Jules de Brayer.

Marguerite Wilson-Pelouze in 1875

Blanche-Adélaïde Vasnier

The von Meck family, *circa* 1875
Left to right, front row: Sonia, Alexander, Maximilian, Michael
Second row: Julia, Ludmilla (child), Nadezhda von Meck, Valdemar, Alexandra (Countess Bennigsen)
Third row: Alexander Yolshin, Karl von Meck, Elizabeth Yolshin (née von Meck), Count Paul Bennigsen
Back row: Alexander Fralovsky (Madame von Meck's brother), Nicholas

Madame von Meck's trio
Left to right: Peter Danilchenko (cellist), Ladislas Pachulsky (violinist), Debussy

particularly *Darling Savishna*, moved me with an intensity of feeling to the point of cruelty, so powerfully expressive is his music. It was an entirely new experience for me to follow his melodic phrases so closely resembling the inflection of the spoken phrase that song and language merge in them and become one.'

Impressions of Moussorgsky by several poets and writers are given in an undated publication, *Moussorgsky en France (1896–1908)* published by the Maison du Lied in Moscow. These writers include Paul Adam, Charles Morrice, Camille de Sainte-Croix, and also Mallarmé. Mallarmé 'was distressed by such heart-rending songs as *Darling Savishna* and the *Songs and Dances of Death* but admired the cycle *Sunless*'. Debussy first mentions Moussorgsky, relating the biographical facts that were then available, in a hitherto unpublished section of a letter to Ernest Chausson of 4 June 1893: 'You probably know that Moussorgsky was almost our contemporary. He was an officer who later retired with a small pension, living almost poverty-stricken in a little village. Since he was very careful about his dress and appearance he must have been fond of luxury. Consequently, if he lived almost as an exile and fled the ready pleasures of the great cities it was because of his musical calling. He died at 39 about 1880–81. [In fact he died in 1881 at the age of forty-two.] I have this information from Brayer who takes on a truly prophetic appearance when he speaks of Moussorgsky whom he places far above Wagner.' Debussy's well-known article on Moussorgsky's *The Nursery* ('No one has been able to reach the best in us more tenderly or more profoundly') was not published until 1901 in *La Revue Blanche*.

Other Russian music was heard in Paris in 1878, when gypsy music was sung by forty 'rossignols de Koursk' at the Trocadéro and when Nicholas Rubinstein conducted four concerts of Russian music, including works by Dargomizhsky, Tchaikovsky, and Rimsky-Korsakov at the World Exhibition. Interest in these new composers began to grow, and between 1878 and 1880 the *Revue et Gazette Musicale* published a long and authoritative series of articles on Russian music by César Cui, issued as *La Musique en Russie* in 1880. In the same year Bourgault-Ducoudray lectured on the new Russian composers at the Paris Conservatoire. It must be emphasized, however, that the Russian composer who was in particular favour in Paris at this time was Tchaikovsky. Between 1878 and 1884 the only orchestral work heard in Paris by a member of 'The Five' was Rimsky-Korsakov's *Sadko*, whereas Tchaikovsky during this same period was represented by his First Piano Concerto, his Fourth Symphony, his first orchestral Suite, *The Tempest, Romeo and Juliet,* and among his chamber works the Third String Quartet and the Trio. Contrary to the general belief, the music of 'The Five' was not at first readily accepted in Paris. Rimsky-Korsakov and Glazounov conducted their works and others by Moussorgsky and Borodin at the World Exhibition of 1889, but it was not until 1893, the year of the opening ceremonies of the Franco–Russian alliance, that these composers became at all well-known.[1] By this time Debussy had written his String Quartet and had almost completed *L'Après-midi d'un faune.*

From all of this we see that the Russian composer likely to have influenced Debussy at this stage was Tchaikovsky rather than Moussorgsky,[2] and particularly Tchaikovsky's Fourth Symphony and his *Romeo and Juliet.* The Fourth Symphony was first given by Edouard Colonne on 25 January 1880, with such success that two movements, the beautiful slow movement and the famous Scherzo with its remarkable *pizzicato* writing for the strings, were repeated a month later. Debussy could certainly have heard it on these occasions. In any case he played this symphony with Madame von Meck, to whom it is dedicated, at the Villa Marguerite at Arcachon in August of the same year,[3] and he played it again with Nicholas von Meck in September of the following year at the Château de Gourievo, the home of Madame von Meck's daughter, the Countess Alexandra

[1] Writing to Chausson in 1893 on the spectacular visit to Paris of a high official of the Russian Fleet, Admiral Avellan, Debussy says: 'I suppose we shall hear a lot of the Russians now because of patriotic feeling. When Admiral Avellan was here it's a pity they didn't invite him to a concert. The bard Tiersot [i.e. Julien Tiersot, the critic and historian] would certainly have said a few words of welcome.'

[2] In a letter to the critic Pierre Lalo of 23 June 1908, on the matter of a supposed affinity between *Pelléas* and *Boris Godounov,* Debussy writes: 'D'avoir mis un peu de clarté dans le débat *Boris Godounov–Pelléas et Mélisande* est un geste élégant de votre part, d'autant plus qu'un certain nombre d'imbéciles y étant intervenus, cela menaçait de prendre des proportions presque diplomatiques. Ne trouvez-vous pas qu'il serait dommage d'aller demander des exemples aux Russes—voire même à Moussorgsky, dont j'ai pu constater, dans un voyage que je fis en Russie, il y a une vingtaine d'années, que personne ne prononce le nom? Ce n'est qu'en France que j'ai commencé à le connaître—ce doit être le cas de beaucoup de Russes.'

[3] On 7 August 1880, Madame von Meck wrote to Tchaikovsky from Arcachon: 'Yesterday for the first time I had the courage to play *our* symphony with my little Frenchman. I am thus today in a terrible state of nerves. I cannot play it without a fever penetrating all the fibres of my being and for a whole day I cannot recover from the impression.'

Bennigsen. On this occasion he made a memorable journey, passing by train through Podolsk and the ancient town of Serpukhov, with its fortress and fourteenth-century cathedral, to the village of Laptevo, about eighty miles south of Moscow, and from there by carriage across the wooded hills in the direction of Ryazan to the secluded country estate of Gourievo. I do not think he could easily have forgotten these experiences of a work of Tchaikovsky with which Madame von Meck was so intimately connected. Something more than an echo of the famous Scherzo is surely to be discerned in the Scherzo of Debussy's Quartet, similarly remarkable for its *pizzicato* writing.[1] As for *Romeo and Juliet*, we cannot fail to hear something of it in *L'Après-midi d'un faune*, namely in the horn writing, voluptuously hovering between two notes in both the love scenes of Tchaikovsky's work and in the central section of *L'Après-midi d'un faune*.

Further light would surely be thrown on the Debussy–Tchaikovsky relationship at the time of Tchaikovsky's numerous visits to Paris if we had been able to solve the mystery of his not having met on any of these occasions the musician of whom Madame von Meck had so frequently written to him. Between 1883 and 1892 Tchaikovsky was in Paris no less than seven times, enjoying the growing success of his works and recording day by day in his diary details of his meetings and conversations with numerous French musicians, among them Debussy's teachers at the Conservatoire and several of his intimate friends. There were meetings with Marmontel and Ernest Guiraud, Debussy's teacher of composition with whom he had an 'intimate talk', with Bourgault-Ducoudray, the 'exalted conversation' running to Glinka and Tolstoi, with Massenet, Delibes, Gabriel Pierné, and Vincent d'Indy. He also records meetings with Debussy's particular friend, the pianist René

---

[1] In the early biography of Debussy by Louis Laloy he is said to have been greatly affected by the gypsy music heard in Moscow and the surrounding country: 'Bien plus que les compositeurs russes, ce sont les musiciens populaires du pays, surtout les tsiganes de Moscou et des environs, qui ont laissé à Debussy un souvenir durable. . . . Au jeune Français qui les écoutait avec ravissement, ils ont appris la fantaisie. . . . Sans eux, il est possible que le *Prélude à l'Après-midi d'un faune* eût chanté moins tendrement. Et le *Quatuor à cordes*, où la musique, obéissante à toute émotion, a l'abondance frémissante d'une source, leur pourrait être dédié.' Since this was written by Laloy nearly thirty years after Debussy's Russian journeys, I am inclined to think that Debussy's recollections, as they were apparently given to Laloy, were by this time somewhat confused. Apart from a recollection of a peasant chorus singing in polyphonic harmony, recorded by Vittorio Gui, we have no first-hand knowledge of the popular music he heard in Russia at this time.

Chansarel,[1] and the cellist Peter Danilchenko with whom Debussy had been associated in Madame von Meck's trio. Of particular interest is the friendship that developed over the years 1886–9 between Tchaikovsky and Gabriel Fauré. Tchaikovsky finds him 'fascinating, charming', lunching and dining with him and, together with Vincent d'Indy, discussing the musical problems of the day at the Café de la Paix. At a reception given on 7 June 1886 by the Russian patroness of music, Madame Bogomoletz, quartets by Tchaikovsky and Fauré were played by the Marsick quartet.[2]

Tchaikovsky's activities in Paris also extended to the social and literary worlds. A Mozartian, though himself almost a character from a Russian realist novel, he devours Maupassant, hears *Figaro* four times in rapid succession at the Opéra-Comique and, between bouts of heavy, solitary drinking, rushes off to the circus with his trusted brother. He visits the Princess Meshcherskaya who was associated with the production of Maeterlinck's *Pelléas et Mélisande* and who, under the name Tola Dorian, was one of the French translators of Swinburne; and he enjoys the lunches with pancakes given by Maria Pavlovna de Benardaky, who cared for nothing but champagne and love, a statuesque woman of commanding beauty, later known to Marcel Proust who remembered her and her extravagant salon in his portrayal of Odette Swann in *A l'Ombre des Jeunes Filles en fleurs*. It is interesting to see the composer of *Eugene Onegin* thus approaching the worlds of Maeterlinck and Marcel Proust, though not all his Paris adventures were so distinguished. On another level he rivalled the triumphs of Gounod and Massenet. The success of his well-known setting of Goethe, *None but the lonely heart* ('Ah qui brûla d'amour peut seul comprendre'), first sung by Pauline Viardot in the 1870s and still striking at the hearts of the new Wagnerian public twenty years later, was so widespread that it was introduced as a central theme in the novel *Le Froc* by Emile Goudeau.[3]

---

[1] On 20 January 1894, at the Société Nationale Debussy and René Chansarel performed an arrangement for piano duet of Rimsky-Korsakov's *Capriccio espagnol*. The posthumously published *Fantaisie* for piano and orchestra is dedicated to Chansarel who was to have given its first performance in 1890.

[2] Fauré's two piano quartets were inscribed to Tchaikovsky in the following terms: Quartet in C minor, Op. 15, 'A Tchaikovsky, hommage et témoignage de la plus vive admiration. Gabriel Fauré'; Quartet in G minor, Op. 45, 'Au cher Maître et ami P. Tchaikovsky, son bien affectueusement dévoué Gabriel Fauré, 15 Mars 1888.'

[3] Emile Goudeau (1849–1906), one of the founders of the cabaret Le Chat Noir at which Debussy in its youth was a pianist, was the author of popular novels of a sentimental or scandalous nature. *Le Froc* (1888) is the story of a priest driven to

It is indeed strange that the French musician who, by 1892, had certainly displayed the stuff of genius, as Tchaikovsky's friend Fauré had by this time openly declared, and who had such good cause to be remembered by Tchaikovsky, is not once mentioned in his voluminous diaries and correspondence. Could there have been some estrangement between them? We have not a clue to this mysterious silence. It is, however, just possible, as we shall see in Chapter 13, that on the occasion of a visit of Tchaikovsky to the Chat Noir Debussy may have been permitted a glimpse of the worshipped composer of Madame von Meck, kept so forbiddingly out of sight.

The Russian influence in France was many-sided, and frequent attempts have been made to identify the features of one Russian composer or another in Debussy's work. In the end they seldom offer more than personal views. These are of course valuable, but unprecise. On the technical plane, in regard to harmony or the use of the pentatonic scale, it is impossible to define this influence with certainty. Vallas, for instance, is constantly discovering an affinity with Borodin, often in the most unlikely places, basing his evidence on nothing more than Debussy's harmonies built on major seconds, which indeed occur most frequently in his work. As for Vallas's contention, repeated unceasingly in programme notes, that the indefinite, flowing theme of Debussy's *Nuages* derives note for note from Moussorgsky's song, *The noisy day has sped its flight*, in the *Sunless* cycle, this, if still likely to be upheld, can only be put down to a peculiar insensitiveness to concepts of melody that were utterly opposed.

The Russian influence was an important phenomenon not only artistically but also socially, and we shall be on safer ground in considering the Franco–Russian entente from a broad social viewpoint. An outstanding work of Debussy conceived in the 1890s is *Fêtes* with its fanfare for trumpets, heard first softly, far in the distance, and gradually magnified into a brilliant ceremonial display. Though he was normally averse to disclosing the associations of his works, or indeed the significance of their many poetic titles, he did, on this occasion, define this episode as representing 'a dazzling, fantastic procession passing through a festive scene and becoming merged into it'. The *Nocturnes*, of which *Fêtes* is the second section,

suicide by the unrequited love of a woman of the world whose heart is, however, eventually softened by a lurid interpretation of this particular song of Tchaikovsky.

passed through many stages; they were originally a triptych entitled *Scènes au crépuscule*, inspired by poems by Henri de Régnier, and as we shall see later there is a passage in these poems that clearly evokes a vision of a procession suggested by this arresting trumpet fanfare. But there is also evidence foreseeing this passage, and perhaps the whole of *Fêtes*, so exuberantly animated, as a musical vision of one of the impressive ceremonial displays held in Paris at the time of the visit of the Tsar Nicholas II, in October 1896, to seal the Franco–Russian alliance.

We have noted that three years earlier the visit of the Russian Admiral Avellan, handsomely fêted together with his squadrons of bearded sailors, did not escape Debussy's notice.[1] Social events of this kind did not leave him unmoved, particularly those of a spectacular or pictorial nature. His correspondence at this time with Pierre Louÿs contains many references to social and political events, notably the death of Bismarck and the Boer War.[2] He could not fail, therefore, to have been greatly moved by the celebrations in Paris marking the Tsar's visit which were of great pictorial appeal and of great psychological significance.

The Tsar Nicholas II and the Tsaritsa Alexandra Feodorovna landed at Cherbourg on 6 October 1896, and drove in procession to Paris from the suburban station of Ranelagh. Designed as a guarantee against renewed German aggression after the Franco–Prussian War, the Franco–Russian alliance, writes Robert Burnand, 'brought forth a display of enthusiasm from the entire nation such as had seldom been known in its history. *Enfin, nous n'étions plus seuls!* . . . The splendour of the reception far exceeded anything to be seen for long afterwards. Excited and impatient crowds had lined the streets during endless hours:

> Pour bien voir le Tsar
> Faut pas rester tard
> Dans son plumard.

[1] In 1893 a Russian squadron under the command of Admiral Avellan anchored at Toulon. In Paris, writes Robert Burnand, 'they were received as if they had brought in their arms both peace and revenge. . . . These happy sailors with their bright new berets and the officers with beards covering their whole chests—there was not a Frenchman, not a Frenchwoman, who would not have wanted to hug them.'

[2] Pierre Louÿs, who was one of Debussy's most intimate friends in the 1890s, was greatly attached to his elder brother Georges Louis, a plenipotentiary in the diplomatic service, known also to Debussy, and with whom Pierre Louÿs frequently discussed political as well as artistic affairs. Director of Political Affairs at the Foreign Ministry in 1904, he was appointed Ambassador at St. Petersburg in 1909.

When the sovereign appeared in a carriage and four driven by two postilions and preceded by a squadron of Arab chiefs on prancing horses, when the Emperor in his great fur hat bowed in acknowledgement to the crowd and the Empress lowered her white umbrella, the cry that rang out, *Vive la Russie!*, was of pride, joy and love.'

Other accounts speak of the streets decked with flowers and of 'the trumpet calls and the strident, joyous fanfares', sounded by the dragoons as another of the processions, preceded by white-cloaked Spahis and Algerian Aghas flashing their scimitars in salute, approached the Arc de Triomphe. At the inauguration during the Tsar's visit of the Pont Alexandre III barges lined with exquisite girls landed from the river to present the Tsaritsa with a huge silver vase filled with orchids, and presently the famous tragedian Paul Mounet, brother of Mounet-Sully, recited to the Tsar a poem, *Salut à l'Empereur*, written for the occasion by José-Maria de Hérédia.

It was at this very time that *Fêtes*, together with the two other sections of the *Nocturnes*, was taking its definitive form. If there is any doubt that Debussy could have been unaffected by these ceremonies it must be dispelled by the fact that Hérédia's poem contained the line, *Car le poète seul peut tutoyer les rois*, emphasizing the right of an artist, even in a republic, to share in the glories of a king.[1]

[1] We have an illuminating account of this occasion in a letter of 18 December 1916, from Pierre Louÿs to his brother Georges Louis, referring to the publication of his poem *Isthi*:

> When I received the published copies of *Isthi* I wondered who might be able to recite these lines. Only one person came to mind, Paul Mounet. I know him slightly. I wrote on the opening page of a copy: 'To P.M. in recollection of 7 October 1896, when I saw in one glance his commanding appearance and the Tsar stupefied at being *tutoyé*.' For an actor the dedication wasn't bad, but I sent him neither the poem nor the dedication. The fact is that, coming from Hérédia, but declaimed with the violence and harshness of Paul Mounet, Nicholas II had been rather startled to hear an actor fling in his face a poem of which the first verse concluded with the line, *Car le poète seul peut tutoyer les rois*. Indeed it is a splendid line, even more like Ronsard than Malherbe. And the fact that it really was recited to the Tsar in front of 500 people is a rather fine poetic anecdote.

The Tsar's visit to Paris was widely commented upon abroad. Among foreign reports quoted by *Le Temps* was one from the London *Daily Telegraph* which spoke of 'The Imperial visit consecrating the revival of France recovered from her mortal blow of 1870. Bismarck's aim to isolate France from the rest of Europe was thus not achieved.' The Republic was justified, the *Telegraph* admitted, amazingly adding at this time 'though it has shown the dangerous tendency to instability which is the vice of all democracies'.

6
Ernest Guiraud

The field open to a musician is not a miserable range of
seven notes. . . .

Marcel Proust

Debussy returned to Paris from the Villa Oppenheim at Fiesole at
the conclusion of the first of his long journeys with Madame von
Meck at the end of October 1880. We have noted the luxury of his
surroundings on this memorable journey. From the sumptuous
Villa Oppenheim he returned to his parents' wretched home, the
two attic rooms at 59bis rue Pigalle, unless by this time they had
moved to slightly larger quarters, a fourth-floor flat in the rue
Clapeyron. Sonia von Meck has described his departure from the
huge solitary mansion, standing on a hill near Fiesole and housing,
besides Madame von Meck's numerous children, suites of tutors and
servants. The floors were mosaic, the ceilings were unbelievably
ornate, and the rich soft furnishings had been left by its former
owner, the Empress Eugénie. Despite such opulence 'life there was
tedious and monotonous', she writes with characteristic ennui.
'Debussy stayed with us until late Autumn, but had eventually to
return to the Conservatoire. When it came to saying good-bye he
wept like a child.'

Two months elapsed before he enrolled as a composition student
at the Conservatoire. On 24 December 1880 he was registered in the
composition class of Ernest Guiraud. Though Guiraud is usually
held to be a minor figure, known chiefly from his associations with
Berlioz, Bizet, and Offenbach, his work is in fact known to everyone
for he is virtually the composer of the splendid *Farandole* in the

[56]

second suite of Bizet's *L'Arlésienne*.[1] An intimate friend of Bizet, he also composed the recitatives for the grand opera version of *Carmen* and, after the death of Offenbach, orchestrated *The Tales of Hoffmann*. His own music, however, is almost forgotten. Born in 1837 at New Orleans, where he spent his early youth, he cultivated in his ballet *Gretna Green* and his light operas, *Piccolino* and *La Galante Aventure*, a slender but attractive style, and in some of his orchestral works, notably the *Danse Persane*, a pleasing exotic vein. As in his orchestrations of the work of Bizet and Offenbach, he showed in these works a highly developed feeling for orchestral colour. He was the author of a treatise on instrumentation published three years after his death, in 1895, which is still worth consulting and which was the first French work of its kind to evaluate the scores of Wagner.

Debussy joined Guiraud's class in the first year of this master's appointment. His co-students were therefore not especially distinguished. They were a future conductor at the Opéra-Comique, Eugène Piffaretti, a harmony teacher, Paul Jeannin, and one Mélanie Bonis who later made a name as a rather frivolous composer. 'A sorry lot', Guiraud laments in his first report, lumping these four students together. Achille's intelligence is commended but he 'needs to be kept in check'; he has 'a strange character' and, at the beginning of his third year, in January 1883, was said to 'write music clumsily' (*écrit mal la musique*). By this time, however, Debussy had written *Nuit d'étoiles* and *Beau soir* on poems of Théodore de Banville and Paul Bourget, and the first of his Verlaine songs, *Mandoline*, and the original version of *En Sourdine*. Guiraud's eyes were later to be opened, and after Debussy's scholastic successes a warm friendship was established between master and pupil. A benevolent figure, Guiraud was an indolent composer, 'so nice, so friendly, but a little soft, a little apathetic', as he is described by Bizet. This vagueness of Guiraud was also noticed by another of his pupils, Paul Dukas. Invariably the long afternoon discussions in his master's spacious studio in the rue Pigalle were suddenly cut short as evening fell, Guiraud with a start realizing that he had almost missed an appointment. The feverish conversation was then pursued down the stairs

[1] Bizet's *Farandole* was originally a short episode of no more than sixty-eight bars. In the second *Arlésienne* suite it was developed by Guiraud into a work four times this length, becoming, in fact, an original work of Guiraud on Bizet's themes. The *Pastorale* and the *Menuet* from the same suite are also largely the work of Guiraud.

and along the pavement until the affectionate professor managed eventually to tear himself away from an interminable clasp of his pupil's hand. Like Bizet, Debussy became greatly attached to this unpractical but warm-hearted musician. They frequently dined out or enjoyed a game of billiards together, and before long Debussy found in him an eager listener to the novel theories with which he was beginning to wrestle on harmony, rhythm, and the function of the music drama.

Maurice Emmanuel saw two personalities at loggerheads in the young Debussy: the law-abiding self-disciplined student, and the independent figure of the later years, sensitive to sham and un-compromising. Closely following the rigorous Conservatoire schedule of competitive trials and examinations, he schooled himself to write academic fugues and choral settings of works by obscure poets. The fugues he was required to write were on themes of Massenet and Gounod. The choral exercises were on texts provided for the diligent Conservatoire students by the Comte de Ségur (*Printemps*, 1882), Jules Barbier (*Printemps*, 1884), and Emile Moreau (*Le Gladiateur*, 1883). In 1882 he won a second honourable mention in counterpoint and fugue, the following year the second Prix de Rome with his cantata *Le Gladiateur*, and in 1884 the coveted Grand Prix de Rome with *L'Enfant prodigue*.

Emmanuel makes it clear that these scholastic successes repre-sented a façade behind which were harboured revolutionary ideas. His account of Debussy's improvisations at the Conservatoire is usually cited as a picturesque episode, which indeed it is, but what Emmanuel meant to emphasize in his precise descriptions of these improvisations was Debussy's awareness at this time that the musical language had grown stale, that perhaps something in it had even been fouled, and that the time had come to listen to the sounds of music afresh, and not only to the sounds of music, but the sounds of the world around us, of nature and of the city too. To the mind of a musician all sounds must strike at some poetry, even, as we shall see, the buses rumbling over the cobblestones of the Faubourg Poissonnière. Writing eight years after Debussy's death, Emmanuel recalled a particular occasion when he was present at one of his improvisatory *séances*. The scene, on a spring morning of 1884, was a dingy classroom with a single window from which could be seen the blackened official emblem of the tricolour:

A dishevelled head peeped through the door, and the student who entered, soon seating himself at the piano, was already the man he was to become. At the piano we heard chromatic groanings in imitation of the buses going down the Faubourg Poissonnière, groups of consecutive fifths and octaves, sevenths which instead of being resolved in the proper way actually led to the note above or were not resolved at all; shameful 'false relations'; chords of the ninth on all degrees of the scale; chords of the eleventh and thirteenth; all the notes of the diatonic scale heard at once in fantastic arrangements; shimmering sequences of arpeggios contrasted with trills played by both hands on three notes simultaneously. For more than an hour he held us spellbound around the piano, his shock of tousled hair constantly shaking as he played. Eventually the supervisor, Ternusse, alarmed by these strange noises ringing through the corridors, burst in and brought our 'lesson' to an end. Debussy was a dangerous 'fanatic' and we were ordered to be off.

Improvisatory features were later deliberately cultivated in Debussy's work—his ideal in the orchestral *Images* was that music 'should seem not to have been written down'—and it was in the course of these improvisations, when the fingers instinctively reached out for new combinations of sound on the keyboard, that some of his novel harmonies must have been discovered.[1] However this may be, some of his harmonic experiments at the Conservatoire had not left the masters there indifferent. Théodore Dubois, a harmony professor who was also organist at the Madeleine, was said to have been so impressed by Debussy's improvisations that he determined to reproduce a certain effect in them on the Madeleine organ one Sunday during Vespers. 'Spinning out a long melody at the keyboard with a single finger,' Léon Vallas writes of this occasion, 'he played no accompaniment, but used instead the mutation stops, adding the cornet, flageolet and mixtures. By this means he embellished each of the notes with harmonics or with an illusory chord, and the strictly parallel succession of these chords thus produced an

[1] Though Debussy did not always compose at the piano, the fluid state of the harmonic language in his time was such that new chords or harmonies could, in fact, only be ascertained, if not first conceived, at the keyboard. Ravel was amazed that his pupil Vaughan Williams was working in a room in Paris containing no piano. 'Comment sans piano', he asked, 'pouvez-vous trouver des harmonies nouvelles?'

effect of consecutive thirds, fifths, and octaves, exactly as in the style of the improvisations of the young Achille Debussy.' If this actually took place as described, it would mean that Debussy had been experimenting with something in the style of the medieval *organum*, and this would thus be the first illustration of the Janus-headed character of his art, of the bridge which it was to build, notably in *Pelléas* and the songs on poems of Charles d'Orléans, between the forgotten practices of the Middle Ages and the harmonic techniques of modern times.

We must link these early keyboard explorations with a more concrete example of Debussy's harmonic concepts. About five years later, in 1889, after hearing Liszt in Rome and *Tristan* and *Meistersinger* and *Parsifal* at Bayreuth, he was to explain in detail to Guiraud an elaborate system which he had worked out of ambiguous chords the aim of which was deliberately to undermine the rigidity of the tonal system and thus, as he believed, to enlarge the range of harmonic expression. Maurice Emmanuel was again present on this occasion and, as a young man of Debussy's own age, was so impressed by the searching mind of his fellow-pupil that he immediately recorded the main features of this disturbing discussion. Emmanuel's notebook, containing this conversation between Guiraud and Debussy in the form of questions and answers, has been preserved and is an invaluable document not only in regard to Debussy's personal ideas, but as evidence of a wide harmonic instability affecting many composers at this time.[1]

In essence Debussy argued that since the octave consists of twenty-four semitones, twelve ascending and twelve descending, arbitrarily reduced to twelve to meet the requirements at the keyboard of equal temperament, any kind of scale could in practice be built without any allegiance to the basic C major scale. This need not disappear, but it should be enriched by the use of many other scales, including the whole-tone scale and what he cryptically calls the twenty-one note scale. (Giving each note the name of its enharmonic counterpart, C sharp D flat, or D sharp E flat, there are in fact twenty-one notes within the octave.) Enharmony should be used abundantly and a plea is made for a distinction between notes of the same enharmonic value, that is to say between a G flat and an F sharp. The major and minor modes are a useless convention. There should

[1] Emmanuel's notes are reproduced *in extenso* in Appendix B.

be great freedom and flexibility in the use of major and minor thirds, thus facilitating distant modulations, and evasive effects should be produced by incomplete chords in which the third is missing or other intervals are ill-defined. By thus drowning or blurring the sense of tonality (*en noyant le ton*) a wider field of expression is ensured and seemingly unrelated harmonies can be approached without awkward detours.

This manifesto on harmony, probably the first conscious renunciation of tonality in favour of an harmonic ambivalence, though Liszt's *Bagatelle sans tonalité* dates from four years earlier, is of the period of *La Damoiselle élue* and the *Cinq Poèmes de Baudelaire*. Tonality was to be submerged; it was not to disappear. And the purpose of this was to secure expression for a richer, not a shrunken, field of associations, transcending the limitations of the mechanical piano like the 'immeasurable keyboard' which Marcel Proust was later to describe, the keys of which were to touch upon myriad sensations and which Proust believed was still, even then, almost unknown.

7
The Parnassians

Le Plaisir est ma loi.
Banville

We must not imagine that the academic success in 1884 of *L'Enfant prodigue* with which Debussy gained the Prix de Rome was of any great artistic significance. It was a resounding success in the official circles of the Académie des Beaux-Arts where to this day this state prize for painting, sculpture, and music is annually awarded by the august members of the Institute, concerned to uphold the traditional artistic canons. Gounod was among the twenty-two out of twenty-eight academicians who voted in favour of the searching young composer. Debussy had deliberately produced for this occasion a work in the style of the acknowledged masters of the day, Lalo, Guiraud, and also Delibes, whose *Lakmé*, performed a few months earlier, he had found extremely pretentious. On 27 June 1884 Debussy played the piano part in the performance of this 'lyrical scene', under the cupola of the French Institute overlooking the Seine. Today only the agreeable *Air de Lia* is known of *L'Enfant prodigue*, the success of which led to a commission, apparently brushed aside, for a three-act ballet to be produced at the Eden-Théâtre.[1]

Behind this academic façade Debussy was nurturing, during these last years at the Conservatoire, ideas that sprang from very different

---

[1] The previous year, when Gounod had presided over the jury at the Beaux-Arts of writers, painters, and musicians, Debussy had won the second Prix de Rome with the cantata *Le Gladiateur*, on a poem of Emile Moreau. From an extract of this score, published in the first edition of Vallas's work, its interest would seem to be entirely academic.

sources. One of his friends studying with Guiraud, Paul Dukas, insisted that the French musical movements of his youth had left him completely indifferent. 'Il faut le poétiser', declared this musician of a philosophical turn of mind, who was at once able to relate the sensibility of Debussy to the spirit that was breaking through in contemporary poetry. To another pupil of Guiraud, Raymond Bonheur, Debussy became bound by a common interest in one of the prominent Parnassian poets. 'We soon became friends', Bonheur notes, 'for I noticed that he happened to be carrying about a volume of Banville, an unusual author for a student to be associated with at that time.' Indeed the works of Banville, a friend and a precursor of Mallarmé, were to have a decisive effect on Debussy's ideas. But before investigating this literary background, steadily being enriched during his later years at the Conservatoire, we should try to see the figures of the friends to whom he was drawn and the circles in which he moved.

Raymond Bonheur (1851–1939), who was to remain one of Debussy's close friends over a period of about twenty years, appears to have been a valuable support to him in his discovery of Banville and Mallarmé. A pupil of Emile Durand at the Conservatoire, his musical output was small and in the latter part of his life he moved chiefly in literary circles and among painters. Like Debussy, he became intimately associated with the family of Ernest Chausson and his brother-in-law, the painter Henri Lerolle, appearing with hem in a large canvas painted by Eugène Carrière. A refined mind, alive to the conflicts between religious principles and the new standards of morality in the work of his literary friends, he figures prominently in the published correspondence of Francis Jammes, Albert Samain, André Gide, and also Eugène Carrière. 'Yes I am a faun, certainly I am a faun, but a faun who will astound you', the Catholic poet Francis Jammes wrote in 1896 to Gide, taunting him for his unrelenting Protestant principles. 'You would make as good a Protestant minister as a poet . . . and as good a pagan faun as a Catholic. . . . And Bonheur belongs to the same species—one of those lepidopterists of goodness, myopic [Bonheur suffered from poor eyesight], but joyfully eyed by the faun as he flits from one happy friendship to another. He and you amount to more or less the same thing.' Jammes was obviously alluding to Debussy's setting of Mallarmé's pagan outburst, L'Après-midi d'un faune, dedicated to

Bonheur, but which was hardly acceptable in the 1890s to artists of such strong religious leanings as Jammes or Gide. Among Bonheur's works are charming settings of seven poems by Francis Jammes, one of which, *Avec les pistolets aux fontes*, was orchestrated by Debussy. The score of this work, dating from about ten years before *L'Après-midi d'un faune*, has unfortunately been lost. Bonheur also wrote the incidental music for Albert Samain's *Polyphème* and an opera, *Mavra*, which has remained unperformed. By about 1900 he appears to have become estranged from Debussy and later planned an opera, *Le Retour*, in collaboration with Gide. Part of the libretto has been published, together with their correspondence.

Sudden estrangements from his friends were to be frequent in Debussy's life. Almost alone among his early Conservatoire friends, Paul Dukas was able to maintain a relationship based on a detached but sympathetic understanding of the emotional and artistic problems with which he was wrestling. The impressions which Dukas dictated to Robert Brussel (published in *La Revue Musicale*, May 1926) are penetrating observations of Debussy's character, anticipating the difficulties that were bound to face his future biographers. 'Capable of alienating affections, he was therefore capable of cultivating them', Dukas argues; and commenting on a dictum of Sainte-Beuve, he maintained that 'since an artist liberates himself and only himself, music cannot exist independently of the man who writes it. . . . Trusting his instinct infallibly, Debussy baffled people unable to measure the intensity of his instinctive reactions.'

Even with his tolerant, philosophical outlook, however, Dukas hardly became one of Debussy's intimate friends. A much closer relationship existed with the eccentric but timid figure of Erik Satie. According to Satie's own recollections his meeting with Debussy took place much later. But I think there is reason to doubt this for they were contemporaries at the Conservatoire from 1879 to 1882. During this period Satie was in the preparatory piano class of Emile Decombes and, like Debussy, he was beginning to frequent at this time the newly established bohemian cabarets in Montmartre. The famous Chat Noir cabaret was opened in December 1881, on the boulevard Rochechouart where, according to the memoirs of Edmond Haraucourt, Debussy was one of the pianists.[1]

[1] Referring to the later establishment of the Chat Noir in the rue Victor Massé, Haraucourt writes: 'En attendant cette ère de splendeurs, nous opérions, musiciens et poètes, dans le mince boyau de la brasserie, entre deux rangées de tables et de banquettes.

Outside the Conservatoire, in the period between his Russian journeys and the award of the Prix de Rome, Debussy gave occasional piano lessons and, recommended by Gounod who had taken an avuncular interest in him, worked as an accompanist to a choral society, La Concordia, and for the singing pupils of Madame Moreau-Sainti. Added to an already crowded list of commitments, these activities indicate the slender resources available for his education. After his sojourns in great houses abroad he was now obliged to earn his living and to pay his way. He seems to have done so with zest. Withdrawn in himself in later years, he was at this early period a vigorous extrovert, fully entering into the activities of a student's carefree life, delighting in company and even conducting, at the Chat Noir, a chorus of bohemian artists and students.

Though he was to become one of the most fastidious of composers, Debussy was at this time prodigal with his gifts. During the years 1880–4 vocal, choral, and orchestral works accumulate. We are hardly able to form a clear assessment of this large juvenile production since few of his early works have been published. Of the remainder many have passed into private hands, others were left behind in Russia where, as we have seen, some of them perished, and of still others we have no trace. But from a knowledge of certain of these works and, more particularly, from the poets to whom he was attracted we can at least follow the broad lines of his early development.[1]

Running through Debussy's entire work is a delicate, sometimes a bitter ironic vein, an attraction to the world of make-believe, the harlequin world in which the love-sick clown watches and amusingly guys himself in frustration. One of his earliest extant songs, attributed to the year 1876, though it was probably written later, is set to the poem of Alfred de Musset, *Ballade à la lune* from his *Contes*

Au fond, Mme Salis, Junon blonde, trônait sur l'estrade du comptoir, ayant le piano à ses pieds. Rollinat, Fragerolle, Delmet, Marie Krysinska, Debussy, tapaient sur l'ivoire et chantaient.'

[1] In 1939 two programmes of Debussy's early unpublished songs were given, not, however, heard since. G. Jean-Aubry and *La Revue Musicale* presented the songs *Coquetterie posthume*, on a poem of Théophile Gautier, and three songs on poems of Paul Bourget, *Silence ineffable*, *Musique*, and *Regret*. At the Salle Gaveau in Paris and later in the year at the B.B.C. Claire Croiza introduced three songs on poems of Théodore de Banville, *O Floraison divine des lilas*, *Souhait*, and *Sérénade*, and a beautiful song, *Jane*, on a poem from Leconte de Lisle's *Chansons Ecossaises*. This group of poems includes *La Fille aux cheveux de lin*, the subject both of Debussy's prelude and another of his early songs, and the poems *Annie*, *Nannie*, and *Nell*, the last being the text of the well-known song of Fauré.

d'Espagne et d'Italie. This is hardly a characteristic poem of Musset, its romantic title belied by a mocking vision of the moon perched above the church steeple like the dot over an 'i':

> C'était dans la nuit brune
> Sur le clocher jauni
> La lune
> Comme un point sur un i.[1]

Something is announced in these lines of the irony of Verlaine, three of whose poems the student Debussy set in 1882, constituting the first versions of *Mandoline, En Sourdine,* and *Clair de lune.* At the same time he was attracted to one of the supreme ironists of the period, Heine, greatly admired in France at this time, whom Debussy knew in the translations of Gérard de Nerval. In 1874 appeared the *Poèmes et Légendes* by Heine, containing the famous *Lyrisches Intermezzo,* its reflections on God and love being compared by Nerval to the Song of Solomon. Debussy's orchestral score and piano duet arrangement of a work entitled *Intermezzo* (dated 21 June 1882) bear an inscription from Nerval's commentary on Canto xxxviii of Heine's work: 'The mysterious island of the spirits was vaguely outlined by shafts of moonlight; delicious sounds emanated from it, nebulous dances floated over it. The sounds became gradually sweeter and the dances whirled on more excitedly.' Debussy could not have forgotten this inscription on his score (followed in Nerval's text by the sombre vision, 'Meanwhile we, both of us, hopelessly drifted on over the vast sea') when years later he wrote his ecstatic piano piece *L'Ile joyeuse.* From the later years at the Conservatoire, too, is the song *Tragédie* on a poem of Heine, translated by Léon Valade. It must also have been at this time that Debussy became acquainted with Heine's early drama *Almansor* (which had appeared in Nerval's *Drames et Fantaisies* of Heine in 1864), providing him with the subject *Zuleima* on which he worked in Rome a few years later. In this drama, dealing with the persecution of Moors in Spain, the Moorish beauty Zuleima, converted to Christianity, is betrothed to a Christian knight. Almansor ben Abdullah, determined to win Zuleima, carries her off on his horse, but his Christian enemies overtake them and, dismounting from their horse, the couple plunge to their death in a

---

[1] The poem of a second song, apparently lost, from the same collection of Musset, *Madrid, Princesse des Espagnes,* is a satirical vision of the women of Madrid and Andalusia.

ravine. The central theme of this play is the supremacy of earthly as opposed to sacred love. In regard to a contemporary choral work, *Invocation*, on a religious text of Lamartine and written as one of the compulsory exercises at the Conservatoire in 1883, it is significant that Debussy told his friends that he was unable to identify himself with its religious sentiment.

Throughout his later years at the Conservatoire Debussy was closely following the latest literary publications. His first setting of Mallarmé, the song *Apparition*, dates from 1883, the year of the first publication of this poem. It is a youthful attempt, but we observe that no time was lost in the effort to establish in music itself the musical ideal towards which the literary minds of this time were striving. In the course of the previous year, 1882, Paul Bourget, known for his dramatic criticisms, psychological novels, and his revealing studies of Stendhal and Flaubert, published a volume of poems entitled *Les Aveux*. The style of this slender volume (divided into three sections, *Amour*, *Dilettantisme*, and *Spleen*) is charmingly sentimental and affecting. Debussy knew Bourget personally and also his beautiful mistress ('It is not that she is so beautiful', he comments, 'but that she has such a delicious manner of calling him Paul') who inspired Bourget's poems set by Debussy, *Beau soir* and *Paysage sentimental*. In all, Debussy set seven poems from *Les Aveux* of which only three (the two just mentioned and *Voici que le printemps*) have been published. Among those still in manuscript are *Musique* and *Romance d'Ariel*, the first of his many attempts to set Shakespeare. Bourget's poem for this song is based on *The Tempest* and contains the lines:

> Dans l'âme d'Ariel une musique vibre
> —O Miranda,—c'est la musique de ta voix,—
> Qui lui donne un regret du lien d'autrefois
> Et la haine de l'heure où le Duc l'a fait libre.[1]

Bourget's literary and dramatic criticisms, published between 1880 and 1882, contain many novel views on the problems of psychology and poetry in the theatre, including one of the first interpretations of Hamlet as a typical introspective character of the end of the century. Debussy was strongly drawn to this interpretation of Hamlet who might have been impersonated by Pelléas,

---

[1] The remaining two songs on poems from *Les Aveux* are *Silence ineffable* (September 1883) and *Regret* (February 1884).

Roderick Usher, or even the young Marcel Proust.[1] It was probably also from Bourget, who had travelled widely in England, that Debussy derived his interest in other English poets. Several of the poems in *Les Aveux* are headed by quotations from Shelley and Tennyson. Debussy must also have been sympathetic to Bourget's amusing *Paradoxe sur la Musique*, published in 1882, in the form of a dialogue with a musician, alarmed by the growing popularity of the concert as an institution, and by what he considered an artificial attempt on the part of the concert public to identify itself with music remote from its own experience.

At this point we may consider Debussy's relationship with Blanche-Adélaïde Vasnier (*née* Frey), the amateur singer whom he had met when accompanying the pupils of Madame Moreau-Sainti and for whom most of his songs of this period were written. We know rather less about this inspiring figure than of the women with whom he had earlier been associated, Madame Wilson-Pelouze and Nadezhda von Meck. As she appears in the portrait by Paul Baudry, Madame Vasnier was a woman of commanding presence, with reddish hair and greenish eyes. She was married to Eugène-Henry Vasnier, a respectable civil servant, clerk to the Board of Works, eleven years her senior, by whom she had two children, Marguerite and Maurice. 'Debussy asked my parents if he could come and work at our home', writes Marguerite Vasnier, 'and thenceforth he was treated as one of the family.' Debussy himself speaks of the Vasniers as 'my second family'. He was a daily visitor to their home at 28 rue de Constantinople, where most of his music of this period was written, and in the summer to their country house at Ville d'Avray. Madame Vasnier had a soprano voice of a high tessitura, which accounts for the agile high-range passages in the song *Mandoline* and in the manuscript fragment *Choeur des brises* for solo voice and chorus.[2] In association with Madame Vasnier, Debussy made his first public appearance as a composer. On 12 May 1882 a concert was given by the violinist Maurice Thieberg at the Salons Flaxland

[1] Commenting on the inability to act, characteristic of his generation, deriving from what he maintained was a nervous heredity, Bourget wrote: 'Il y a du Hamlet dans chacun de nous, de ce prince douteux, inquiet, qui raisonne au lieu de frapper, et chez qui l'événement extérieur n'est qu'un contre-coup très diminué de l'événement intérieur.' Hamlet was the answer given some years later by both Debussy and Proust in a questionnaire asking them to name their favourite dramatic character.
[2] *Le Ménestrel* wrote of Madame Vasnier: 'Her vocalizations were carried off with a perfection not often met with among professionals.'

in Paris 'graciously assisted by Madame Vasnier and M. Achille de Bussy'. Debussy accompanied Madame Vasnier in an aria of Auber and also Thieberg (possibly a student or a violinist visiting Paris from abroad) in works of Beethoven and Vieuxtemps as well as in pieces by the Polish, Moravian, and Hungarian composers, Lipinski, Ernst, and Miska Hauser. He also accompanied four pieces of his own, a *Nocturne* and *Scherzo* for violin and piano, and two songs, *Les Roses* and *Fête galante*, sung by Madame Vasnier. The latter is probably the song bearing this title on a poem of Théodore de Banville.[1]

We may gather something of the nature of this attachment from the several dedications to Madame Vasnier from Debussy:

'May you always be remembered as she who has realized the ideal of musicians and who has given delight with the poor music of one who will always be your friend and composer' (on a fragment of music written as a New Year greeting). 'Anything of any value in me is here—judge for yourself' (on the song *La Fille aux cheveux de lin*). 'To Madame Vasnier. These songs which she alone has brought to life and which will lose their enchanting grace if they are never again to come from her singing fairy lips. The eternally grateful author' (on an album of songs on poems of Verlaine and Paul Bourget).

Illuminating Debussy's literary development from another aspect are his settings of numerous works of Théodore de Banville. Banville was an important figure in the Parnassian movement who encouraged Verlaine and Mallarmé to develop their musical imagery. Assessing Debussy's choice of poems and extracts from plays of Banville, Madame Souffrin-Le Breton points out that he must have been aware of the significance of certain of Banville's literary innovations. The play of rhythms in Banville's poem *La Dernière Pensée de Weber*, known as *Nuit d'étoiles* in Debussy's setting, almost itself suggests a musical composition. The subject of *Le Triomphe de Bacchus*, an early orchestral work, is based on another

[1] The *Katalog der Musikautographen-Sammlung Louis Koch*, edited by Georg Kinsky (Stuttgart, 1953) has the following entry: 'Lied. "A Madame Vasnier. Fête Galante. Poésie de Th. de Banville. Musique Louis IXV [*sic*] avec formules 1882 p [ar] Cl. Debussy." 2 pp.' The first verse of this pastiche song opens with the line 'Voilà Sylvandre et Lycas et Myrtil'. Other songs for Madame Vasnier in this pastiche manner were a *Rondel Chinois* 'from contemporary manuscripts', and a *Chanson espagnole* for two voices, sung by Debussy and Madame Vasnier at a fancy-dress ball. An arrangement of the *Nocturne* and *Scherzo* for cello, bearing the date 14 June 1882, is listed in the *Collection André Meyer* (1961).

poem by Banville, *Le Triomphe de Bacchos à son retour des Indes*, presenting an unusual version of the myth of Dionysus. As for Debussy's setting of Banville's play *Hymnis*, we may see here, Madame Souffrin-Le Breton suggests, in one of the dialogues between Hymnis and Anacreon, a reflection of the maternal security Debussy found in his association with Madame Vasnier. 'Etre fière de ton génie', Hymnis sings of Anacreon,

> T'environner comme un enfant
> Qu'on encourage et qu'on défend.

I do not think this is looking too far. It was also in *Hymnis* that Debussy found his celebrated reply to the registrar of the Conservatoire. 'What rule do you follow?' this austere gentleman had asked. 'Mon plaisir!' the pupil shamelessly replied. Illustrating the aesthetic of the Parnassian poets breaking through into music, Debussy's words were taken from the reconciliation scene in Banville's play:

ANACREON: Hymnis!
HYMNIS: Le Plaisir est ma loi!
ANACREON: Viens ma colombe!
HYMNIS: Laisse-moi!
ANACREON: Chère Hymnis!
HYMNIS: Effeuillons des roses
    Le remède aux ennuis moroses
    C'est la volupté!
ANACREON: C'est l'amour![1]

The third play of Banville on which Debussy worked during his student years, *Diane au bois*, was carried further than either of the others and was cherished by Debussy long after *Pelléas et Mélisande* and *La Mer*. In 1909 he disclosed to his first biographer, Louis Laloy, the opinion of Guiraud to whom *Diane au bois* had been shown in its early stages. 'This is all very interesting', the good-natured master declared, 'but you must put it away for later or you will never have

---

[1] Debussy's manuscript of this scene of *Hymnis* was listed as in the possession of Arturo Toscanini in *Census of American Music Manuscripts* by Otto E. Albrecht (University of Pennsylvania Press, 1953). The entry reads: 'Ode bachique [sic], tirée d'*Hymnis*, 11p. Duet with piano accompaniment.' The text is the entire scene vii between Hymnis and Anacreon. The manuscript of Debussy's setting of the opening strophes of *Hymnis*, 'Il dort encore, une main sur la lyre', belongs to the collection of Dr. Martin Bodmer in Geneva.

the Prix de Rome.' This work was begun towards the end of Debussy's period at the Conservatoire, but does not really belong to our survey at the moment. We shall return to it in the next chapter on the Roman period, where it properly belongs.

Some writers, enlarging on Debussy's relationship with Madame Vasnier, have suggested that there was a physical relationship between them. This would be an important matter to establish, but we have no first-hand evidence of any value. There is nothing in Debussy's cordial correspondence from Rome with Monsieur Vasnier to suggest that their attachment developed to this point, though there may be some significance in the fact that the correspondence with Madame Vasnier has been either lost or destroyed. It is presumed that Debussy's several flights from Rome were made with the intention of rejoining Madame Vasnier in Paris. Here again evidence is lacking. On the other hand, an interesting letter written by Debussy from Rome to his friend Claudius Popelin does indicate, assuming that it refers to Madame Vasnier, a deepening bond. He writes in this letter: 'Need I tell you that in these two months I haven't changed in the least, that certain of my feelings have only become more acute? . . . As I've told you, I've allowed her image to sink too deeply into my every action and thought. I'm sorry to make this confession for it doesn't suggest that I've been able to follow your advice to turn away from this mad, blinding love and to rediscover our relationship of friends.'

Our picture of Debussy's attachment to this amateur singer, obviously a figure of great inspiration whose spirit he projected into the large number of works of this early period, is admittedly incomplete. Yet in view of the sensibility peculiar to the young Debussy, developed, as we have seen, by his wide but fastidiously chosen readings, he would have been incapable of repressing a free and ready response. Love for such a nature is not an idealized romantic love; it is love that is easily and constantly awakened, nourished by sensations. Leaving for Rome six months after the award of the Prix de Rome, when he was still no more than twenty-two, Debussy might have recalled Banville's *Contes pour les femmes* which had appeared in 1881. Here, in the tale entitled *Premier Amour*, we read of a realistic and wholly unsentimental outlook: '"Madame," said the poet, "you ask me at what age love begins. It never begins for being in love is part of the man himself, like being a negro or having an aquiline nose. Those who are destined to fall in love have always been in love."' In the following tale, *La Fin de la fin*, the poet describes an equally encouraging prospect: '"I have told you, Madame, that the age of falling in love never begins. Nor does it end, and for the same reason. The true lover would be a lover on a desert island."'

8

Rome

Occupez-vous un peu à faire élargir les portes de ma prison.

Letter to Eugène Vasnier

Reluctantly, on 27 January 1885, Debussy left the active literary and musical circles of Paris for the Villa Medici in Rome. At the age of twenty-three he was leaving France for the sixth time. The opportunity, in the form of a state scholarship awarded to holders of the Prix de Rome, to work peacefully in the great Renaissance villa near the Piazza di Spagna must appear ideal. In fact, few of the French composers provided with this privilege were able to benefit from it. They were often skilled and original composers yet they were required regularly to submit the works they had written, the so-called *envois de Rome*, for academic approval. Debussy's life in Rome was poisoned by these bureaucratic regulations. He may have suffered from the rupture of personal relationships, and certainly he felt uprooted from his fertile surroundings. But his correspondence of these years shows that he suffered even more from intolerable restrictions on his widening artistic outlook.

At Marseilles, on the way, he was already homesick. No sooner is he in Rome than he tells Monsieur Vasnier how much he misses his warm, understanding friendship and the family life to which he was admitted. He finds the Villa Medici, with its commanding view over Rome, a forbidding, loathsome place, and he is lost in the dark enormous room he is given, known to the scholars as 'the Etruscan Tomb', so sparsely furnished that 'one has to walk a league from one piece of furniture to another'. His good Conservatoire friends whom he rejoins in Rome, Gabriel Pierné, Paul Vidal, and Georges

Marty, he now finds stiff and conceited. Particularly distasteful, he emphasizes, is the social life in this artists' colony, with its petty rivalries, demanding, if one were to take part in it, a callous indifference which is foreign to him. His main desire, as he unburdens himself to Monsieur Vasnier on his arrival, is to return to Paris as soon as possible.[1]

Throughout the two years spent in Rome he becomes more and more oppressed by life among a colony of prize-winning artists. He is 'crushed and annihilated' by Rome, the Villa Medici is a 'prison' and the director, the painter Ernest Hébert, a paternal guide to the state scholars, is a 'jailor'. He becomes obsessed with the idea of 'escape' and although anxious to avoid censure from his benevolent mentor, who in all good faith emphasizes the many advantages open to him, he hands in his resignation after his second year, having in the meantime made no less than three flights to Paris.[2]

It was with the utmost reluctance that, under the influence of Vasnier, he brought himself during his stay to complete two works, *Zuleima* and *Printemps*, duly submitted to the Académie des Beaux-Arts and reported upon, both of them adversely. A mystery surrounds the composition of *Zuleima*, dramatizing, as we have seen, the central figure in Heine's play *Almansor*. Shortly after his arrival in Rome, on 4 June 1885, he tells Vasnier that '*Zuleima* is decidedly not for me. It's too old and fusty. The great silly lines—great only in length—bore me and my music would be stifled by them.' Later, two of the three sections were surely written for we read: 'I don't say that I shan't return to it, but the first two sections will have to be very much revised.' The following year, on 19 October, he writes emphatically that '*Zuleima* is dead and I shall certainly not be the one to bring her to life again. It's not the kind of music I wish to write. . . . It's too much like Verdi and Meyerbeer.'

[1] Wide intervals separate the twelve letters to Monsieur Vasnier partially published in *La Revue Musicale* (May 1926). Their dates are, in 1885, the end of January (two), 4 June, August, 16 September, 24 November; and in 1886, 29 January, 5 May, 19 October, and 30 December. Two letters of 1886 are undated. Other published correspondence of Debussy from Rome consists of a letter to the artist and enameller, Claudius Popelin, of 24 June 1885, published in *La Revue des deux mondes* (15 May 1938), and substantial fragments of letters to Emile Baron, a bookseller in the rue de Rome in Paris, written between 6 November 1886 and 9 February 1887, published in *La Revue Musicale* (January 1934).
[2] The first was in April 1885, the second at the beginning of July in the same year, and the third at the end of the winter 1885-6. The statutory regulations require scholars to remain at the Villa Medici for three years. Debussy finally left at the beginning of his third year, shortly after 9 February 1887.

This can only mean that this work, probably resulting from his earlier attraction to Heine's *Intermezzo*, had been unwillingly completed and despatched to Paris since two months later, on 31 December 1886, the Academy published their opinion of it in the *Journal Officiel*, their first report on Debussy's work in Rome. Amazingly, this vocal work, said by the composer to be in the styles of Italian and French grand opera, is declared to be 'bizarre, incomprehensible, and unperformable'.

Sketches for a setting of Flaubert's *Salammbô* were written in 1886, and the following year *Printemps* was produced, a work for orchestra and small choir singing with closed lips. Written hurriedly shortly before the final departure from the Villa Medici in February 1887, it was conceived as 'a work in a very special colour, covering a great range of feelings', its subject being 'the slow miserable birth of Nature, a gradual blossoming and finally the joy of being born into a new life'. Despite this momentary enthusiasm, Debussy apparently set no store by this work since he allowed it to be forgotten until the end of his life, its first performance taking place as late as 1913 in a re-orchestrated version made from the piano duet score by Henri Büsser. It must have been the frequent use of chords of the ninth that caused the Academy unaccountably to condemn 'its vague impressionism, one of the most dangerous enemies of works of art'. Before leaving these two works we may note that the Academy's report on *Printemps* was based on the piano score only, the full score, it was stated, having been destroyed in a fire at the binders. As for *Zuleima*, the entire music of this work has completely disappeared. With our knowledge of Debussy's opinion of these works at the time and his disdain for officialdom, it is impossible not to suspect his deliberate destruction of them.

His stay in Rome was not, however, entirely wasted. The work in which he placed his greatest hope was his setting of Théodore de Banville's play, *Diane au bois*. He worked on this score, representing the main exploration of his early youth along the borderlands of poetry and music, throughout the major part of his stay in Rome, from his arrival at the beginning of 1885 until four months before his departure. Though unfinished, the manuscript reveals the origin of features of Debussy's style in works from the *Poèmes de Baudelaire* and *L'Après-midi d'un faune* onwards.

The subject of Banville's comedy, derived from Ovid's

Metamorphoses, is the conquest by Eros of Diana who, though loving Endymion, had expelled one of her nymphs for having broken the vow of chastity. As a punishment she is made to suffer the true pangs of love and, in the final scene of seduction, succumbs to Eros who appears in Endymion's guise. Debussy's novel approach to this subject is described in highly significant passages in his correspondence with Vasnier. 'I don't think I shall ever be able to confine my music within too strict a mould', he writes, contrasting the subjects of Heine and Banville, on 4 June 1885. 'I am not referring to musical forms; this is a literary question. I shall always prefer a subject where, in some way, dramatic action is sacrificed to a wide range of inner feelings. It seems to me that in this way music becomes more human, more true to life and its expressive power becomes deeper and more subtle.'[1] Later he hopes to characterize Diana by a musical idea 'of a beautiful coldness', and explains that as she gradually gives way to love this idea 'must undergo transformations and yet retain its shape'. The problem was perplexing. 'One day I think I've found what I want; the next I fear I'm mistaken.' He confesses that he 'has never been so disturbed'. Large cuts must be made in the play to enable the 'thousand feelings' of the characters to be conveyed 'as precisely as possible'. In the end one scene was written 'but it is not at all in shape and I am very little pleased with it'. With remarkable self-knowledge he writes in a letter of 19 October 1886: 'I had undertaken a task which was perhaps beyond my powers. It has no precedent and I am obliged to invent new forms. Wagner could be of use to me, but I needn't tell you how absurd it would be even to try. I could use his system in the transitions from one scene to another, but I should want to keep the line lyrical and not allow it to be absorbed by the orchestra.' Debussy's knowledge of Wagner at this time must have been limited to a performance of *Lohengrin*, heard in Rome, and to the vocal scores of *Tannhäuser* and *Tristan*, yet this judgement clearly anticipates the Wagnerian impact shortly to be made on deeper levels of his sensibility.

The manuscript of twenty-nine pages, for soprano, tenor, and

[1] The original French text of this passage, beautifully expressed, deserves reproduction: 'J'aimerai toujours mieux une chose où, en quelque sorte, l'action sera sacrifiée à l'expression longuement poursuivie des sentiments de l'âme. Il me semble que là, la musique peut se faire plus humaine, plus vécue, que l'on peut creuser et raffiner les moyens d'expression.'

piano accompaniment set out on three staves, is a setting of parts of scenes iii and iv of the second act leading to the seduction of Diana. It has imperfections, principally in some of the modulations and part-writing, but the intentions are clear enough. The harmony is boldly chromatic, the texture is admirably clear, with contrasted contrapuntal designs between the voice parts and the bass or an inner instrumental part. Evocative rhythmic calls were probably foreseen for horns or woodwinds, and there is a profusion of trills and delicate arpeggios. The harmonic scheme rejects a unifying tonality. The scene opens in C sharp minor, soon leading to C sharp major. The following sections alternate between D major, B flat minor, C sharp minor, and E major. The concluding duet is in G flat major. Two main motives are associated with Eros and Diana. The writing for the voices is supple, following the poetic prosody. The main flaw is the formal duet at the end, a piece of great lyrical charm but in a surprisingly conventional manner.

Debussy's ideas in this experimental score were enmeshed with those of Banville. In her study of Debussy's knowledge of this poet, Madame Souffrin-Le Breton describes the action of *Diane au bois* as taking place as in a dream, 'a blurred landscape after the manner of Verlaine'. At one point Banville requires the stage to be 'entirely in shadows'. The moon rises over the forests and lakes of a scene of Watteau, and the air is filled 'with an ambrosian perfume'. The characters communicate with each other 'in magic words'. Something of the character of the Forest of Arden in *As You Like It* was in Banville's mind and it is significant that during his stay in Rome Debussy was strongly attracted to this play of Shakespeare and contemplated setting a version of it. In *Diane au bois* the images of poetry and music were already intercrossed. Debussy's imagination was nourished by poetic images, but Banville resorts to music to portray his characters.[1] Eros catches a distant horn call or idles away his time, playing rippling figures on the flute of Silenus:

---

[1] Anticipating the symbolist aesthetic of Mallarmé, Banville, as early as 1872, stated that 'music must necessarily and inevitably return to its function in Greece and the ancient civilizations of the Orient where it was the twin sister of poetry'. In the seduction scene in *Diane au bois* music plays a predominant rôle:

> Silène, heureux magicien
> Assembla ces roseaux selon son art ancien.
> La Nymphe que les bois nomment avec mystère
> Accourra par l'effet d'un charme involontaire
> Au son de cette flûte. Eveillons ses accords.

From another viewpoint Banville's play was a sophisticated modern comedy. Seduced by Eros, Diana lifts up her gaze to the stars in the heavens and sees each one of them twinkling at her defeat. But she is not to be humiliated. Since she is a goddess, she argues, she has eternity in which to repent. The setting is alive to Banville's irony:

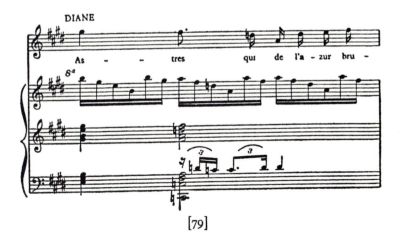

Gabrielle Dupont in August 1893 at the home of Pierre Louÿs.
Photo by Louÿs

Draped studies of Gabrielle
Dupont taken in August 1893
by Pierre Louÿs

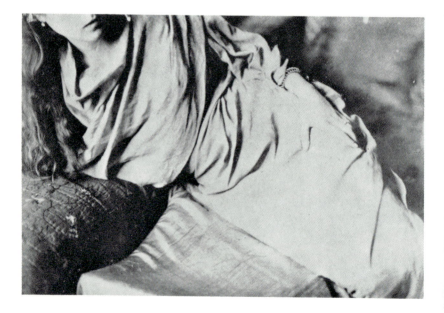

- lleurs.   é-tei-gnez-vous

ᴍuch of *Diane au bois* was written away from the Villa Medici, at the country home of Count Giuseppe Primoli at Fiumicino, a bathing resort near Rome at the mouth of the Tiber. In the summer of 1885 Debussy spent several weeks there in solitude, the Count, absent in Paris, having placed his house at his young friend's disposal. It was delightfully furnished, Debussy reports, 'like the English cottages described by Bourget. . . . I was able fully to satisfy my primitive instincts, talking to no one except at meal times (which was trouble enough), walking and working almost satisfactorily.'

The son of Charlotte Bonaparte and brought up at the Tuileries in Paris, in the circle of the Empress Eugénie, Count Primoli was a patron of the arts well known for his hospitality. He was a most sympathetic friend to Debussy in Rome. Anxious to promote Franco-Italian artistic relations, he later introduced d'Annunzio to Paris and opened the way to the triumph of Eleanora Duse. Perhaps it was not a coincidence that at the time of the composition of *Diane au bois*, with its sophisticated Watteau-like scenes, Debussy should have been associated with this generous patron who possessed the largest private collection of the works of Watteau, numbering at his death in 1927 over two hundred.[1]

At least as significant as Debussy's association in Rome with Primoli was his meeting with Liszt. Their meeting must have taken

[1] Though welcomed almost as a Frenchman in the circles of Alphonse Daudet, the Goncourts, and others, Primoli sometimes surprised his French friends by his directness of approach, such as the gift to a friend of a cast of the beautiful breast of his great-aunt Pauline Borghese. 'Charmante Italie', comments Fernand Gregh, 'si férue du beau qu'un Bonaparte y peut apporter en cadeau à une amie le sein de sa grande tante!'

place in Rome in November 1885. In the last year of his life Liszt took a benevolent interest in the young French composers at the Villa Medici. Pierné improvised with him on two pianos, and Vidal and Debussy played to him the *Valses romantiques* for two pianos by Chabrier. This must have been something of a revelation to the aged composer for I have discovered no record of Liszt, who missed none of the works of the forward-looking musical minds of his day, having previously been acquainted with Chabrier's original piano music. However this may be, Debussy certainly owed a musical revelation to Liszt, perhaps the most memorable impression made on him in Rome. Writing of his friendship in Rome with Liszt, Vidal states: 'The most interesting religious music I heard was at S. Maria Maggiore and S. Maria dell' Anima which I visited on the advice of Liszt.' It is clear that Debussy's visit to S. Maria dell' Anima, the church of the German Catholics in Rome, where he heard, probably for the first time, the music of the Renaissance composers Palestrina and Orlando di Lasso, must also have been made at Liszt's suggestion. It is entirely in keeping, moreover, with Liszt's adventurous outlook that, as his last act of encouragement to the younger musicians of his time, he should have opened Debussy's eyes to Renaissance music. On 24 November 1885 Debussy wrote to Vasnier:

I must tell you of the single time I went out this month. I went to hear two masses, one of Palestrina, the other of Orlando di Lasso at a church called S. Maria dell' Anima. I don't know if you know it—it is hidden away in a maze of awful little streets. I like it very much as it is very simple and pure in style, unlike so many of the others filled with sculptures, pictures and mosaics all so theatrical. The statue of Christ in these churches looks like a lost skeleton sorrowfully wondering how it came to be placed there. The Anima is the only place to hear such music, which is the only church music I can allow. That of Gounod and company seems to me to derive from an hysterical mysticism and produces the effect of a sinister farce.

The two above-named people are masters, especially Orlando who is more decorative and more human than Palestrina. The effects they produce entirely from their great knowledge of counterpoint are tremendous feats. You probably are not aware that counterpoint is the most forbidding thing in music. In their

[82]

work, however, it is wonderful for it is made to underline the significance of the words of which it brings out incredible depths; and sometimes there are winding melodic lines that recall illuminated manuscripts and ancient missals.

Nowhere in Debussy's correspondence from Rome does he speak so enthusiastically. This introduction to the music of the Renaissance 'was the only time', he concludes, 'when *le monsieur à sensations musicales* came to life in me again'. It is interesting to see the young agnostic musician thus inspired, through the agency of Liszt, by the sacred music of these as yet hardly known Renaissance composers.

Liszt, with 'his shock of hair like a willow tree', as Banville remembered him in his later years, also played to Debussy, though what he played we are not told. He might conceivably have played some of his late piano compositions, the impressionist *Nuages gris*, the *Bagatelle sans tonalité*, or *La Lugubre Gondola*, though it is unlikely or Debussy would have recalled these startling revolutionary pieces in his later comments on Liszt. Debussy, writing years later, merely says of Liszt's playing in Rome that he used the pedal sparingly, 'as a form of breathing', in the manner, as he remembered having been told by Madame Mauté, that Chopin used the pedal. There were, of course, many musical matters on which Liszt and Debussy may have agreed. In 1879 Liszt made an arrangement of Tchaikovsky's *Eugène Onegin*, followed the next year by Debussy's arrangements from the *Swan Lake*. Liszt's knowledge of Russian music in the last years of his life was immense, much more extensive than that of the young Debussy, and he believed in its future. Yet there was also a fundamental divergence between them. Liszt was a Byronic figure stimulated by the outside world. Quoting *Childe Harold*, he wrote on the score of one of his piano works: 'I live not in myself but I become portion of that around me.' However much a product of his time, Debussy suspected the march of events by which an artist is submerged. 'The ideal is to remain unique, without a blemish', declares Monsieur Croche, the imaginary interlocutor of Debussy's critical essays. 'The period acclaim of an artist tends to spoil him for he is likely to become merely the expression of his period.'[1]

[1] The account given by André de Ternant of Debussy's meeting with Liszt in Rome, widely reproduced, as also Ternant's accounts of supposed meetings with Brahms and other musicians, has no foundation. The hoaxes of André de Ternant are dealt with in Appendix C.

Though little was achieved and though he was constantly planning to return to Paris, Debussy hardly wasted his time in Rome. The letters to the bookseller Emile Baron contain orders for the latest publications in Paris and, judging by the long lists he sends, he must have read voraciously. Among the authors probably new to him are Huysmans, of whose *Croquis Parisiens* he orders a de luxe edition, and Jean Moréas, of whom he reads *Les Cantilènes* and the famous *Le Thé chez Miranda*. Rosicrucian literature is represented by Albert Jounet's *Rose-Croix*, and there is evidence that he was impressed by the first French translation, by Félix Rabbe, of the complete works of Shelley.[1]

His outlook was surely widened by these Paris publications, but after the abandonment of *Diane au bois* his stay at the Villa Medici seemed more pointless than ever. He now finds Rome insufferable. It is 'positively ugly—a town of marble, fleas and boredom'. Urged to visit the museums, he insists that he 'is not in the right frame of mind', though out of Rome, at Orvieto, he is enormously impressed by Signorelli's *Resurrection of the Dead*. If he visits the Sistine Chapel it will be 'as a man dragged to the scaffold'. Glimpses of the Roman scene slipped into his letters are enlivened by sardonic humour. Watching from his window the priests in black and red robes winding their way in processions through the streets, they seem to him 'like black radishes and roguish pimentos'. The perpetual blue sky is monotonous, and so is the terracotta colour of the ruins. Thank goodness, he says, for a snowfall, covering up their hard outlines.

He perpetually shuns his fellow prize-winners who accuse him 'of having picked up some philosophy in the *brasseries* of the Boulevard St. Michel'. He guys in his letters the pontificating director, Hébert, 'who lifts his eyes to heaven whenever he speaks of Michelangelo or Raphael'. In order to ensure that he shall not attend receptions to visiting notabilities he declares that he was obliged to sell his evening clothes. Probably he visited the opera for he inveighs also against 'operatic cavatinas and pantalooneries'.

Behind the invective and caricature an ideal is buried that he is

[1] Volume I of this translation appeared in 1886 and volumes II and III in 1887. This was not a highly accomplished translation, but it was an important addition to the French translations of nineteenth-century English poets then becoming widely appreciated. In his study *Shelley et la France*, Henri Peyre gives an interesting account of the early French enthusiasts of Shelley, all of them known to Debussy, some of them intimately. Debussy's knowledge of Shelley is discussed in Chapter 13 in relation to his interest in Keats and Goethe.

gradually able to define. Responding to Wagner and the music of the Renaissance, he keeps before him a vision of music that should be 'supple and adaptable to fantasies and dreams'. 'Que ton vers soit la bonne aventure', came the call from Verlaine, 'Et tout le reste est littérature'. Music had not yet set out on its adventure. 'A dissonant chord would almost cause a revolution!' Debussy exclaims. The crisis was inevitable. He is determined to return to Paris if only 'to see the pictures of Manet and hear Offenbach'. He can no longer wait for 'the moment of deliverance' and in February 1887, after the hasty completion of *Printemps*, he handed in his resignation and left for Paris for the last time. According to Count Primoli one of his flights, possibly the last, was engineered by a threat of suicide. He impressed upon Vasnier that he could 'no longer drag out this monotonous, easy life'. In Rome he 'would come to nothing'; his 'mind was dead'. He broke with the Villa Medici and was shortly to break with the Academy in Paris.

PART II

Maturity
1888-1902

9
Bayreuth

'Komm! . . . Es ist billig!'

With Debussy's return to Paris in February 1887 we enter upon a
period hitherto obscure, but which can now to a large extent be
illuminated. He lived at the home of his parents at 27 rue de Berlin,
though an unpublished letter of about 1888 suggests that for some
time he stayed at 76 Boulevard Malesherbes at the home of Etienne
Dupin, a wealthy financier and patron of music who was later to be
mysteriously assassinated in Mexico. He returned without any means
of support, with no support in view, and to make matters worse on
12 April 1887, barely two months after he was back, Manuel
Debussy was abruptly dismissed from his post at the Compagnie de
Fives-Lille. The family was clearly relying on Achille's success. So
much we may deduce from the conventional character of two large-
scale works, the *Fantaisie* for piano and orchestra and the opera
Rodrigue et Chimène, the latter written under parental pressure, and
also from a letter of five years later, dated February 1893, to Prince
André Poniatowski, a French-born diplomat and industrialist of
Polish origin who provided him with material support. Debussy says
here: 'My family has been affected by several regrettable matters in
which I couldn't help being involved. They find me far too un-
productive, at any rate in regard to the glory they expect to be
reflected on them, and they have consequently opened a pin-
pricking offensive against me, partly for sentimental reasons and
partly from anger. They are aware that the castles in Spain they had
built out of my prospects have come to nothing!'

[89]

In the meantime, with the support of Etienne Dupin, two journeys had been made to Bayreuth. In 1888 Debussy heard *Parsifal* and *Meistersinger* at Bayreuth, and in the following year these operas again and also *Tristan*. These form part of a series of Wagner operas which he heard in Bayreuth and Paris over a period of six years, from 1887 to 1893, culminating in a performance of extracts of *Das Rheingold* at the Opéra, the first introduction of this opera in Paris, in which Debussy himself took part, followed by the first French performance of *Die Walküre*. We may best judge the important impact of the Wagner operas at this still impressionable period by setting out the performances which Debussy attended:

3 May 1887	*Lohengrin*, Eden-Théâtre, Paris, conducted by Charles Lamoureux.
Summer, 1888	*Parsifal* and *Meistersinger*, at Bayreuth.
Summer, 1889	*Parsifal*, *Meistersinger*, and *Tristan* at Bayreuth.
22 March 1893	*Lohengrin*, Paris Opéra.
6 May 1893	*Das Rheingold*, Paris Opéra. (Extracts performed in concert form with Debussy and Raoul Pugno at two pianos.)
12 May 1893	*Die Walküre*, Paris Opéra.

The gap of four years between Debussy's second visit to Bayreuth and the performance of *Lohengrin* in 1893 does not mean that during this interval there was no further opportunity to become acquainted with Wagner's works. This was the period when the Wagnerian fever in Paris was at its height, important Wagnerian extracts being regularly given at the Paris symphony concerts, chiefly under the direction of Charles Lamoureux and Jules Pasdeloup.[1]

We see from this table that Debussy was closely associated with the fervent Wagnerian movement in France from its inception. The notorious *Tannhäuser* scandal at the Opéra occurred in 1861, the year before his birth, but the first Paris performance of *Lohengrin*, in 1887, was hardly less of a fiasco. A few days before the performance France and Germany had been on the brink of war on

---

[1] Robert Burnand in *La Vie Quotidienne en France* notes: 'At the conclusion of the Wagnerian excerpt at the Pasdeloup concerts Debussy would conspicuously stand up and leave the hall before the Beethoven symphony with which the concert usually concluded.'

account of the Schnaebelé incident, a trumped-up charge against a French official arrested in Germany as a spy, with the result that there were hostile demonstrations against Wagner and the production was hastily withdrawn. Six years later the introduction in Paris of *Rheingold* took a quaint form, again hardly calculated to advance Wagner's interests. On a sunny spring afternoon Catulle Mendès, a pretentious literary figure, poet, journalist, and librettist, gave a lecture on this work at the dark, cavernous Opéra, preceded by his recollections of the *Tannhäuser* scandal and including an analysis of the entire *Ring*. Mendès, seated at a table on the covered orchestral pit, read his script under a green lampshade. Debussy and Raoul Pugno, a well-known piano virtuoso, were at his side at two grand pianos together with the six soloists who had entered arm in arm. Behind him, inappropriately enough, was the scene of the bridal chamber of *Lohengrin*. Debussy and Pugno played the Prelude, the single, prolonged E flat major chord of which it consists surely having sounded very odd in this form, and accompanied the six soloists in extracts. Debussy's comments on this truncated version, in a letter to Chausson of 21 May 1893, were scathing:

I'm rid of the *Rheingold*. This is a nuisance so far as the gold is concerned, but it is good to have done with the Rhine. The performance was a terrible bore. Catulle Mendès spoke on the *Walküre* in such a way that the mothers who had naïvely brought their daughters were frightened away by the wicked priest's fiery words. The month of May, it appears, is henceforth to be the month of the *Walküre*, for some simple-minded people believe that this work announces the spring of a new music and the death of the old worn-out formulae. It's not what I think, but that doesn't seem to matter.

We must beware of reading too much into the sarcastic tone of these remarks. Debussy's anti-Wagnerism was to some extent a pose, designed to conceal both his admiration and his fear of Wagner. There is no evidence that Wagner's huge, sensuous philosophy left him indifferent. Very strong feelings were aroused. He is 'the old poisoner', the 'ghost of old Klingsor', language which indicates an obsession with a nature fundamentally too similar, and also too ruthless, to be ignored.

We have unfortunately no first-hand evidence of Debussy's impressions of the Bayreuth performances. Nowadays when there is an unending series of festivals in towns and villages all over Europe we have some difficulty in reconstructing the religious conception of a pilgrimage associated with the Bayreuth festivals. The journey was undertaken precisely in this sanctified spirit, particularly by the numerous French visitors for whom the music of Wagner, especially after *Parsifal*, filled the new religious need. Not all the French musicians, however, who flocked to the Bayreuth temple submitted to the spell. At the first Bayreuth performance of *Parsifal*, in 1882, the disciples from Paris included Ernest Chausson, Jules de Brayer, who later introduced Renoir to Wagner,[1] Catulle Mendès, his ex-wife Judith Gautier, and Vincent d'Indy. Rather unexpectedly, the French contingent at the first performance of *Parsifal* also included Léo Delibes, who scandalized d'Indy by his unforgivable irreverence.[2]

In 1888, the year of Debussy's first Bayreuth pilgrimage, a French lawyer, Emile de Saint-Auban, one of the faithful, but seemingly also a Daumier character, shrewdly observant at the cosmopolitan shrine, gives an ironic picture of the extravagance of the Wagnerian cult:

The sight of the station, on arriving at Bayreuth, was most odd. Such a mass of people were waiting, excitedly walking about or rushing forward, waving handkerchiefs, it was like a crowd at a harbour greeting the arrival of the steamer. I stepped down on to the platform.

---

[1] Three years earlier, in 1879, Brayer had published the first French translation of *Parsifal, Essai de traduction analytique sur le Parsifal, pièce d'inauguration théâtrale*. The meeting at Palermo in 1882 between Renoir and Wagner, arranged by Brayer and resulting in the several portraits of Wagner by Renoir, is the subject of an exhaustive study by Willi Schuh, *Renoir und Wagner* (Zurich, 1959). It was on this occasion that Renoir wrote in a letter to an unnamed friend a long and picturesque description of his meeting with Wagner, in the course of which he says, 'Nous avons parlé des Impressionistes de la musique.' One wonders of whom Renoir could have spoken to Wagner as a musical Impressionist. Surely not of Debussy, known neither to Renoir nor to Brayer at this time. Possibly he attempted to describe to Wagner the work of Fauré, Duparc, Chabrier, or Chausson.

[2] 'Asked for his opinion of *Parsifal*', d'Indy writes, 'Delibes declared that he adored the second act "parce qu'il y avait des petites femmes, et que, les petites femmes c'est toujours amusant."' Shocked by this confession, d'Indy adds, with puritanic contempt: 'Thus the composer of *L'Omelette à la follembuche* dared to speak of the *Blümenmädchen*!' *L'Omelette à la follembuche* is a one-act operatic farce by Delibes given at the Théâtre des Bouffes-Parisiens in 1859.

'*Komm, mein Herr!*'

Who is this soprano piping these words into my ear? I turn round, and a delicate little hand catches hold of my arm. Is this charming damsel a customs official? I am not aware of having done anything illegal, to be set upon in this way.

'*Komm! . . . Es ist billig.*'

Well, it can't be the customs. But surely I have read something of this sort in *Parsifal* with the difference that the Pure Fool is assured that his experience will cost him nothing at all! Can it be, by any chance, that the Flower Maidens scene is to be enacted on the station platform? My Flower Maiden, however, with her skinny figure and her hair neatly plaited round her temples, is hardly a rose.

'*Komm! Es ist billig!*'

What, another!

'*Komm!*'

A third?

'*Komm mein Herr!*' suddenly growls a deep bass.

Upon my word, this must be Klingsor! At last it all becomes clear. We are being offered rooms. It is not a competition of Flower Maidens, it is a competition of hotel keepers, which is much more to the point. Since, then, we are to be put up and not seduced let us make a choice. Klingsor is a pleasant enough fellow. I decide for him and I stay in the Rue Richard Wagner.

Pictures of the master, this witty Wagnerian goes on to tell us, are everywhere, in everything, on everything. Curtains display images of Lohengrin and the swan. *Leitmotive* are embroidered on shirt fronts, on the cambric of handkerchiefs. The 'Theme of the Last Supper' is embroidered in red and gold silk against a blue background on a dressing-gown. The festival theatre at Bayreuth is lit by gas. Despite the formalities of the sacred occasion, the orchestral musicians are in shirtsleeves, their jackets rolled up on the floor, and within hand's reach are pint tankards: 'Their fawn-coloured brown sparkles in the candle light with metallic reflections and mingles with flashes from the nearby brass instruments in the intimacy of things destined for one and the same aim.'

The lists of French visitors to Bayreuth from 1876 to 1896, established by Debussy's teacher at the Conservatoire Albert Lavignac, form a fascinating document. At *The Ring* in 1876 Ernest Guiraud, Debussy's composition teacher, was present with Madame Wilson-Pelouze, Catulle Mendès, and Saint-Saëns. *Parsifal* and *Tristan* in 1886 were attended by Debussy's friends, Raymond Bonheur, Paul Bourget, and Paul Dukas, as well as by Massenet and Messager. Not only musicians but writers and painters were prominent visitors. Pierre Louÿs and Maurice Barrès were present at *Parsifal*, *Tristan*, and *Tannhäuser* in 1891, and in 1896 Colette heard *The Ring* at Bayreuth as did Renoir and Rolland. Lists of English visitors, if ever they could be compiled, would be equally illuminating. Both George Moore and Bernard Shaw were deeply moved by *Parsifal* at Bayreuth, the latter in 1889 when Debussy was also there. Delius was at Bayreuth in 1894, apparently in the same year as Walter Crane, who made a charming drawing of the Wagnerian devotees. Swinburne heard Wagner at Munich. Among the Bayreuth visitors in later years, Stravinsky was intolerably bored by *Parsifal*, presumably his only acquaintance with this work.

Visitors in 1888, the year Debussy made the journey to hear *Parsifal* and *Meistersinger*, included Hugo Wolf and the twenty-eight-year-old Gustav Mahler. They were of course not known to Debussy, but it is interesting to reflect that both Wolf and Debussy were able to absorb the Wagnerian force, whereas Mahler, despite his thorough knowledge of Wagner, which even at this early age he had acquired as a conductor of his works, appears by contrast to have been reluctant to receive Wagner's shattering influence.[1] Hans Richter and Felix Mottl were the conductors of *Parsifal* and *Meistersinger*, Parsifal was sung by Ernest van Dyck and Walter by Heinrich Gudehus. The production of *Parsifal*, with its wonderful transformation scenes, was said by the French visitors to be deeply enchanting, except for the Flower Maidens scene, the monstrous blooms of which, in harsh, brutal tones, reminded Lavignac of provincial hotel decorations in the worst possible taste. In the following year Debussy heard these operas again at Bayreuth, and also

---

[1] In 1887 Mahler, at the age of twenty-seven, deputized for Nikisch as conductor of *The Ring*. In his searching study, *Mahler: The Early Years*, Donald Mitchell writes convincingly of Wagner's influence on Mahler's early works, *Das Klagende Lied*, *Des Knaben Wunderhorn*, and the first three symphonies. Yet in Paris, the stronghold of Wagnerism, where, between 1900 and 1910, there had been several opportunities of hearing Mahler's works, his admirers could find no trace of Wagner. When his Second Symphony was performed there in 1910 Alfredo Casella, his boldest champion in Paris, declared that 'it was a work written as if Wagner had never existed'.

Tristan, in which the principal parts were sung by Heinrich Vogl and Rosa Sucher.[1]

Of all the works of Wagner relished by Debussy *Parsifal* had the deepest influence, and it was to remain the work to which he responded more and more acutely until the end of his life. It is possible that at this stage of his development he was hardly equipped to assimilate the entire force of Wagner's allegory with its complex psychological symbols of the spear, the Grail, and the wound. A lifetime's experience is indeed necessary to come to terms with the struggle between the spirit and the impulse, so powerfully expressed in *Parsifal*, by comparison with which the earlier *Tristan* represents an almost immature stage in Wagner's development.[2] We have some evidence of Debussy's experience of *Parsifal* at Bayreuth from the contemporary score of *La Damoiselle élue*, completed in 1888. But certain of the later works, the interludes of *Pelléas et Mélisande*, *Le Martyre de Saint Sébastien*, and aspects of the orchestration and the melodic designs of *Jeux* show that, even though Debussy was not to hear a stage performance of *Parsifal* again until 1914, his musical imagination had been suffused with its spirit.

In his article on *Parsifal* in *Gil Blas*, 6 April 1903, republished in the collection of critical essays, *M. Croche antidilettante*, Debussy

[1] French visitors to Bayreuth in 1888 included Edouard Dujardin, editor of *La Revue Wagnérienne*, Robert Godet, Jules de Brayer, Vincent d'Indy, Charles Lamoureux, and André Messager. Among Debussy's friends at Bayreuth in 1889, participating in the experience of *Parsifal*, *Meistersinger*, and *Tristan*, were Madame Wilson-Pelouze, Chausson, Robert Godet, the lawyer Paul Poujaud, the portrait-painter Jacques-Emile Blanche, and Chabrier. One of the most fanatic of Wagnerians, Chabrier, an intimate friend of the Wagnerian singer Ernest van Dyck, had travelled widely in Germany, where his works were conducted by Felix Mottl, and had earlier heard *Tristan* at Munich. On this occasion, according to Vincent d'Indy, 'he burst into sobs of despair before even the first note of the Prelude. To his friends who enquired whether he was ill he could only reply, "Oh that open A on the cello! Fifteen years I've been waiting to hear it!"'

[2] The effect of *Tristan* on many people, not only French, at the end of the century is described by another visitor to Bayreuth, Mark Twain: 'I know of some, and have heard of many, who could not sleep after it, but cried the night away. I feel strongly out of place here. Sometimes I feel like the one sane person in the community of the mad.' The hypersensitive artists who had developed under the combined influences of Wagner and Poe were easily provoked to tears by music, as was Debussy himself at the performance of his own *Martyre de Saint Sébastien*. The physical effect of *Tristan* on Debussy was described by a friend after a performance at the Théâtre des Champs-Elysées in 1914: 'He literally shook with emotion.' The impression made by *Parsifal* is described in several novels of the period, among them *La Lueur sur la cime*, published by Jacques Vontade (pseudonym of Madame Bulteau) in 1904, in which the writer Etienne Marken weeps throughout the whole performance. Two characters in this novel, André and Jacqueline, converse on the Wagnerian revelation: 'Je puis résumer aisément l'impression générale que me fait la musique de Wagner: elle me donne une envie excessive de vous embrasser à fond.'

makes some caustic comments on the characters of *Parsifal*—
'Amfortas, that melancholy knight of the Grail, who whines like a
shop-girl and whimpers like a baby. . . . Kundry, a sentimental
draggletail for whom I have little affection'—which lead him to
condemn Wagner's allegory as representing 'moral and religious
ideas that are completely false'. Klingsor, he mockingly declares, 'is
the finest character in *Parsifal*, a one-time knight of the Grail, sent
packing from the Holy Place because of his too pronounced views
on chastity'. It is admittedly difficult to reconcile such views with
his conviction that *Parsifal* is nevertheless 'one of the most beautiful
monuments ever raised to music', that it is 'incomparable and
bewildering, splendid and strong'. There is, of course, the simple
explanation that the psychology of *Parsifal*, as opposed to the music,
is abstruse, though in view of Debussy's keen literary imagination
this is hard to admit. Perhaps he was writing in the spirit of Poe's
The Imp of the Perverse, deliberately misleading his readers. 'There
lives no man,' says Poe in this tale, 'who at some period has not been
tormented by an earnest desire to tantalize a listener by circum-
locution.' It is certain that Debussy's attitude to Wagner was
complex, compounded of love and fear, displaying many contradic-
tions and compelling him to lash out with ironic jibes at the object
of his admiration. So much we gather from his published articles.
His letters and his music tell another story. When Richard Strauss, in
the company of Romain Rolland, heard *Pelléas et Mélisande* in Paris
it was the Wagnerian elements he noticed.[1] Later, at the time of the
composition of *Le Martyre de Saint Sébastien* and *Jeux*, Debussy
seems almost to have been haunted by memories of *Parsifal*. When
Pelléas was revived at the Opéra-Comique in 1914, coinciding with
Weingartner's performance of *Parsifal* at the Théâtre des Champs-
Elysées, he tells the impresario Henry Russell that 'I couldn't possibly
compete with such an attraction', and begs for tickets for the second
performance. The orchestration of *Jeux*, he tells André Caplet, is
required to produce 'an orchestral colour illuminated as from behind
of which there are such wonderful effects in *Parsifal*'. And it is again
this opera that he mentions to Stravinsky in speaking, of all works,
of *Petrouchka*. The *tour de passe-passe* in *Petrouchka* 'has a kind of

[1] In his *Fragments de Journal* (*Cahiers Romain Rolland* No. 3) Rolland writes of the
performance of *Pelléas* he heard with Strauss at the Opéra-Comique in 1907: 'He
didn't let a single Wagnerian imitation pass without remarking on it, and not in
praise. "But that's the whole of *Parsifal*", he said of one passage.'

Debussy in 1894 at the home of Pierre Louÿs.
Photo by Louÿs

Zohra, in Moorish costume, and Debussy in 1897.
Photo by Louÿs

sonorous magic . . . an orchestral infallibility that I have found only in *Parsifal*', a comparison, incidentally, which was hardly calculated to please Stravinsky and which, as we shall see when dealing with the Debussy–Stravinsky relationship, indicates the parting of the ways between these composers. As opposed to Stravinsky, Debussy felt that music was to be kept alive by some sort of allegiance to the ideals of Wagner.[1]

Two incomplete works, written after the second visit to Bayreuth, should help us to assess the earlier influence of Wagner. They are the opera *Rodrigue et Chimène*, of which the manuscript is in the possession of Alfred Cortot, and a scene from *Axel*, the play of Villiers de l'Isle Adam, mentioned by Vallas without any indication of the owner of the manuscript.[2]

The grand opera *Rodrigue et Chimène* was begun about 1889 and absorbed most of the next two years. The libretto, based on Corneille's *Le Cid*, was by Catulle Mendès, who had published in *La Revue Wagnérienne* a fatuous conversation, 'Le vieux Wagnériste et le jeune Prix de Rome', believed to have been between himself and the young Debussy. The admiration of Mendès for Wagner was uncritical and unbounded. Mendès had known Wagner personally, but quarrelled with him following Wagner's attack on France at the time of the Franco–Prussian War, and became celebrated for his line, 'Je lui refuserai la main qui l'applaudit.' Jean Cocteau, who knew Mendès towards the end of his life, grandiloquently describes

[1] In the chapter dealing with Debussy's pronouncement on Wagner in his book *Les idées de Claude Debussy, musicien français*, Léon Vallas quotes many passages from Debussy's articles of a seemingly chauvinistic nature, suggesting that Wagner was wholly foreign to French dramatic ideals. As we see this problem today from a longer distance of time Vallas's emphasis can no longer be accepted. In Romain Rolland's *Journal des années de guerre* and other sources there is much evidence that Debussy became aware of his national mission only during the calamities of the first World War and even then, in view of the German onslaught, his inevitably hostile feelings were much milder than those of other French musicians or, for that matter, of Stravinsky. Earlier he had been particularly free from chauvinistic tendencies. Writing in 1887 to Pierre Louÿs, he attacked the nationalistic tendencies expressed by Emile Zola and Alfred Bruneau on the subject of their opera *Messidor*: 'Have you detected their deplorable patriotism, as if they had said, "it may be bad, but in any case it's French!"' Nor were his musical interests insular. Encouraging Monsieur Barczy, his host in 1910 in Budapest, to investigate the sources of Hungarian popular music, he claims the right to do so for the reason 'that I have an infinite love of music, not only French music!'

[2] No trace has been found of the owner of this manuscript whose identity Vallas concealed: 'Avant d'entreprendre la composition de *Rodrigue et Chimène* . . . [Debussy] avait pensé à mettre en musique un drame d'une esthétique toute différente. . . . Il avait même mis en musique une scène d'*Axel*; ce document, certainement d'un haut intérêt, gît inconnu dans une collection particulière.'

him as 'a defunct figure who trailed behind him the august ruins of Romanticism and the purple of its gods', and goes on to give this satirical portrait:

Catulle Mendès was fat and walked lightly. His hips and shoulders undulated. A sort of airship roll propelled him along. The crowd parted in surprise as he passed. He was like a lion and a turbot. His cheeks, eyes and little fish-like half-moon mouth seemed to be imprisoned in some sort of jelly which kept him at a distance and put some mysterious transparent trembling thickness between him and the rest of the world. He had the same little curls, waves and reddish moustache as a lion, the same proud mane and the same tail, formed by the tails of his black dress-suit hanging down below the short putty-coloured coat which was left untidily open. His coat bore the red ribbon of the Legion of Honour and revealed his loose white cravat, his shirt front stained with coffee, his shirt showing between his dress waistcoat and his trousers which hung in countless folds over tiny pointed boots. In his charming pale plump hands he carried a Chaplinesque walking stick.

He appeared wearing a carnival mask with a lace border, explaining 'that he had had a fall the day before on the Boulevard Malesherbes. The mask was to keep in place a plaster on his nose.'

There is something grotesque about Debussy's association with this picturesque character. According to Alfred Cortot, Mendès, passing the time playing dominoes at the Café Napolitain, had struck up a chance acquaintance there with Debussy's father, Manuel. Since Debussy's works had found little favour at the Académie, Manuel was anxious to develop an association with Mendès, who was known for his influence at the Opéra. Thus arose the ambitious project for an opera on Corneille's *Le Cid*. Three acts were sketched out when the odd story was put out that the table on which Debussy had been working by the fireside had accidentally overturned, the entire score going up in flames. The score of *Printemps* was similarly said to have been consumed in a fire. It later transpired that there had been no truth whatever in the story about *Rodrigue et Chimène*. The score was bought by Alfred Cortot after Debussy's death and is now in his private collection.

[98]

The descriptions of the score by Léon Vallas and Gustave Samazeuilh show that Debussy was temperamentally incapable of meeting the demands of an exteriorized, theatrical subject. He made it clear to his friends that he abhorred the whole project—not surprisingly in view of the text, quoted by Vallas, of one of the drinking songs:

> Du vin! du vin! Videz les caves
> Du vin de Burgos et d'Irun!
> Par Saint-Jacques, les hommes braves
> N'entendent pas la messe à jeun!

In the conventional tradition the finale of the last act is preceded by a soldiers' chorus. Significantly, it is here that Debussy's score breaks off.

Rodrigue et Chimène was thus added to the long list of failures and misfires. Before approaching the important association with Villiers de l'Isle Adam we must consider another discarded work, the *Fantaisie* for piano and orchestra, begun in 1890 and destined for performance at the Institute. Despite his stormy career at the Villa Medici Debussy was due in 1890 to be fêted by an official concert of his works before the academic judges. So many projects had been discarded or left unfinished that a representative programme could hardly be established. *Printemps* had been condemned, *Zuleima* destroyed. The *Fantaisie* was accepted and so was *La Damoiselle élue*, written between 1887 and 1889. To precede these two works Debussy was required to write an overture. Sceptical of official functions, he refused to comply with this request, the whole project came to nothing and his connexions with the Academy were severed.

The subsequent history of the *Fantaisie*, a work of considerable power and beauty, despite its conventional lay-out in three movements, is illuminating. Engraved at the expense of Catulle Mendès as an inducement for co-operation on *Rodrigue et Chimène*, it was ready to be published in 1890 and the first movement was to be performed by René Chansarel in the same year at a concert conducted by Vincent d'Indy. These plans, too, came to nothing. Debussy was unwilling to allow only a truncated version to be performed, and at the end of the rehearsal removed the parts from the stands. It has been assumed that in later years he was anxious to forget this youthful academic work. Recently published facts show that this is not entirely true. In 1893 he planned to have it played in New York and he later intended to re-orchestrate it. It was not heard, however, until after Debussy's death, in 1919, when it was given on the same day in its original version by Marguerite Long in Lyons and by Alfred Cortot in London.

Though it would be fascinating to see the music that Debussy wrote for Villiers de l'Isle Adam's play *Axel*, written shortly after his return from the Bayreuth performances of *Parsifal*, a knowledge of this musical score is not essential to an understanding of the development of his ideas. The fact that at this time Debussy was sufficiently attracted to this play to write music for it is itself highly significant since *Axel*, like *Parsifal*, is a study of renunciation. Like *Parsifal* too, it had an immense influence. Villiers de l'Isle Adam, Rémy de Gourmont wrote, 'opened the doors of the unknown with a crash, and a generation had gone through them to the Infinite.' Its theme is that since reality can never reach the imaginative heights of the dream any attempt to find a reflection of the dream in real life can only result in a compromise. Consequently the true dreamer, if he is to remain loyal to his ideal, must reject an exteriorization of it. Death is thus seen to be the justification of his loyalty to the dream. Axel, in the play, is a man of 'virile beauty', living like the heroes of Poe or Wagner in an isolated medieval castle. He possesses great wealth, the use of which, however, he denies both to himself and to the Rosicrucian nun Sara who is in love with him. In an impassioned, grandiloquent speech Sara attempts to entice Axel into a life of exotic pleasure, evoking visions that include a porcelain dwelling on the Japanese lakes, the bazaars of Bengal, the fjords of Norway, and even a glimpse of a romantic London fog. She offers him sensuous pleasure ('Cover yourself with my hair and inhale the ghosts of perished roses!') and sadistic pleasure ('I will force you to stammer out upon my lips the confession that gives most pain, and all the dreams of your desire shall pass into my eyes to multiply your kiss'). But it is all to no avail. 'These dreams', Axel convincingly argues, 'are so beautiful, why should we realize them?' Reality must be paltry by comparison with such visions. The earth on which Sara proposes the enacting of their dreams is merely 'a dross of frozen mud, whose Time is but a lie set in the face of heaven'. Nor, for the dreamer, can life itself be acceptable. 'Live?' asks Axel. 'Why should we live? Our servants will do that for us.'

Sponsored by Princess Meshcherskaya,[1] *Axel* was given at the Théâtre de la Gaîté on 26 February 1894, in the year following the first production of *Pelléas et Mélisande*, also sponsored by the Princess. The music, not by Debussy but by his friend Alexandre Georges, was somewhat in the style of Erik Satie. Though an orchestra and choir of some fifty musicians were provided, the music consisted only of a single phrase harmonized in different ways.[2] W. B. Yeats, present at the first performance and moved, as apparently was Debussy, by its religious symbolism, notes that not everyone in the audience received the message of the play with due reverence. Princess Meshcherskaya was in a box with her three divorced husbands, and 'one fat old critic, when the Rosicrucian magician began to denounce the life of pleasure and to utter the ancient doctrine of the spirit, turned round with his back to the stage and looked at the pretty girls through his opera glasses'.[3]

Villiers was a contributor, as were many friends of Debussy including Gabriel Mourey and Robert Godet, to *La Revue Wagnérienne* which appeared under the editorship of Edouard Dujardin between 1885 and 1887. A sardonic as well as a spiritual writer, Villiers had known Wagner and had discussed religious matters with him, notably the omission of any reference to God in *Tristan*. But he was not afraid of presenting a bold caricature of the Bayreuth cult. Wagner at Bayreuth, he writes in *La Revue Wagnérienne*, is 'our great Grocer to whom dukes and kings come from the four corners of the earth, deserting their families, their homes, and their countries', to pay homage to 'MY MU-SIC'. Elsewhere he enigmatically says of Wagner, 'Il est cubique', an expression apparently borrowed from Villiers by Debussy who, in a letter to Robert Godet, applies it to the Wagnerian conductor Charles Lamoureux ('ce chef d'orchestre cubique'). Indeed, Wagner acquired so many different interpretations, being endowed with a different significance for each of the conflicting symbolist groups,

[1] Princess Meshcherskaya, one of the friends in Paris of Tchaikovsky, was better known under her pseudonym Tolia Dorian, one of the first French translators, with Debussy's friend Gabriel Mourey, of Swinburne.
[2] The *Aubade* by Alexandre Georges from *Axel* was published in *L'Illustration* (*Supplément musical*) of 17 March 1894.
[3] Published in its final form in 1890, the year after Villiers' death, *Axel* had earlier appeared in serial form in the *Renaissance littéraire et artistique* (1872), *La Revue Indépendante* (1880, alternative versions by Rémy de Gourmont), *La Vie artistique* (1882) and *La Jeune France* (1885-6). Possibly Debussy's setting was based on extracts in the last of these reviews.

that after the third year of its publication *La Revue Wagnérienne* could no longer claim to represent Wagner's interests exclusively. Robert Godet, who wrote one of the last articles to appear, deplored the break-up of the Wagnerian religion. 'Happy are those who are able to go to Bayreuth', he concluded with youthful enthusiasm, 'to revive their faith in *Parsifal. Heil dir, Licht!*'

IO
Wagnerian Friends

Aime-t-on mieux la fin de *Tristan* ou celle de *Katia?* Il *faut*
choisir.

Robert Godet

Robert Godet enjoyed a long and intimate friendship with Debussy
dating from their visits to Bayreuth in 1888 and 1889 and tested by
the subsequent Wagnerian crisis in Debussy's development. Half-
brother of the theologian Georges Godet and of the writer and
political figure Philippe Godet, Robert Godet came from a distinguished Swiss family of Neuchâtel, where he was born on
21 November 1866. Having settled in Paris in his youth, he became
during the 1890s the foreign political editor of *Le Temps*, and
was also for a short time its London correspondent. A fervent
Wagnerian, he supported at this time the pan-German views
of Houston Stewart Chamberlain, the British-born political philo-
sopher who later married Wagner's daughter Eva, and translated
into French Chamberlain's notorious *Foundations of the Nineteenth
Century*.

At the same time he was able to claim, with his friend Jules de
Brayer, to have been one of the first critics in France to recognize
the genius of Moussorgsky and was the author of an important study
of the historical background of the characters in *Boris Godounov*.[1]
Attracted to exotic civilizations, he travelled in his youth to Java and
other countries in the Far East, offering to Debussy on his return
theoretical treatises on the music of the Orient and the Sunda

---

[1] He possessed the original edition of *Boris Godounov*, with autograph annotations
by Moussorgsky, which he left to the Bibliothèque Cantonale at Neuchâtel.

Isles.[1] His interest in the Orient persisted, and towards the end of his life he translated aesthetic and historical works on India and Mohammedan civilization by Alfons Vaeth and Edward Westermarck. A remarkable linguist and a figure of wide culture with an encyclopaedic knowledge of philosophy and the arts, he was also a composer, though he refused ever to reveal his works, which included songs with orchestral accompaniment and an unfinished symphony. After his death, in Paris in 1950, his musical manuscripts were deposited by his friend Aloÿs Mooser in the University Library of Geneva.

With his unrelenting gaze through steel-framed spectacles and his enormous square-cut beard, this highly accomplished figure, the last of the humanists, as Mooser held, had something of the appearance of Rimsky-Korsakov or of Vladimir Stassov. Though he had the confidence of several of his contemporaries besides Debussy, notably Rodin, Ernest Bloch,[2] and Ernest Ansermet, and published critical studies of great perspicacity, he remained on the periphery of the artistic movements of his time, a shy, erudite scholar, buried in his books. Yet he was at the same time a man of powerful convictions, uncompromising in his ideals and quick to annihilate any sign of a debasement of them. Life-long friends who failed to live up to his image of them were ruthlessly cast aside. In a dispute which threatened to turn into a duel Debussy offered, with the poet Camille de Sainte-Croix, to act as one of his seconds. A man of outstanding intellect in many spheres, Godet was also throughout his long life a staunch mountaineer. At the age of seventy, accompanied by his two daughters but without a guide, he climbed to the summit of Mont Blanc.

In 1888, at the age of twenty-two, Godet published in Paris an autobiographical novel entitled *Le Mal d'aimer: Etats d'âme*, a source of great value, hitherto unexplored, in assessing the nature of Debussy's relationship with him. In this *roman à clef* Jacques Arnal is

[1] They were offered to him but apparently Debussy had little use for theoretical treatises. Godet writes: 'On eut l'occasion de soumettre à l'auteur d'assez nombreux documents recueillis en divers lieux d'Asie et des Iles de la Sonde, cela dans le pieux souci d' "orienter" (c'est pour une fois le mot propre) sa mémoire ou sa fantaisie. De ces beaux documents on concevait quelque orgueil parce qu'ils ne couraient pas les rues, et encore que l'on n'eût aucune part à leur impressionnant appareil scientifique. Eh bien! l'ingrat n'y prit pas même un pauvre petit point de repère acoustique. Il considérait d'un oeil méfiant . . ."ces monuments d'érudition où la lettre, si par hasard elle était juste, tuerait d'autant plus sûrement l'esprit".'

[2] Godet's correspondence with Ernest Bloch has been deposited in the Library of Congress, Washington, to be made available twenty-five years after Bloch's death.

a Swiss musician, Godet himself, earning a living in Paris by giving lessons in musical theory, correcting proofs for music publishers and writing music and dramatic criticism. Turned in upon himself, Arnal had long suffered from the silent intimacies of reflection, and though he was capable of enjoying the company of friends, he remained haunted when alone by his addiction to self-analysis (*les vieilles manies d'analyse*), which compelled him to seek the origin of his ideas in what he recognized as a terrifying emptiness. Then the idling in cafés was resumed, together with the same sterile discussions, and Arnal would suddenly become seized by an inability to utter a single thought. Words then, as a means of communication, seemed to him useless. It was vanity, he says, to believe that words could convey the workings of the imaginative mind, and even if they could, can any verbal expression be expected to have the same significance for two people? In his youth he remained in a constant state of hesitation and indecision. Every theory, even an artistic theory, appeared to him the expression of a limited mind, and from his long nightly discussions he returned, having exhausted his friends, wearied by his own silence, sinking eventually to sleep in a state of mind sickened by half-truths.

Love, however, remained an ideal of Jacques Arnal, but more than love, friendship. 'I feel,' he writes, 'that love—the feeling that, to a certain extent and in regard to certain specific matters, life can be shared—drives one to put into life the greatest possible intensity. But I find the same in friendship with, however, less violence and extravagance, without the mysterious attraction of "eternal womanhood", but also with less fluctuation, a more comforting peace of mind, and perhaps with more confidence.'

Godet presented Debussy with a copy of *Le Mal d'aimer* in July 1889, shortly before their visit that year to Bayreuth. He immediately received a warm acknowledgement: 'I have been reading you throughout the night! Don't be hurt if I tell you of my sympathetic response to what you call your unfortunate prose. I have had the rare feeling of reading about genuine people whose sufferings I know well enough . . . I hardly dare say more, and forgive the meagreness of these lines as a tribute to our cherished friendship.'

The description of Arnal's musical allegiances in the year 1888 shows a mind alive to the new spirit that was breaking through and contains, besides a moving account of the three operas of Wagner that Godet was to hear at Bayreuth with Debussy, a view, novel and wholly independent at that time, of Moussorgsky.

Although when he was weary of life Jacques felt that nothing could ever fill the emptiness within him, he responded to music with great fervour. His feelings had been deeply aroused by Bach and Beethoven. In Chopin he had discovered certain morbid harmonies. Liszt and the Russian composers, among them the sublime, unknown Moussorgsky, had allowed him to see how the simple poetry of the people could move the distressed, complex, contemporary soul. But more than all the others, two figures had become associated with his joys and sorrows and became his true friends. Schumann was the first to have disturbed him, the first perhaps to have awakened that element of madness, likely at some moment to explode in us all. Through Schumann he came to understand the fantasy of Hoffmann and the moving and ironic works of Heine, and Schumann's music drew from his youthful heart a tenderness too other-worldly, too beautiful and delicate to be absorbed in the hard life of reality. Wagner, whom Jacques came to know later, after studying his works over a long period, continuously amazed him at every page. Even then, when he was thoroughly familiar with the master's works, his amazement persisted. Exploring the fierce, uncontrollable passion of *Tristan*, and in *Meistersinger* the charm of medieval German life, Jacques was unable to conceive how a single mind could produce a work as serene as a moonlit night under the linden trees, when not lit up in brilliant sunshine, and at the same time a poem of anguish recoiling in hatred from daylight. This was perplexing enough, but Jacques felt utterly incapable of grasping the size of Wagner's genius when, after the selfish passion of *Tristan*, he produced in *Parsifal* an expression of the supreme beauty of compassion.

Godet's steadfast friendship for Debussy and the moral and aesthetic support which he unceasingly offered him was based on a temperamental affinity, but I think it may also have been based on a temperamental divergence. The central plot of *Le Mal d'aimer* concerns a crisis in Godet's early life which he interprets in terms of an antithesis between the philosophy of *Tristan* and that of Tolstoy. Jacques Arnal is in love with a Russian singer, Ludmilla Nemerowsky, whom he has heard in a concert performance of the first and third acts of *Tristan*. At the climax of the novel he had been reading the early story of Tolstoy, *Family Happiness* (of which the French title is *Katia*), renouncing primitive desire for domestic fidelity. Torn between his urge to seduce Ludmilla and the observance, prescribed by Tolstoy, of traditional morality, he is caught in an uncontrollable conflict and dreams of killing Ludmilla to satisfy his conception of the sacrifice of love. 'Aime-t-on mieux la fin de *Tristan* ou celle de *Katia*?' he desperately asks. 'Il *faut* choisir.' Choosing the solution of Tolstoy, he abandons Ludmilla and eventually marries an unassuming Dutch girl as, in fact, Godet did in real life. 'I shall have the strength now to live,' he tells her, 'and to renounce the dream world for ever.' 'Hais l'idéal plutôt que d'en faire un vain songe' runs the quotation from Maurice Boucher at the head of *Le Mal d'aimer*. We see here the basis of the friendship between Godet, who had renounced the outer world, and Debussy, the adventurous, creative artist. When faced with similar dilemmas Debussy invariably chose the fearful solution that only for a moment Godet had dared to contemplate. Three of Debussy's Verlaine songs are dedicated to Godet, who was his oldest and his most faithful friend, having known intimately Debussy's parents, his first and his second wife and his daughter 'Chouchou'.[1]

If Godet's relationship with Debussy was rooted in their common admiration of *Parsifal*, or rather the dual aspect of *Parsifal*, another life-long friendship was born from a common experience of *Tristan*. In the *Revue Wagnérienne* of 15 January 1887, Gabriel Mourey wrote in his poem *Tristan et Isolde*,

> Avoir le ciel entier pour soi, n'être plus qu'un
> Et deux pourtant; fondre mon être dans ton être;
> Devenir azur, nuage, étoile, parfum,
> Loin des hommes, loin des demain, loin des peut-être!

Twenty-two years later, in 1909, Mourey and Debussy revived their youthful experience of *Tristan* in a projected opera based on Mourey's adaptation of Joseph Bédier's edition of the medieval chronicle, *La Légende de Tristan*. Though this project remained unrealized, Debussy firmly pursued what he intended to be an original setting of the Tristan legend and went so far as to sign a contract with Giulio Gatti-Casazza for its production at the Metropolitan Opera in New York. A letter from Debussy to

[1] The published letters from Debussy to Godet extend from 1889 to 1917. The letters from Godet to Debussy have unfortunately been withheld from publication.

Mourey of 20 February 1909 goes some way to explaining the failure of this undertaking. There was a sharp divergence of views. 'You take the matter of a musical setting of this work too lightly. In the first place we can't have singers who act the parts as well. Singers have no more idea of acting than the wooden leg of a table; and as for a combination of spoken verse and sung verse, this is frightful. The result is that they both sound wrong. I'd rather have opera without any poetic ambiguity.' And he puts forward an extraordinary vision of the medieval Tristan legend, 'a choreographic version with choral accompaniments written in a particular manner'.

Born at Marseilles in 1865, Gabriel Mourey had published a volume of verse, *Voix éparses*, at the age of eighteen and became a typically versatile figure of the age, poet, novelist, playwright, critic of literature and painting, and translator. A confirmed anglophile, he created his reputation with translations of two works which made a profound impression on the young Debussy and were of great significance in French letters. In 1889 he brought out the first French translation of the complete poems of Poe; and in the same year he published a long study on Swinburne in *La Revue Indépendante* including translations of some of the *Poems and Ballads*. Its success encouraged him to translate the entire collection, which he issued in 1891, the first volume of Swinburne in French, with a preface by Maupassant drawing attention to the revelatory depths of Swinburne's sensuality.[1] Godet recalls that in an early discussion Debussy was haunted by Poe's ailing women, always about to become disembodied, their very names, Lady Madeline, Ligeia, and Morella, striking deep into his imagination, and he remained haunted by them until the end of his life. He was similarly drawn to Swinburne of whom, before 1890, he knew the play *Chastelard*,

[1] 'Il est impossible de nier', Maupassant writes in this preface, 'que cette œuvre appartienne à l'école sensuelle, à la plus sensuelle, à la plus idéalement dépravée, exaltée, impurement passionnée des écoles littéraires, mais elle est admirable presque d'un bout à l'autre. Sans doute les amateurs de clarté, de logique et de composition s'arrêteront stupéfaits devant ces poèmes d'amour éperdus et sans suite. Ils ne les comprendront pas, n'ayant jamais senti ces appels irrésistibles et tourmentants de la volupté insaisissable, et l'inexprimable désir, sans forme précise et sans réalité possible, qui hante l'âme des vrais sensuels.
'Swinburne a compris et exprimé cela comme personne avant lui, et peut-être comme personne ne le fera plus, car ils ont disparu du monde contemporain, ces poètes déments épris d'inaccessibles jouissances. Tout ce que la femme peut faire passer d'aspirations charnellement tendres, de soifs et de faims de la bouche et du cœur, et de torturantes ardeurs hantées de visions enfiévrantes pour nos yeux et pour notre sang, le poète halluciné, l'a évoqué par ses vers.'

based on the algolagnic nature of Mary Queen of Scots, the *Poems and Ballads*, and *Laus Veneris* with its *Tannhäuser* associations.

Mourey's friendship with Debussy inspired numerous theatrical projects. Among Mourey's wide circle of friends were Huysmans, the occultist Jules Bois, for whose play, *Les Noces de Sathan*, Debussy entertained the idea of writing incidental music,[1] Mallarmé, and Marcel Proust. He corresponded with Villiers de l'Isle Adam and he was later on intimate terms with Gabriele d'Annunzio who, at the time of his co-operation with Debussy on *Le Martyre de Saint Sébastien*, confesses to having been affected by Mourey's Swinburne translations. In his fascinating book on England, *Passé le Détroit* (1895), Mourey describes his visit to Swinburne at Putney and his discovery of Turner, later proclaimed by Debussy as 'the greatest creator of mystery in art'. They were bound in their admiration of other painters. Mourey was one of the chief historians of the Art Nouveau movement of which, as we shall later see, there are musical parallels in *La Damoiselle élue* and other of Debussy's early works. In 1890 and again in 1908 he wrote remarkable studies of Odilon Redon whose finest canvases were inspired by subjects of Poe and who produced portraits of two of Debussy's intimate friends, Ernest Chausson and Ricardo Viñes.

In *Passé le Détroit*, known to Debussy some eight years before he first visited England, there are moving pages on a visit to St. Paul's Cathedral, reached through an impenetrable London fog, which might have been written by Huysmans or even by Poe himself. Waves of dense yellow fog fill the vast interior of the church, penetrating its very walls or appearing to be descending upon the church below from the great dome. Even the huge statue of Wellington is obscured. Suddenly the scene vanishes as the fresh, spring-like voices of a boys' choir evoke a vision of Montsalvat.

[1] *Les Noces de Sathan* appeared in 1890. Debussy had been asked to write the music for this esoteric drama of which the characters are Satan, Mephistopheles, Faust, Adam and Eve, and Psyche. In an undated letter to Bois from the rue de Londres Debussy mentions 'a bad adventure' and states that after due consideration the music for *Les Noces de Sathan* cannot be supplied. Was he referring to one or other of the occult religious practices common in Paris at that time, instituted by the 'Pagans', the 'Satanists', and the 'Gnostics'? Jules Bois was the author of several works on occult practices, among them *Les Petites Religions de Paris* (1894) and *Le Satanisme et la Magie* (1895), the latter, with a preface by Huysmans, containing detailed descriptions of the Black Mass and the wide practice at this time in Paris of depraved cults. Shortly after his project with Debussy, Jules Bois successfully co-operated with Erik Satie. His story, *La Porte héroïque du ciel*, was published in 1894 with Satie's prelude and illustrations by Antoine de la Rochefoucauld, the accredited painter of 'The Cult of Isis'.

Mourey imagines Parsifal at St. Paul's, stepping forward in a white tunic of initiation, and Amfortas with his expiatory wound bleeding from his breast, in remorse and pain and in the throes of death. 'Amfortas, Amfortas,' he hears the cry, 'show us the Holy Grail!' 'I cannot, I cannot,' Parsifal replies. 'I am unworthy. I am a sinner. I have loved the woman who was a sinner. I suffer, yet in my very suffering my desire is unappeased.' The chant of the boys' choir is as suddenly concluded, and the charm is over. Outside, London, swarming with life, is of some ghastly pale colour, 'everything enshrouded in a funereal fog through which penetrates the light of the dawn of the last day of the world.'[1] Though Debussy later knew the London fogs himself, and also their portrayal in the pictures of Monet, he must surely have remembered this charming book when writing his piano prelude *Brouillards*.

The earliest of Debussy's projects with Mourey dates from about 1890. In his one-act play, *Lawn-Tennis*, published in 1891, Mourey announced as in the press a later play, *L'Embarquement pour ailleurs* 'avec glose symphonique de C. A. Debussy'. We know nothing of the history of this project which presumably did not materialize. But *Lawn-Tennis*, dealing in a bold manner with a lesbian theme, was obviously known to Debussy, and the subject may have returned to his mind in 1913, at the time of the composition of the ballet *Jeux*, the scenario of which is similarly concerned with lesbian associations.[2] Later at the Théâtre des Arts Mourey wished to promote a stage performance of *La Damoiselle élue*, a scheme which Debussy enthusiastically endorsed, but which came to nothing for the reason that Antoine was only remotely interested in the musical aspects of his productions, as Debussy discovered when he was approached by Antoine to write incidental music for *King Lear*. A tragic subject, *Huon de Bordeaux*, and two fantasies, *Le Marchand de rêves* and *Le Chat botté*, were among other passing projects of Mourey and Debussy, none of which was to materialize.

[1] Besides chapters in this book on the Pre-Raphaelites and other movements, Mourey describes with great sensitiveness many characteristic scenes. 'Voilà un livre à garder, pour le relire', Huysmans commented, 'car il est vraiment intéressant et nous fait au moins connaître à quelques-uns des casaniers comme je suis les Préraphaélites d'Angleterre. . . . Et dans vos motifs londoniens, la page exquise, de touchante beauté, sur les prostituées!'

[2] Written for production at the Théâtre des Arts, *Lawn-Tennis* was published after a private performance with an introductory letter from the producer, André Antoine. Mourey's sensibility and perception are praised by Antoine who, however, considers the subject and its treatment over-bold for public presentation.

The long correspondence with Mourey offers glimpses into many corners of Debussy's mind. At the beginning of 1909 he told Mourey that he was becoming obsessed by deep-seated hesitations. He describes 'a curious compulsion to leave works unfinished'. In August of the same year he writes to André Caplet of the same phenomenon, indulging in an ambiguous state of mind which he describes as 'le délicieux mal de l'idée à choisir entre toutes'. He was at this time concerned principally with his two operas on tales of Poe. Though also engaged at this time on the great *Images* for orchestra, a Wagnerian influence was still active, but on a deeper plane. At the same time he was hoping to find a new interpretation of the ancient myths not of northern Europe, but of the classical Greek figures of Psyche and Orpheus. The idea of a ballet on the subject of Orpheus had been planted in his mind at the time of his early association with Paul Valéry,[1] and his interest in this theme was

[1] Writing to Debussy about 1900 on the subject of a ballet they had discussed, Valéry throws out an arresting idea: 'I had incidentally thought of the myth of Orpheus, that is to say the animation of all things by a spirit, the fable dealing essentially with movement and order.' Valéry's letter is an interesting document showing a poetic conception of the ballet in the minds of Valéry and Debussy at least ten years before the arrival in Paris of the Diaghilev ballet. Valéry writes:

Mon cher Debussy,
Je pense à vous et aux ballets.
Nul sujet déterminé ne m'est encore venu. Peut-être faudra-t-il en causer, car, atmosphère, coloris général, tout cela doit monter du musicien, le librettiste réservé à projeter seulement une correspondance entre le mouvement et l'orchestre.
Mais j'ai un peu rêvé de dansantes questions depuis dimanche.
A mon avis il faut faire le plus clair ballet du monde, celui sans programme, car il ne voudrait dire que ce que les jambes et les instruments permettent.
Seulement, pour varier l'action pure, je joindrais aux danseuses quelques mimes féminines.
Les danseuses, dans leur tutu et maillot éternel.
Les mimes—voiles légers, complets, non loin de ceux des figurines grecques.
Aux premières le mouvement, le déplacement simple avec toutes les grâces qu'elles pourront.
Aux autres, les gestes, sourires et anecdotes désirables.
Voilà mon alphabet et déjà un peu de ma syntaxe.
Notez que je considère rigoureux les rôles à attribuer à ces deux escadrons ou moyens. Au fond ce sont deux langues différentes en tout,—et qui n'ont de commun que,—le silence.
J'ajoute une énormité. La musique—la vôtre—peut-elle pas être également *double* et, sous l'unité apparente du son, distincte entre elle-même,—comme s'éloigne de l'entre-chat,—la physionomie? Mais ceci est dit au hasard.
J'avais songé incidemment au Mythe d'Orphée, c'est-à-dire l'animation de toute chose par un esprit,—la fable même de la mobilité et de l'arrangement.
Voyez-vous quelque chose dans cette direction? Notez que je dois penser à vous tout le temps, donc je tâtonne, donc je vous écris.
Cette spéculation m'amuse beaucoup—elle a pour moi l'inattendu d'une pointe.
Tous mes hommages à votre femme et mille amitiés,
                                                    Paul Valéry

revived in 1907 in the form of a project with Victor Segalen for the opera *Orphée-Roi*. Orpheus, he then declared, was 'the original and the most sublime of the Misunderstood'. ('Possibly he saw himself as a modern Orpheus,' André Schaeffner comments, 'an Orpheus not so much seeking Eurydice as pursued by her.') To Mourey, who had suggested that he write a score for his play *Psyché*, he writes with humility, 'What kind of genius is required to revive this ancient myth from which all the feathers of the wings of love have been plucked!' Eventually he managed to write for Mourey's play a flute solo, *Flûte de Pan*, later called *Syrinx*, as exquisitely and as lovingly designed as the flute solo for Mallarmé's mythological faun. It was the one project that was not allowed nebulously to float about in his mind during their long friendship.

II

The Orient and the Art Nouveau

J'aime les images presque autant que la musique.
Letter to Edgard Varèse

Bayreuth was a lasting impression of the years immediately following the return from Rome, but in 1889, when *Tristan* had been heard at Bayreuth, there was also an opportunity to hear an immense variety of exotic music at the Paris World Exhibition held on the Champ de Mars. Coinciding with the centenary of the French Revolution, this was the most spectacular of the several Paris Exhibitions, the Tour Eiffel having been erected on the Champ de Mars to mark the occasion. We can hardly overestimate the impact made on Debussy at this still formative period by the revelation of this entirely novel exotic music. Arresting accounts of his experience are given by three of Debussy's friends, Robert Godet with whom he had been to Bayreuth, Julien Tiersot the critic and historian, and Judith Gautier the former wife of Catulle Mendès.

Many fruitful hours for Debussy [Godet writes] were spent in the Javanese *kampong* of the Dutch section listening to the percussive rhythmic complexities of the gamelan with its inexhaustible combinations of ethereal, flashing timbres, while with the amazing Bedayas the music came visually alive. Interpreting some myth or legend, they turned themselves into nymphs, mermaids, fairies and sorceresses. Waving like the ears of corn in a field, bending like reeds or fluttering like doves, or now rigid and hieratic, they formed a procession of idols or, like intangible phantoms, slipped away on the current of an imaginary wave.

Suddenly they would be brought out of their lethargy by a resounding blow on a gong, and then the music would turn into a kind of metallic galop with breathless cross-rhythms, ending in a firework display of flying runs. The Bedayas would then remain poised in the air like terrified amazons questioning the fleeting moment, the secrets of love and life.

But they are amazons only for a moment; now they are water-spirits or birds or flower-maidens weaving festoons, or butterflies of all the colours of the rainbow. A flute run flashes out and each of the Bedayas beats its wings, or flutters its petals, and once again they come to life in rhythm paying homage to their hidden god. The feline grace of their youthful bodies suggests an entwining creeper; their nervous, flexible limbs are the colour of jasmine; their tiny, nodding heads are crowned with fabulous flowers through which are glimpsed the sparkle of their gold head-dresses and their jet black hair.

Memories of these oriental visions were later evoked, Godet believed, in *Pagodes*, *Et la lune descend sur le temple qui fut*, and perhaps also in the prelude, *Terrasse des audiences au clair de lune*. Everyone crowded in to see this sensuous oriental spectacle, and the associations aroused were endless. 'According to his leanings,' Julien Tiersot writes, 'each compared the Javanese dancers with some heroine of his choice. One imagines *Salammbô*, another the Queen Rarahu. One of my fellow music critics actually thought of the flower-maidens in *Parsifal*. One of the dancers—Wackîem is her name—with her sweet, serious face, her shoulders and bronze arms emerging from under a curiously draped gold-embroidered costume and wearing on her head either a gold helmet or white lotus flowers, is the living image of a little Indian divinity. Another is Tamina, almost Pamina of *The Magic Flute*; and indeed an association with Mozart's masterpiece, with its mysterious ceremonies and its invocations to Osiris and Isis, is by no means out of place.'

The visual and literary imagination was abundantly fed by these dancers from the oriental harems; and so was the musical imagination. Using the pentatonic scale and employing only a single string instrument, the *rebab*, the other instruments being all metallophones, gongs, xylophones and bells, struck with hammers and mallets thickly padded to avoid all shock, the gamelan from Jogya, sent to

Paris in 1889, produced a full and powerful orchestral tone. At the Exhibition of 1900, also attended by Debussy, Judith Gautier notes that the gamelan, apparently the Solo gamelan from Bali, produced a more limpid texture. The music played by both of these gamelans has distinct technical resemblances to the music of the Renaissance: the *rebab* plays a fixed chant around which the percussion instruments weave a complex polyphony. 'Do you not remember the Javanese music,' Debussy wrote in 1895 to Pierre Louÿs, then travelling to Spain, 'able to express every shade of meaning, even unmentionable shades and which make our tonic and dominant seem like ghosts?' Recollections of the Jogya and Solo gamelans were alive in his mind still when, in 1913, he wrote in the *Revue S.I.M.*:

There were, and there still are, despite the evils of civilization, some delightful native peoples for whom music is as natural as breathing. Their conservatoire is the eternal rhythm of the sea, the wind among the leaves and the thousand sounds of nature which they understand without consulting an arbitrary treatise. Their traditions reside in old songs, combined with dances, built up throughout the centuries. Yet Javanese music is based on a type of counterpoint by comparison with which that of Palestrina is child's play. And if we listen without European prejudice to the charm of their percussion we must confess that our percussion is like primitive noises at a country fair.

An unforgettable impression was also made at the 1889 Exhibition by the travelling theatre from Cochin China, appearing in Europe, like the gamelan, for the first time. Here a subject is given to the actors on which they improvise to the accompaniment of a four- or five-piece instrumental ensemble. We have from Tiersot a precise description of this ensemble. It consisted of 'a gong suspended from a wall; two kinds of drums; a bowed instrument called a *dong-cô* with two strings strung in a very curious fashion; a kind of oboe called a *song-hi* with eight holes; a flute with an embouchure in the middle of the instrument; and another bowed instrument called a *lion*. The *song-hi* has very harsh, shrill sounds. On the other side of the stage is an enormous percussion instrument, a kind of bass drum on which a sixth player now and again strikes with great fury.'

It is amusing to see that in recalling, in 1913, his impressions of this Chinese theatre, Debussy makes an ironic reference to Bayreuth: 'The Annamites presented a lyric drama in embryo, foreshadowing the structure of *The Ring*. In the Chinese theatre there were simply more gods and less scenery.' Possibly, also, in speaking of the degree of terror created by a gong he was thinking of Stravinsky's *Sacre du Printemps*, heard that very year: 'A shrill little clarinet [i.e. the *song-hi*] sets the mood and a sense of terror is created by a gong. No need for a special theatre or a hidden orchestra. The artistic instinct is enough. Which makes one wonder how much our civilization has suffered from professionalism.'[1]

The 1889 Exhibition also greatly encouraged an interest in the decorative arts of the Orient, Japanese painting and the batik designs of Java, and in the interesting movement known as Art Nouveau. This movement, an offshoot of Impressionism and closely allied with the Nabis, advocated that works of art should include not only paintings but utilitarian objects, bookbindings, furniture, metal craft, tapestries, and murals. The fascinating aesthetic of this decorative art, deriving in part from the Arts and Crafts movement of William Morris and the vogue in France of the English Pre-Raphaelites, has only recently received the attention it deserves. We are amused today at such a typical product of the Art Nouveau as the Paris Métro stations with their fantastic vegetative ornaments, but in fact this extravagant sense of design sprang from deep symbolical sources. Writing of this symbolism on the occasion of the exhibition of Art Nouveau at the Museum of Modern Art in New York in 1960, Peter Selz quotes the statement of Walter Crane, president of the Arts and Crafts Exhibition Society: 'Line is all important, let the designer therefore, in the adaptation of his art, lean upon the staff of line—line determinative, line emphatic, line delicate, line expressive, line controlling and uniting.' And he goes on to explain

[1] Transcriptions of the music of the Chinese theatre and also of the gamelan music are to be found in *Les Musiques bizarres à l'Exposition* by the composer Louis Bénédictus, friend of Judith Gautier, published in 1889 by Debussy's publisher and benefactor Georges Hartmann. A study of Debussy's works influenced by the 1889 Exhibition, 'Pentatonism in Debussy's Music', was undertaken by the eminent ethnomusicologist, Constantin Brailoiu, who aptly described Debussy's orchestra, particularly that of the *Nocturnes* and *La Mer*, as a *gamelan stylisé*.

A complete set of gamelan instruments had been presented by the Dutch Government to the Paris Conservatoire in 1887, its pentatonic features recalling to Brailoiu those of *La Fille aux cheveux de lin*. André Schaeffner has suggested that Debussy may have tried over oriental scales on these percussion instruments with Bourgault-Ducoudray, professor of musical history at the Conservatoire and composer of a *Rapsodie cambodgienne*, performed in 1889.

the significance of designs associated with the lily and the peacock adopted by the French from the English Aesthetic movement:

> The peacock's tail feathers occur more often than the whole bird, and soon the water-lily pad and stem take precedence over the flower. The tendril of the vine is more interesting than its leaves, the bud more intriguing than the blossoms. . . . Almost to the exclusion of men it is the woman who dominates the Art Nouveau world, and the aspect of woman which preoccupies the artist is her hair—long, flowing hair which may merge with the drapery or become part of a general wavy configuration. . . . Loïe Fuller's serpentine dances, *The Butterfly*, *The Orchid*, *The Fire*, *The Lily*, enjoyed the highest popularity and can be seen as the most apt expression of certain art impulses at the time. Her veils performed the same erotic function as the flowing tresses of the Art Nouveau female. The girl-woman, to a great extent descended from the hothouse creatures of the Pre-Raphaelites, has the same ambivalent eroticism of a small-breasted, narrow-shouldered, virginal, indeed often boyish creature. Almost emaciated, her body is yet extremely languorous in its sexually suggestive poses . . . The interest in the bud and the young girl suggests that the Art Nouveau artist . . . seemed to prefer a melancholy nostalgic expression to unbridled gaiety and joy.

Maurice Denis, who was to have illustrated Debussy's *L'Après-midi d'un faune*, and Bonnard, who wished to undertake the decor for *Pelléas et Mélisande*, were associated with this movement; and so were Toulouse-Lautrec, influenced, as he himself declared, by William Morris, Gustave Moreau, Gauguin, Seurat, and Picasso (notably in his *Courtesan with Jewelled Collar* of 1901) who made sketches for the decor of *L'Après-midi d'un faune*. The serpentine dances of Loïe Fuller and her elaborate use of veils were well known to Debussy. At the time of Debussy's association with the Diaghilev ballet, Loïe Fuller presented her choreographic version of the *Nocturnes*, using a profusion of shining, flame-coloured veils.

Allied to this conception of decorative symbolism in the line—upward-moving lines were held to be expressive of joy, downward-moving lines were inhibiting and depressing—was the studied preciosity of the Art Nouveau artist. He has a fetish for articles of clothing, a necktie or a hat; he develops a cult for the single beautiful object, a vase, a jewel, or more often a book exquisitely bound and typographically unique. In Oscar Wilde's *The Picture of Dorian Gray* and its French prototype, Huysmans' *A Rebours*, there are frequent examples of handsomely bound books ravishing the eye. Dorian Gray has as many as nine copies of his favourite book bound in different colours and styles each to suit a particular mood. Huysmans' Jean des Esseintes was as stimulated by the appearance of the original edition of Mallarmé's *L'Après-midi d'un faune* as by its contents. Its covers in Japanese felt, 'as white as curdled milk', were fastened with silk cords, one China pink, the other black, knotted together in a rosette, the appearance of the wonderful book producing a note of velvety softness, 'a suspicion as of Japanese rouge, a suggestion of love and licence'.

We have much evidence showing that Debussy's musical and artistic sensibility at this stage was a reflection of the theories of the Art Nouveau movement. His conception of melody as an 'arabesque' was the direct musical counterpart of these theories. He saw the music of Bach deriving entirely from the 'capricious' or the 'adorable' arabesque. 'The musical arabesque or rather the principle of the ornament', he wrote in *La Revue Blanche*, 1 May 1901, 'is at the basis of all forms of art. The divine arabesque was used by Palestrina and Orlando. They discovered its principle in Gregorian chant and provided support for its interlaced designs with strong counterpoint.' Similar views of symbolical design in the visual arts were stated by Maurice Denis ('depth of feeling derives from the capacity of lines and colours to explain themselves'), and by Gustave Moreau ('my aim is to express thought by the line and the arabesque'). Debussy was an admirer, as were Maeterlinck and Pierre Louÿs, of the art of Walter Crane, widely known on the Continent, with its swirling floral ornamentation and its female figures enmeshed in creepers. He was a reader of the luxurious German magazine *Pan* (founded by Julius Meier-Graefe in 1895) devoted to the most significant art movements throughout Europe and prominently displaying the work of the Art Nouveau painters. Apparently the illustrations in *Pan* were associated in his mind with the use of the term *Image* for a musical composition.[1]

[1] In 1911 when Edgard Varèse had asked him to contribute to another magazine named *Pan* Debussy replied: 'Is this the same *Pan* that appeared some fifteen years ago? It was then a very well illustrated review. . . . If you could send me a copy I should be

Debussy certainly cherished the single exquisite object in the manner of the heroes of Huysmans and Oscar Wilde. 'Desire is everything', he confesses in a letter of February 1893 to Prince Poniatowski. 'One has a mad but perfectly sincere craving for a work of art.' The work of art, he explains, may be a 'Velasquez, a vase of Satsouma or a new kind of tie. What joy the moment one possesses it! This is really love.' His finely shaped handwriting, his monogram consisting of mysteriously entwined initials, his pre-occupation with the decorative features of his publications, particularly the colours and spacing of the title page, the furnishings of his humble home in the rue Cardinet ('your Art Nouveau den', as Pierre Louÿs described it)—all this indicates that Debussy was deeply affected by specific trends in the visual arts.[1] A design in pastel of a woman with flowing hair, made by Debussy as a frontis-piece for a novel by his friend René Peter, could be mistaken for an early Gauguin or a Maurice Denis. Not for nothing was the first concert devoted entirely to Debussy's works given, on 1 March 1894, in the gallery of La Libre Esthétique in Brussels, then the main centre of the Art Nouveau movement. The gallery, temporarily turned into a concert hall, displayed not only the freshly painted canvases of Pissarro, Renoir, Gauguin, and Signac, together with posters of Toulouse-Lautrec, but William Morris's illuminated books of the Kelmscott Press, Aubrey Beardsley's illustrations for Oscar Wilde's *Salomé*, and buckles and bracelets designed by the London Guild of Handicraft.

pleased and I'll see if I can subscribe to it for I love *les images* almost as much as music.' (Letter to Edgard Varèse of 12 February 1911.) The use of the term *Image*, a generic term that may be applied to the bulk of Debussy's work, dates from as early as 1894 when it was applied to the original versions of the *Sarabande* (from *Pour le Piano*) and *Jardins sous la pluie* (from the *Estampes*).

[1] They included trends penetrating far into the hinterland of the Art Nouveau movement. Answering a questionnaire in 1889, Debussy stated that his favourite painters were then Botticelli and Gustave Moreau. Botticelli was not interpreted at this time as he is today. Associated with the Pre-Raphaelites and through them with the Art Nouveau style, he made a highly sensuous appeal to the artists of the *fin-de-siècle*. 'Ah, les bouches de Botticelli', writes Jean Lorrain in his book *Rome*. 'Ces bouches charnelles, fermes comme des fruits, ironiques ou douloureuses, énigmatiques en leurs plis sinueux sans qu'on puisse savoir si elles taisent des puretés ou des abominations.' Significantly, Gustave Moreau, whose *Salomé* caused a sensation, was discovered by Huysmans. 'Dans l'œuvre de Gustave Moreau', we read in *A Rebours*, 'conçue en dehors de toutes les données du Testament, des Esseintes voyait enfin réalisée cette Salomé surhumaine et étrange qu'il avait rêvée. . . . Elle devenait, en quelque sorte, la déité symbolique de l'indestructible Luxure, déesse de l'immortelle Hystérie, la Beauté maudite, élue entre toutes par la catalepsie qui lui raidit les chairs et lui durcit les muscles.'

Among the works played at this concert was *La Damoiselle élue* conducted by Eugène Ysaÿe.[1] Despite its obvious associations with Wagner's *Parsifal* and the music of Eva in *Meistersinger, La Damoiselle élue*, written between 1887 and 1889 and published in 1893 by the exclusive *Librairie de l'Art Indépendant*, was a typical product of the Art Nouveau. Rossetti's poem *The Blessed Damozel*, which appeared in Gabriel Sarrazin's *Les Poètes modernes de l'Angleterre*, greatly attracted the Art Nouveau artists, characteristically drawn to English poetry. What they admired in Rossetti's painting of the Blessed Damozel was again the symbolism of line or arabesque. They cherished, apart from the melancholy of her greenish-blue eyes, the peculiar curve of her sensual protruding upper lip, her copper-coloured locks and the curvature of her swan-like neck repeated in the draperies of her celestial gown.[2] The publication of Debussy's score was illustrated by Maurice Denis, in black and several shades of gold, showing the Blessed Damozel at the gold bar of Heaven.

The score of this work brings us very near to a purely visual conception of music: the decorative Pre-Raphaelite curves are projected or translated into the long sinuous arabesques of the Damozel's aria. Vallas was entirely wrong in imagining that the limited edition of the work indicates the composer's 'little hope' of frequent performances of his work. A mere one hundred and seventy copies of the vocal score were printed, not available to anyone of course but, like the rare publications described by Wilde and Huysmans, to be reserved for the initiate, the esoteric few. At the first performance, on 7 April 1893 at the Salle Erard in Paris, the

---

[1] The other works of Debussy given at this concert were the String Quartet, played by the Ysaÿe Quartet, and two of the *Proses lyriques*, sung by Thérèse Roger, Debussy's fiancée, accompanied by the composer. The numerous references to painting in the Belgian criticisms of this concert were, of course, prompted by the works of the Impressionists seen by the audience on the walls of the gallery during the performance. Reminded of the impression made on him by oriental scenes at the 1889 Exhibition, Maurice Kufferath wrote of the Quartet: 'Une œuvre? Nous ne savons. De la musique? Peut-être, mais à la façon dont sont de la peinture les toiles des néo-japonisants de Montmartre et de sa banlieue belge.' *La Damoiselle élue* suggested to him 'le sentiment grave d'une maladie du sens auditif, pareille à celle que la vision de certains peintres manifeste dans le sens de la vue'.

[2] Mr. Tschudi Madsen shows that there was 'an uninterrupted sequence running from the Pre-Raphaelites' enthusiasm for Botticelli's lines via Walter Crane's linear aesthetic to Beardsley's elegant play with surfaces and curves'—those especially, one might add, of his illustrations for Wilde's *Salomé*. It was in the same year as the publication of *La Damoiselle élue*, 1893, that Wilde's *Salomé* appeared in Paris, and under the imprint of the same exclusive publishers, *L'Art Indépendant*. Bound in seductive purple covers, it was dedicated to Pierre Louÿs, then Debussy's most intimate friend, who, with others, had helped Wilde to write the play in French.

principal soloist was Thérèse Roger who, the following year, was to become Debussy's fiancée. Flatteringly, the witty music critic Willy (Colette's husband whose appearance was later to remind everyone of Edward VII though Colette insisted that he was more like Queen Victoria) declared that Debussy could now claim to be *le damoiseau élu*.

An even smaller edition had been published in 1890 of Debussy's *Cinq Poèmes de Baudelaire* on poems from the *Fleurs du Mal*: a mere one hundred and fifty copies on several different kinds of Japanese and other art papers were issued by subscription, again by *L'Art Indépendant*. Needless to say, neither of these expensive publications, underwritten by Debussy's friends, Ernest Chausson and Etienne Dupin, was designed as a commercial proposition. If one believes in art for art's sake one must believe what it says: one does not publish to make money.[1]

[1] It is interesting to see that the *Poèmes de Baudelaire* were admired at the time of their publication by Gabriel Fauré, who ungrudgingly declared them to be the work of a genius. This opinion was all the more disinterested on Fauré's part since his famous song-cycle *La Bonne Chanson* (1892–3) met at first with a poor reception. We find an assessment of the current feelings on the songs of Debussy and Fauré in a letter of the summer of 1894 from Marcel Proust to Pierre Lavallée: 'Do you know that the young musicians are almost unanimous in not liking *La Bonne Chanson* of Fauré? It appears that it is needlessly complicated and so on, very inferior to his other songs. Bréville and Debussy (who, they say, is a great genius far superior to Fauré) are of this opinion. It makes no difference to me for I adore this cycle and what, on the other hand, I do not like are his earlier songs which they prefer.'

12
Chausson, Régnier, and Laforgue

Fille de l'onde et mère de l'amour.
Swinburne

Upholding the uniqueness of the artistic creation, Debussy craved attachments in his personal life that should similarly be exclusive. He cultivated an intimacy with his friends that was intense, ecstatic, and possessive. 'I was utterly demoralized and felt that leaving you was an irreparable disaster', he agonizingly confesses to Ernest Chausson after spending a country holiday with him at Luzancy; and with child-like candour he admits, 'I am afraid of working in the void.' Casual friendships were not unknown to him, but they either un-accountably vanish or deepen into an intimate type of personal intercourse with an overwhelmingly strong emotional basis. He several times tells a friend that he is the only one with whom he can be in harmony. He demands solitude, but with a friend's reassurance in the background, and in the special use he makes in his correspondence of the word 'sensibility' ('In the name of sensibility, mother of us all') we see him more than usually conscious of the physical element underlying personal attachments.

Music was thus in some way related to an esoteric union. 'My music has no other aim', he tells Robert Godet, 'than to melt in the minds of predisposed people and to become identified with certain scenes or objects.'[1] This sense of exclusiveness sometimes compelled

---

[1] 'Du reste cette musique n'est pas faite pour d'autres buts: se mêler aux âmes et choses de bonne volonté.' (Letter to Robert Godet of 25 December 1889.) This Pan-like declaration, novel in French music, reaches back to an earlier literary source. It recalls the final passage from Flaubert's *Tentation de Saint Antoine*: 'Je voudrais . . . couler comme l'eau, vibrer comme le son, briller comme la lumière, me blottir sur toutes les formes, pénétrer chaque atome, descendre jusqu'au fond de la matière—être la matière!'

him to resort to child-like intrigues. His mutual friends were often unknown to each other or seemed to be unaware of the degree of intimacy reached with one or another of them; and though normally candid and even brutally frank, he was sometimes amusingly mystifying. In a letter to the young playwright associated with Marcel Proust, René Peter, which he had been solemnly ordered to burn, we read: '(1). I had asked you not to say that I dined with you Tuesday last and you kept your promise. (2). I gave myself away and spoke in the most casual way of our evening at the Funambules. (3). So we did, in fact, spend the evening together, *and I didn't for a moment think of asking you to keep it a secret.*'

Relatively few of his friends were musicians and even those that were, such as Chausson and Satie, were also deeply involved in other contemporary artistic movements. On the face of it, his friendship with Chausson was a rose-coloured idyll. 'No more Russian music, no more boating, no more billiards', Chausson regretfully wrote at the end of a holiday at Luzancy. 'What a nuisance you are to have gone!' Gone were those happy days, they had gone. And the lilac time had gone too, and the roses and the carnations had faded. There were the indulgent sighs of Chausson's songs. And there, too, caught on the screens of their cameras, are the bearded young composers with their slender canes and their straw hats. *Le temps des lilas ne reviendra plus ce printemps-ci.* 'The time of our photography is over and of our gastronomic conversations too', Chausson goes on, guying this title of his well-known song, 'and the time of our playing with balloons!' The billiard table, boating on the lake, and playing like children with balloons: it is almost the setting of a Maupassant story.

Debussy found in Chausson 'a big older brother'. Associated for hardly more than two years, from 1892, they discuss Moussorgsky and Wagner, and also the warm clothes needed by Debussy for the coming winter months and the amounts of his unpaid bills. The wealthy son of a banker, Chausson lived in a luxurious apartment, 22 Boulevard de Courcelles, decorated by his brother-in-law Henri Lerolle[1] and housing a collection of paintings by Renoir, Gauguin, Redon, and Degas. He possessed a country house at Luzancy and also the Château des Moussets at Limay, near Mantes. The visitors

[1] Henri Lerolle (1848–1929) was a painter of academic landscapes and portraits, notably one of Loïe Fuller, and several paintings on religious subjects including *The Communion of the Apostles* in the church of the Capuchin monks in Paris.

to his Paris home were the most brilliant figures in the arts. They included Renoir, Manet, Degas, Redon, and Rodin, also Albert Besnard and Eugène Carrière, both of whom painted Chausson's portrait, the hazy Carrière drawing out the remote look in his melancholy grey eyes. Among the musicians were Chabrier, whose famous collection of Impressionist paintings included Manet's *Bar aux Folies-Bergères*; César Franck and his disciples Vincent d'Indy and the tragic Henri Duparc; Gabriel Fauré and his future pupil Charles Koechlin; the young Erik Satie; Eugène Ysaÿe, the generous and disinterested sponsor of Debussy, Fauré, Chausson, and d'Indy; and the celebrities of the following decade, Alfred Cortot and Jacques Thibaud. In this company were also the aristocratic Henri de Régnier with monocle and drooping moustache, André Gide, looking like the young Liszt, the faun-like Mallarmé,[1] and, peppering the conversation with caustic quips, Colette and her husband Henri Gauthier-Villars, the witty music critic who signed his pieces 'Willy' or 'L'Ouvreuse' (the elderly usherette who avidly awaits a few sous for showing people to their seats).[2]

A family man, happily married, Chausson took a paternal interest in his impecunious friend. He was able to introduce him into the aristocratic circles of the Faubourg Saint-Germain, frequented at this time by the young Marcel Proust, where Debussy conducted an amateur choir, accompanied his songs, and played Wagner. At the beginning of 1894, at the house of Henri Lerolle, an evening was arranged at which he steeled himself to playing and singing the whole of the first act of *Parsifal*, presumably in the translation of Judith Gautier, for which he received the considerable sum of a thousand francs. ('Some people said they couldn't hear the words', Lerolle truthfully reported of this ordeal to Chausson. 'I'm not surprised! You know how he articulates. We consider ourselves

---

[1] In addressing the envelopes of letters to his friends Mallarmé used to amuse the postman as well as the recipient with a charming rhyme. A letter to Chausson was addressed thus:

> Arrête-toi, porteur, au son
> Gémi par les violoncelles,
> C'est chez Monsieur Ernest Chausson,
> 22 Boulevard de Courcelles.

[2] A study of Chausson's salon, if ever the relevant letters and documents could be assembled, would be a valuable addition to the memoirs of the period. His Impressionist collection and his library alone deserve attention. Literary works dedicated to him include Camille Mauclair's *Le Soleil des Morts*, one of the most illuminating commentaries on the ideas and the personalities of the artists associated with Mallarmé.

fortunate if he sings anything but *tra ta ra ta ta*.') For a time—it could hardly have been for more than a few months from the end of 1893—Debussy's life appears to have been greatly eased by the handsome financial rewards of these ventures.[1] But he soon becomes intolerant of the Faubourg Saint-Germain snobbery. 'How stupid these people are!' he explodes in a letter to Chausson. 'One would have to be a very weak-minded individual to fall for any of this!'

Chausson was a pupil of César Franck, and it is significant that an important work written at the time of Debussy's association with him was based on Franck's novel theory of the cyclical musical form. This is the String Quartet, completed in February 1893, and performed in Paris by the Ysaÿe Quartet at the end of the year, on 29 December. On the face of it, this venture into chamber music is surprising. Planned to be followed by a piano and violin sonata and a second string quartet (a section of which was announced in March 1894 as having been written), it represents a temporary renunciation of literary and pictorial allegiances and the adoption of a traditional outlook to which, very much later, there was to be an enthusiastic return. In 1915 Debussy told Stravinsky that the works he had recently written, the *Etudes* and the sonatas, were all examples of 'pure music'. We see that he was similarly drawn to the idea of pure music at the very time when he was engaged on his most important works issuing from the Symbolist aesthetic, *L'Après-midi d'un faune*, the *Proses lyriques*, and an early form of the *Nocturnes*.

The title-page of the Quartet baldly states: 'Premier Quatuor en sol mineur, Op. 10.' This is possibly an ironic concession to the meticulous methods of classifying chamber works, since no other work of Debussy bears anything so prosaic as an opus number or indication of key. However this may be, the Quartet shows Debussy with one foot in the academic world of Franck and the other in the dream world of *L'Après-midi d'un faune*. It presents a fusion of the cyclical form and the variation form. Transformations of a single

---

[1] He occasionally accepted strange commissions. At his humble lodgings, about 1891, Debussy received a call, unannounced, from a distinguished Scottish officer, General Meredith Reid. Speaking not a word of French, he thrust before the bewildered composer his elegant visiting card. Composer and general thereupon faced each other in a dumb-show of perplexity, until an interpreter was discovered in a nearby tavern, where the commission was happily received to arrange and orchestrate a march traditionally associated with the general's ancestors, the ancient Earls of Ross, known also as the Lords of the Isles. The original edition of this *Marche écossaise* bore the title, 'Marche des anciens comtes de Ross, dédiée à leur descendant le général Meredith Reid, grand'croix de l'ordre royal du Rédempteur'.

theme predominate throughout the four movements. There is a minimum of thematic development; many prismatic changes of harmony; minute variations pieced together in the form of a mosaic; and constant recastings of the germinal theme in rhythm and mode. The expressive opinion of one critic was that Debussy was 'rotten with talent'. Another, alluding to Oriental imagery in French literature at the time, wrote of the flying *pizzicati* in the Scherzo: 'Here is something for which I would willingly give everything that Pierre Loti ever wrote.' Debussy was greatly indebted to Franck in regard to the cyclical form of the Quartet yet there was a gulf between them. Franck's comment on an earlier work of Debussy, the *Ariettes* of 1888, 'C'est de la musique sur les pointes d'aiguilles' (idiomatically, 'the split hairs of music' or 'the nerves of music'), though meant to convey his irritated censure of Debussy's style, defines precisely its compelling, nervous appeal, as it had now developed.

Though immediately successful, the Quartet was received by Chausson with unaccountable reservations. 'I must tell you that for some days I have been greatly upset by what you said of my quartet', Debussy wrote in his last published letter to Chausson, of February 1894. 'I felt that in the end it only resulted in your being attracted to certain aspects of my work to which I attach little importance.' In a generous spirit of compromise he undertook to write for Chausson a second quartet, 'in a more dignified form'. On the matter, however, of this abandoned second quartet and the later stages of Debussy's relationship with Chausson our knowledge is limited. We know only that early in 1894 the friendship with Chausson was abruptly broken off.[1] Chausson died on 10 June 1899, as the result of a mysterious bicycle accident, following a period of acute depression, and in which there may well have been a suicidal element. Though he had been estranged from Chausson for over five years, Debussy attended the funeral, together with many well-known figures in the arts, among them Duparc, Fauré, Albeniz, Degas, Rodin, Redon, Henri de Régnier, and Pierre Louÿs.

An early friendship with Henri de Régnier, a close associate of Mallarmé, leads us to consider the original form of the three

[1] In a letter to me of 15 May 1959, Chausson's daughter, Madame Etiennette Lerolle-Chausson, has kindly provided me with a possible explanation of the rupture: 'Financial questions played a part in their estrangement, particularly as there appeared to be an element of double dealing.... My father was also very annoyed by the strange engagement, fortunately but very unpleasantly broken off, with our friend Thérèse Roger.'

Nocturnes for orchestra. Debussy enjoyed a fruitful friendship with this passionate and luxuriant poet. He played to him, before its performance, a piano version of *L'Après-midi d'un faune*, which Régnier found 'as warm as in an oven', and they were drawn together by an independent view of literary and musical symbolism. 'When he spoke to me of the debasement through usage of certain words in the French language,' Debussy notes, 'I thought that this also applied to certain chords which had become vulgarized in the same way.' It was Régnier who approached Maeterlinck on Debussy's behalf for the use of *Pelléas* as a libretto, and Debussy's respect for his judgement was such that he submitted to him his four poems, which he was about to use as texts for the *Proses lyriques*. Régnier recommended two of these poems, *De Rêve* and *De Grève*, to be published in the review, *Entretiens politiques et littéraires*, edited by his friend Francis Viélé-Griffin.[1]

Among the works which Debussy was prepared to introduce on his projected tour of the United States in 1892 he mentions to his sponsor, Prince Poniatowski, '*Trois Scènes au Crépuscule*, almost finished, that is to say that the orchestration is entirely laid out and it is simply a question of writing out the score'. This triptych is none other than the three well-known *Nocturnes* for orchestra which, although they were to undergo several transformations before reaching their final form, were inspired by one of Régnier's most original works. The *Scènes au crépuscule* are a series of ten poems forming part of Régnier's *Poèmes anciens et romanesques*, published in 1890. Like Mallarmé's *L'Après-midi d'un faune* and *Hérodiade*, they are the product of an imaginary theatre of the mind in which action is sacrificed to poetic associations. Twilight is neither hopeful day nor deathly night; it represents disillusionment. A play (*soir de fête*) emerging from a dream is enacted on a 'strange meadow'. The players are deflowered maidens in 'faded robes' (*robes défleuries*). Pride is 'broken as in a sword clash'; hopes 'are killed like blue birds bleeding through the night'. Memories are stirred by 'the bright shout of the trumpet' (*le cri du buccin clair*) piercing the vision (*trouant la toile du décor*). The imagery of the first poem is associated with musical instruments, trumpets, and flutes, suggesting Debussy's *Fêtes*, and also with a female choir, as in *Sirènes*. It is true that the

[1] Régnier's private papers, which may well contain many further references to Debussy, have been deposited in the Bibliothèque Nationale but are not yet available for consultation.

flutes in Régnier's poem, 'deep flutes weeping in vanity', do not suggest the brilliant opening of *Fêtes*. But contrasted with the flutes and trumpets is a 'wan choir' (*chœur qui s'étiole*) which may well have planted in Debussy's mind the idea of the female choir in *Sirènes*. Elsewhere in this collection, not in the *Scènes au crépuscule* but in *La Vigile des grèves*, there are even closer parallels with *Fêtes*. Here Régnier speaks of 'a procession of flutes' and 'the brilliance of angry tambourines and sharp trumpet calls'. We have earlier suggested an association of the fanfares in *Fêtes* with the military processions in Paris at the time of the Franco-Russian alliance. These fanfares are also suggested by the line in *La Vigile des grèves*, 'Will love proclaim its voice in fanfares':

> L'amour sonnera-t-il par sa voix des fanfares
> En rapts brusques mordus de baisers et de cris,
> Ou chantera-t-il, glorifiantes et graves,
> Des promesses d'hymens et de rites fleuris?

Debussy surely knew the *Poèmes anciens et romanesques* at the time of their publication in 1890; and he would also have known the copy belonging to Pierre Louÿs, Régnier's brother-in-law, which bore at the head of the *Scènes au crépuscule* the inscription in Louÿs's handwriting, 'So sweet that joy is almost pain' from Shelley's *Prometheus Unbound*.

The score of the *Scènes au crépuscule*, though near completion in 1892, has disappeared. A later form of the work is similarly unknown: in 1894 the three orchestral scenes inspired by Régnier were surprisingly recast in the form of a violin concerto to be played by Eugène Ysaÿe. 'Debussy is writing a concerto for you,' Chausson casually writes to Ysaÿe. 'I don't know it and do not now wish to know it.' The 'concerto' is without doubt the 'three *Nocturnes* for violin and orchestra' described by Debussy in a letter to Ysaÿe of 22 September 1894: 'The orchestra of the first consists of strings; of the second, flutes, four horns, three trumpets and two harps; of the third, of both of these groups. It is an experiment with the different combinations that can be obtained from one colour—like a study in grey in painting.' Significantly, this letter, with its remarkable pictorial reference, was written only a few months after Debussy's return from Brussels where, as we have seen, on 1 March 1894 an entire concert of his works, consisting of the String Quartet, two

A boating party at Luzancy on the Marne in 1893
Left to right: Ernest Chausson, Raymond Bonheur,
Debussy, Madame Chausson

Georgette Leblanc

Mary Garden as Mélisande in 1902

of the *Proses lyriques* and *La Damoiselle élue*, was given in the art gallery of La Libre Esthétique hung with pictures of Gauguin, Renoir, Pissarro, Sisley, and other Impressionists. The analogy of 'a study in grey in painting' no doubt applies to *Nuages*, though it is difficult to say which painter or painters Debussy had in mind. Later he says of *Nuages* that it is the musical equivalent of 'grey tones lightly tinged with white'. Turner was known to him at this time, and also Monet. As for *Sirènes* it is possible that this was suggested not only by Régnier's *Poèmes anciens et romanesques* but by his later poem *L'Homme et la Sirène*, on mermaids and mortals,[1] or by Swinburne's poem *Nocturne*. Debussy was greatly attracted to Swinburne to the extent, about 1890, of having established for his friend René Peter a short bibliography of Swinburne in French translation. Swinburne's *Nocturne* had appeared in *La République des Lettres* in 1876, written by him in French but revised and corrected by Mallarmé. Like Debussy's *Sirènes*, a seascape in which the wordless female choir evokes mermaids, Swinburne's *Nocturne* is also a poem of the sea, or rather a poem of love symbolized by a mermaid arising from the sea. In the *envoi* to this poem we find the idea, expressed by many artists at the end of the century, Régnier, Mallarmé, and Debussy chief among them, of the vast enveloping sea as a mother figure:

> Fille de l'onde et mère de l'amour
> Du haut séjour plein de ta paix profonde
> Sur ce bas monde épands un peu de jour.

The influence of Régnier is discernible in another of Debussy's works of this period, *De Rêve*, the first of the four *vers libre* poems[2] for the songs *Proses lyriques*, published as a tribute to Régnier in the review of Francis Viélé-Griffin. In the manner of the dream poem of the *Scènes au crépuscule* and with memories, too, of *Parsifal*, knights in quest of the Grail collide in a nightmarish association with

---

[1] Published in Régnier's *Aréthuse* (1895), *L'Homme et la Sirène* is in the form of a dramatic scene in three parts. In the first, *Le Veilleur de Proue*, the Watchman says:

> A travers mes songes j'y vois clair
> Et moi seul
> Je sais la mer
> Toute la mer
> Et qu'il y a des Sirènes sur la Mer.

[2] Debussy had earlier been associated with Marie Krysinska, one of the originators of the *vers libre* at Le Chat Noir (*see* page 144).

mocking Flower Maidens. The text of each of these poems offers an instructive view of the several Symbolist factions with which Debussy was associated about 1893. In *De Fleurs* Debussy rather overboldly experiments with the typical floral imagery of the Art Nouveau—entwining stems, purple irises, and the long, scented pistils of white lilies. Characteristically, these suggestive images are enshrouded in darkness ('Mon âme meurt de trop de soleil.'). Elsewhere in the texts of this cycle there are attempts to emulate the irony and the masterly treatment of ennui in the work of Jules Laforgue, *notre Jules* as he is called in the letters to Robert Godet. Debussy's attraction to Laforgue, whose caustic but delicate humour conceals an element of impotence, was not a superficial attraction. In later years, as he probed into deeper levels of the musical imagination, he frequently came near to Laforgue's vision of despair, *les usines du néant*, and in the last months of his life at the approach of death, he finds refuge in the irony of Laforgue's lines:

> Les morts
> C'est discret
> Ça dort
> Bien au frais.

In Debussy's *Proses lyriques* two themes are prominent, deriving from Laforgue, innocence and boredom. This combination is curious and its significance is not at first apparent. The dancing white horses in the crepuscular seascape of *De Grève* unexpectedly evoke the laughter of exuberant schoolgirls, and in *De Soir* these same innocent schoolgirls cheerfully sing their simple roundelays, unable, however, to dispel the heavy gloom associated no less in France than in England with Sunday observance.

Several poems entitled *Dimanche* were written by Laforgue which he calls, in English, 'the ever spleen day' and in which he mocks a death-like emptiness. The innocent girls in his poems, like those in Debussy's *Proses lyriques*, are endowed with the virtues of chastity not on moral grounds, but for the pathetic reason that Laforgue had become a victim of his own charming timidity and sensitiveness.[1]

[1] In London Laforgue married Leah Lee, having earlier declared: 'Vous savez qu'il y a trois sexes, l'homme, la femme et l'anglaise. Le type de l'adorable, de l'aimée unique, pour moi, est par exemple, l'Anglaise. Elle n'a pas, pour moi, d'organes sexuels. Elle est tout Regard—toutes les autres sont les chiennes.'

Laforgue's story, *Lohengrin fils de Parsifal*, ends with a chaste union of Lohengrin and the emaciated Elsa 'her breasts easily covered by saucers'. The pillow on which their heads rest is changed into a swan that flies into the altitudes of metaphysical love.

Though less mature than other songs of this period (the *Trois Mélodies* on poems of Verlaine and the first set of *Fêtes galantes*) the *Proses lyriques* reveal a new musical element: effects in the elaborate piano accompaniment of bells, chimes, and echoes which seem to call for an orchestral transcription. Two of the songs, *De Grève* and *De Soir*, were, in fact, orchestrated, the scores having remained undiscovered.

Another work of approximately the time of the *Proses lyriques* was *Nuits blanches*, conceived as a set of five or six songs, again on poems written by Debussy himself. This cycle was announced as due to appear on the cover of the *Nocturnes*, published by Fromont in 1900. Nothing, however, is known of the music. The sketches for the poems are contained in a small eight-page notebook formerly belonging to Madame Texier-Debussy. They were consulted by Léon Vallas who published an extract from them in *Les Nouvelles Littéraires* (15 April 1933). By comparison with the *Proses lyriques*, their imagery of drapery and dreams appears to be elementary, not to say sentimental. The following lines, published by Vallas, were merely a sketch left incomplete and with many erasures:

Ce soir, il m'a semblé que le mensonge
Traînait dans les plis de sa jupe,
Et ses petits pieds ont foulé
Mon coeur sans merci.
Dans le lourd silence de la nuit
Il y a quelqu'un derrière moi,
Quelqu'un venu à travers mes songes
Dont mon coeur rompu,
La fièvre de mon sang
Rythment le doux nom.
Voici qu'une main s'est posée sur mon épaule
Petite main qui noue ou dénoue à son gré
Le fil de ma destinée.
Lorsqu'elle est entrée il m'a semblé
Que le mensonge traînait aux plis de sa jupe;
La lueur de ses grands yeux mentait
Et dans la musique de sa voix
Quelque chose d'étrange vibrait. . . .

Shortly after the appearance of the *Proses lyriques* Debussy temporarily embarked upon writing plays and even contemplated the founding of a literary review. About 1890 he had become acquainted with the brothers René and Michel Peter, sons of a prominent figure in the medical world, Dr. Michel Peter, the adversary and also the cousin of Pasteur. Ten years Debussy's junior, René Peter had aspirations as a playwright and from 1894 onwards published several light comedies and tales written in association with Georges Feydeau, Robert Danceny, and others. He was a friend of Marcel Proust, who mentions him in endearing terms in his correspondence with Reynaldo Hahn: 'He is delightful, full of ideas which I had never suspected in him and extremely kind.' René Peter lived with his family at Versailles. When staying at Versailles in 1906, Proust conceived a plan in co-operation with Peter about a husband, who, torn between his attraction to his wife and to prostitutes, is driven to suicide. Proust subsequently admitted that he lacked the courage to write this play, but the idea was used in *Swann's Way*, in the episode where Swann repairs to brothels in the hope of understanding Odette.

In his recollections of his friendship with Debussy, Peter states that, having been impressed by the judicious use of words in Debussy's conversation and by the help he had received from him on his play *La Tragédie de la Mort*, for which Debussy also wrote a *Berceuse*, he had the strange idea of becoming a pupil of Debussy in dramatic art. Over a period of about four years, Peter claims, Debussy gave him lessons twice weekly in drama. These lessons, he says, provided him with little orthodox skill as a playwright and he was obliged to confess that they were disappointing.

Nevertheless at least three comedies were undertaken by Debussy and Peter in co-operation, *L'Herbe tendre*, *L'Utile Aventure*, and *F.E.A.* (*Les Frères en Art*). The dates of these strange ventures, the first two of which were probably not completed, are approximately between 1895 and 1899. Of the first we know nothing but the title. Negotiations for the production of the two later plays were pressed forward and were almost successful. In regard to *Les Frères en Art* Debussy, according to Peter, judged the play to be too unprofessional and was in any case reluctant to appear as a dramatic author before the production of *Pelléas et Mélisande*. Also, according to Peter, this play, though accepted for production, was left far from complete. In fact, it was very nearly completed. The three rambling acts, written entirely in Debussy's hand, were discovered after his death and are now in a private collection. It is in the nature of a *roman à clef* in which real people, including Debussy himself and Rosalie Texier, his first wife, appear under fictitious names. The subject deals with the rivalry that persists among artists when faced with the formation of a benevolent society, *Les Frères en Art*, to prevent the commercial exploitation of their work. Significant references are made in the discussion between critics, painters, and musicians to Monet, Bonnard, Rodin, Mallarmé, Ibsen, and Ruskin. The part of an English critic, Redburne, is apparently meant to portray Swinburne. An annotated publication of this play, illuminating Debussy's changing theories and ideas at this period, remains to be undertaken.[1]

Yet another literary project belongs to these years. An ephemeral project of a literary review, if we are to believe the contents of an undated letter to René Peter, was to have been undertaken by Debussy with the support of certain academic figures: the historian Ernest Lavisse, the Greek scholar Victor Bérard, and the authority on Oriental literature André Chevrillon. Since this project, which never materialized, was also associated with the renowned courtesan Liane de Pougy and the sophisticated journalist Jean Lorrain, one would be inclined to look upon it as a practical joke were it not for the fact that in Paris at that time, even more than in London, scores of little reviews were constantly springing up as organs of an entirely personal aesthetic outlook.[2]

[1] Some five or six years after these plays were embarked upon René Peter introduced Debussy to André Antoine, the director of the Théâtre Libre, with a view to his writing the incidental music for Antoine's production of *King Lear*. In the entry under the date 8 January 1904 in *Mes souvenirs sur l'Odéon et le Théâtre Antoine* (1928), Antoine notes: 'Il me faudra une musique de scène pour *Le roi Lear* mais je voudrais quelque chose ayant du caractère. Mon ami René Peter m'a suggéré Claude Debussy; ce serait le rêve si le jeune maître voulait accepter.' In a letter to Antoine of 20 September 1904 Debussy demands at least thirty musicians and in any case cannot undertake to have the score ready by 1 October. He mentions two pieces, which were eventually published in 1926 under the title *Musiques pour le Roi Lear*, consisting of a *Fanfare* for trumpets, horns, drums, and two harps, edited by Roger-Ducasse, and *Le Sommeil de Lear* for two flutes, four horns, harp, drums, and strings. They were not used in the production and from the evocative nature of these short pieces one greatly regrets that the project was not completed. The first performance of *Lear* at the Théâtre Antoine, in which the great actor himself took the part of Lear, took place on 5 December 1904, and was an outstanding event. 'Pour la première fois chez nous,' Antoine notes, 'on a eu la sensation complète du drame shakespearien.'

[2] On the fascinating phenomenon of the 'Little Reviews' Rémy de Gourmont writes: 'At that time the only way freely to publish one's ideas was to establish for oneself a little review. A few people got together, collected a little money and sought out a printer. . . . The writers of my generation who finally established themselves had truly to struggle against the entire world.' Several of the famous works of Verlaine and Mallarmé, not to speak of the almost equally fine works of many lesser figures, did, in fact, first appear in quite obscure reviews.

Peter was not Debussy's only pupil at this time. To eke out a living he gave harmony and piano lessons, often to quite untalented amateurs, and coached singers. One of his earlier pupils, Marguerite Vasnier, makes it clear that he was nothing of a teacher, having not the slightest patience and being incapable of seeing a student's elementary requirements. He expected his simple-minded pupils to be thoroughly conversant with everything he was required to teach them. We know the names of very few of these casual pupils. Mademoiselle Worms de Romilly, to whom the *Prélude* of *Pour le Piano* is dedicated, received a piano lesson from Debussy on the morning of his marriage to Rosalie Texier, his only means of paying for their modest wedding breakfast. From the gross terms used in his correspondence when mentioning his pupils (*la volaille à laquelle je donne des leçons*) we may judge that the relationship between teacher and pupil was not always smooth. Alone among his pupils, Nicolas Coronio, a wealthy amateur to whom the *Toccata* of *Pour le Piano* is dedicated, was able to profit from his tuition and wrote songs which Debussy admired.

13
Reynold's and the Chat Noir

L'homme pauvre du coeur est-il si rare, en somme?
Verlaine

Not all the lanes and by-paths of the literary and musical worlds in which Debussy moved in the closing years of the nineteenth century have been fully explored, but as documents and memoirs accumulate much of the background of his activities during these years comes to life—a background that in Debussy's works is frequently brought into the foreground.

Among the cafés which he frequented about 1895 were the Taverne Weber, in the rue Royale, and the nearby Irish and American bar called Reynold's. The Taverne Weber had something of the reputation at that time of the present-day Café des Deux Magots. Everyone in the arts had been there at one time or another. It was here that Debussy met Marcel Proust. Utterly different in their social, though not in their artistic, outlook, they had been for some time on distant but courteous terms. One evening Proust offered to drive Debussy home in his four-wheeler. The long, flowing sentences of Proust's conversation, as of his writing, interspersed with many pointed anecdotes, were hardly appreciated by Debussy. Nor was Proust entirely at ease. Nevertheless, with his renowned hospitality, Proust offered to organize a party in Debussy's honour, unaware that his guest was the least gregarious of people. 'Forgive me,' Debussy frankly explained. 'I am really just a bear. Perhaps it would be best if we went on meeting casually, as we do.'

Weber's was frequented by the *élite* of the artistic world, but the company at Reynold's Irish and American bar was of another class altogether. A favourite haunt of Toulouse-Lautrec, this was the rendezvous of stable lads, jockeys, trainers, and coachmen, mostly English, wearing loud check tweeds, *les gens à carreaux*, as Debussy persisted in calling them. Running along the long narrow bar was a polished mahogany rail ('the colour of Rembrandt', said Lautrec), and customers lined the wall at a single row of tables. Music on the banjo and mandoline was provided by an Englishwoman and her coloured son. The proprietor, Achille Picton, had a soft spot for his namesake Achille Debussy, and also for the stunted Toulouse-Lautrec whom he respectfully addressed as *Monsieur le Vicomte Marquis*. Drinking was heavy among the jockeys and trainers and the long periods of silent, steady intoxication would suddenly turn into violent, drunken brawls with tables overturned, mirrors smashed, and the boulevard girls screaming with fright.

Intrigued by these horsy English exiles who had made their home in the rue Royale, Debussy relished 'the decidedly aesthetic environment of Reynold's'. Popular figures there were the corpulent Tom, coachman of the Rothschilds, and his spirited wife, who delighted Debussy by her impersonation of Queen Victoria. Another local celebrity was May Belfort, an Irish singer known by the several drawings and paintings of her by Lautrec and who appeared at Reynold's in 1895, at the very time when Debussy was frequently there. May was known to be given to certain vicious practices, but at Reynold's she was anything but vicious. Cuddling a black kitten and dressed in a child's bonnet and a Kate Greenaway dress, she was able to put the company in a sweet humour by singing with a childish lisp the well-known English music-hall song, *Daddy wouldn't buy me a bow-wow*, containing the lines,

> I've got a little cat,
> I'm very fond of that.

But the main attractions at Reynold's were the famous clowns Foottit, one of the older English exiles (originally Foottit, the spelling presumably changed to avoid the pronunciation 'foutie')[1] and his inseparable Chocolat, a Spanish negro who had only to appear in the circus ring in his cherry-red suit and say *Chocolat, c'est moâ* to bring the house down. Calling in after their tiring performances at the Nouveau Cirque, Foottit and Chocolat were happy

---

[1] George Foottit, born in Manchester in 1864, was the most celebrated English clown of his time. His reputation was entirely created in Paris where he died in 1921.

to go on singing and tap-dancing. Like Lautrec, who did numerous drawings of them, Debussy opened his heart to this lovable pair. Over a glass he discussed with these subtle and intelligent clowns life in the circus, the technique of the flying trapeze, the significance of the clown's sugar-loaf hat, music, philosophy, and poetry. To Footitt he quoted Banville's fantastic poem, *Le Saut du Tremplin*, in which the despised sorrowful clown, daubed in white, yellow, green, and red, and about to somersault from his springboard, dreams of defying the law of gravity, of finding wings and flying away for ever from his heartless admirers, the glum grocers, notaries, and bespectacled stock-exchange gamblers, to find peace in the firmament, among the stars:

> Enfin, de son vil échafaud,
> Le clown sauta si haut, si haut,
> Qu'il creva le plafond de toiles
> Au son du cor et du tambour,
> Et, le coeur dévoré d'amour,
> Alla rouler dans les étoiles.

Debussy never forgot this introduction to the eccentricities and the broad but subtle fun of circus-life and the old-time music-hall. In later life he frequently visited the music-hall. In London, after spending four nights at Covent Garden overwhelmed by *The Ring*, he spent the fifth night at the Alhambra music-hall, 'as a reward for good behaviour', as he put it. Later, at the Théâtre Marigny on the Champs-Elysées, he saw the celebrated American comic juggler Edward la Vine, 'General Ed La Vine, the Man who has Soldiered all his Life', as he was announced, though actually more of a tramp than a warrior, and who was said to appear at least nine foot high. Not only *General Lavine eccentric*, but *Minstrels*, *The Golliwog's Cake Walk*, and parts of *La Boîte à Joujoux* are all wonderful circus pieces, musical counterparts of the most satirical Toulouse-Lautrecs and rooted in the tap-dancing of Footitt and Chocolat amidst the brawls of coachmen and check-coated jockeys at Reynold's in the rue Royale.

We may see these memories fertilizing deeper layers of Debussy's mind. Towards the end of his life, when the circus pictures of Toulouse-Lautrec had been succeeded by the studies of Picasso and Rouault, penetrating to the depths of the clown's desperate soul, when Colette had written her moving *L'Envers du music-hall*, Debussy revived, in the serenades of his 'cello and violin sonatas, the same Harlequin that in his early youth he had seen through the sophisticated eyes of Watteau, Banville, and Verlaine. Here, however, he has the courage to face an ultimate disillusionment and emptiness, never far below the surface of make-believe, and which every artist who would flee the world like Banville's clown flying into the firmament, is brought in the end to embrace.[1]

It must have been at the period that Debussy knew Footitt and Chocolat, about 1895, that he met Colette and her husband. Colette provides us with one of the most lively portraits of Debussy at this time. We see him among musicians, not in any way remote from them but, on the contrary, a dominating figure, amusing the company with outlandish pranks, including a prophetic vision of something in the nature of *musique concrète*.

Whenever I met Claude Debussy [Colette writes] it was in the warm, rather feverish atmosphere of people wholly enamoured of music. At the piano, a composer. His elbows on the black expanse of the grand piano, propping up his head, a tenor. Glued to her armchair, a soprano, head upturned, effortlessly pouring out her vocal line like the smoke of a cigarette. No sooner did Louis de Serres leave the keyboard than his place would be taken by Pierre de Bréville, or by Charles Bordes, or by Déodat de Séverac. The absent-minded Vincent d'Indy, reclining on a sofa, would break into an astonishingly vulgar waltz, suddenly cutting himself short, struck with shame. It would then be the turn of Gabriel Fauré and André Messager, finding themselves rivals for once, to improvise a duet at the keyboard. Off they would start in a perilous rhythm, watching out for the trap of each modulation on the way.

[1] The works of Debussy's later years related to the psychology of the circus, the music-hall, and the *commedia dell'arte* include *Gigues*, the first panel of the great orchestral *Images*. This is based on one of Verlaine's most affecting poems, *Streets*, written in Soho in a café on the corner of Old Compton Street and Greek Street:

> Dansons la gigue!
> J'aimais surtout ses jolis yeux,
> Plus clairs que l'étoile des cieux
> J'aimais ses yeux malicieux.

The history of this work and of other later works of this kind will be dealt with in the subsequent volume.

At times like these music seemed to intoxicate Debussy. Warm and dark of complexion, his Pan-like head surmounted by entangled locks of hair needed only the background of a grapevine. He was set trembling by some inner excitement. In his unrelenting gaze the pupils of his eyes seemed momentarily to dart from one spot to another like those of animals of prey hypnotized by their own searching intensity. He responded to music as a bell-shaped crystal awaits the shock of vibration to produce its perfect purity of tone.

We were together one Sunday evening, having heard the first performance in France of *Antar*, unless I am thinking of *Sheherazade*. Overcome by the work, Debussy was turning it over in his mind in an attempt to reconstruct it. He started with some kind of low buzzing, then presently lingered on a high-pitched note like the sound of vibrating wires at a telegraph pole, groping all the time in his memory for the line of one of the themes. Suddenly his forbidding expression lit up. 'Just a minute, just a minute', he exclaimed, 'it goes like this ... mmmm ... and then presently ... mmmm. ...' One of us leaped at these snatches of a forgotten theme and went on to develop it. 'That's it, that's it!' Debussy agreed, 'and while that goes on, the cellos in the bass have mmm ... and the drums, directly they come in, very softly, there's that sudden explosion on the brass, and then ... and then. ...' Humming, and soon caterwauling, when it came to imitating the violins, and eventually panting, he seemed to be almost annihilated by the battle of instruments in his mind. Grasping a poker, he hammered away with it on the lid of the piano, and while still holding on to it he discovered another sound by running his fingers along the window pane. [In another version he provides a *pizzicato* on the basses by hurling a cork at the window pane.] Smacking his lips, he produced the sound of a xylophone, and went on in a crystalline voice to imitate the liquid sounds, *doug doug*, of the celesta.

There he stood in front of us all, using his voice, his arms and his feet while his two spiral locks of black hair danced wildly about on his forehead. His laugh of a faun found no echo in our own laughter; it was the expression of something within him, and I drew in my mind the vision of the great master of French music inventing before us the music of the jazz band.

[139]

At an earlier period, from about 1889 onwards, Debussy had frequented at least three of the literary and artistic cafés then coming into vogue: the Taverne Pousset at the Carrefour Châteaudun, Vachette in the Latin Quarter, the rendezvous of Jean Moréas and André Gide, and the Chat Noir in Montmartre.

Pousset's, a small mock-medieval restaurant with sombre furnishings and stained-glass windows, was primarily a meeting-place of journalists who, by two in the morning, had each devoured at least six hard-boiled eggs washed down by the tavern's celebrated Munich beer. At this gossip centre at the foot of Montmartre several picturesque characters were temporarily taken up by Debussy. They included the painter of English extraction, Louis Welden Hawkins, the size of a giant, who was also a boxer and a chiromancer;[1] Raoul Ponchon, friend of Chabrier and Verlaine, an incorrigible noctambulant and writer of brilliant racy poems who became known as the Molière of the comic verse of his time; the serious-minded composers Jules de Brayer and Alexandre Georges, curiously devoted at this time to the masses of Haydn but who were constantly arguing over the relative merits of *Der Freischütz* and *Carmen*; and the portrait-painter and critic Paul Robert, who usually painted at night, whose pages on El Greco brought tears to his friends' eyes and for whom Debussy posed for a charming drawing. Of swarthy complexion and with heavy drooping moustache, Robert resembled a Spanish pirate. An adventurous Don Juan who broke every woman's heart at Maxim's, he had an equally insatiable culinary appetite.[2] He was an original and courageous character, warmly devoted to Debussy on whose behalf he readily engaged in fisticuffs with any detractor of *Pelléas* who came his way.

Another little-known figure at the Taverne Pousset was Henry Mercier, a dreaded duellist whose victims included Jean Moréas, whom he wounded, and the poet Robert Caze, whom he killed. Celebrated in a poem of Verlaine (*Prince des vers et de la prose*), Mercier spent years translating Keats, his efforts unfortunately left

[1] Hawkins, who died in Paris in 1910, was among the painters at Mallarmé's 'Tuesdays' and is portrayed in the stories of Jean Lorrain, author of the satirical *Pelléastres*. His picture, *L'Impossible Alibi*, 'œuvre ténébreuse et aiguë où il y avait comme un atmosphère d'Edgar Poe', is the subject of a tale of Lorrain (in his *Histoires de Masques*, 1900) on the adventures of an anarchist.

[2] The celebrated gastronome Curnonsky, 'Kurne' as he was familiarly called by Debussy, the pseudonym of Maurice Sailland, pays tribute to Paul Robert as 'une grande gueule'. Left unsatisfied by a six-course dinner, he was seen by Curnonsky to round off this gargantuan meal with a copious plate of ham, sausages, and sauerkraut.

unfinished and unpublished. In his correspondence with Godet, Debussy refers to an evening at the home of Mercier towards the end of 1889 at which were recited part of Mercier's translation of *Endymion*: 'It's very beautiful once you accept its particular colour, its watery landscapes and an ethereal Diana (*une Diane très vais m'en aller*),[1] not at all a sharply defined figure.' At about the same time Debussy was closely associated with a group of writers and painters who were discovering Shelley as a rebel and an artist. In Rome he had read the first complete French translation of the works of Shelley by Félix Rabbe, and it is most likely that he knew the prose translation of Shelley's *Alastor* published in *La Jeune France* (September 1884) by Gabriel Sarrazin. This is dedicated as 'un songe étonnant de description et d'invention, de vision et de rêve', to a great Shelley enthusiast of that time, the painter Henry-Julien Detouche, who made one of the first portraits of Debussy. Other friends of Debussy and Sarrazin inspired by the atheism and the lyrical genius of Shelley were Paul Bourget, Elémir Bourges, Maurice Bouchor, Raoul Ponchon, and Emile Goudeau, the poet of the Chat Noir. Years later, when writing the Prelude, *Ce qu'a vu le vent d'ouest*, Debussy must have remembered Rabbe's translation of Shelley's lines from the *Ode to the West Wind*:

> Thou
> For whose path the Atlantic's level powers
>
> Cleave themselves into chasms, while far below
> The sea-blooms and the oozy woods which wear
> The sapless foliage of the ocean, know
>
> Thy voice, and suddenly grow gray with fear,
> And tremble and despoil themselves: oh, hear!

At Vachette's in the Latin Quarter Debussy met Jean Moréas, the Greek-born leader of the *Ecole Romaine* which sought a return to the Greco-Roman sources of French culture. Their conversations on two occasions are reported to have turned on Schopenhauer, who

---

[1] The allusion is to the remarkable poem of despair, *Rescousse*, in *Les Amours Jaunes* by Tristan Corbière, concluding with the verse:

> Si de mon âme
> La mer en flamme
> N'a pas de lame,
> —Cuit de geler . . .
>
> Vais m'en aller!

about 1892 became the idol of several of the Symbolist schools, and on Goethe's *Faust*, Part II. Here we may observe Debussy's admiration for a certain aspect of *Faust*, read in the translation of Gérard de Nerval, which he shared with André Gide and Pierre Louÿs, a hedonistic aspect which may be surprising to readers of *Faust* today. Having quoted voluminously from Part II of *Faust*, Moréas was infuriated by Debussy who, according to the report of their conversation, insisted that there was one character in this work more significant than all the others, a classical character whom Moréas, though by birth a Greek, had failed to understand. '*Foumiste!*' thundered Moréas in his Greek accent. '*Avant dé vénir mé voir, il sé docoumente!*' This character was the relatively minor figure of the watchman Lynceus whose duty in the play is to proclaim from his watch-tower the rising of the sun in the east. The humble servant has had a vision of another sun, rising in the south, a vision of pure beauty, symbolical of Helen, by which he is overcome to the extent of forgetting his vigilant duties. Brought in chains by Faust before Helen, he is forgiven by her and set free. 'The evil that I caused I may not punish,' Helen proclaims. Goethe's theory here is that beauty alone has the power of subjugating man, and its pursuit must excuse everything, even moral responsibilities. This was the root Parnassian theory which, long after the decline of the Parnassian movement, persisted as the philosophical basis in the work of artists of many schools. Fauré, in works such as his tender, almost amorous *Requiem*, was bound to this belief, and the discovery by André Gide of Goethe's faithless guardian living in the present, in the eternity of the single moment, had a great influence on his early works, notably his *Nourritures terrestres*.[1]

Exactly when Debussy began to frequent the Chat Noir, the first

[1] In the translation of Philip Wayne, the lines of Lynceus in *Faust*, Part II, Act III, which made such a strong impression on Debussy and Gide are:

> All forgotten was my duty,
> Warden's oath and trusted horn;
> Though your threats destroy me. Beauty
> Stronger is than wrath or scorn.

Debussy, according to Robert Godet, was also impressed by the famous lines of Faust in Act V:

> Zum Augenblicke dürft' ich sagen:
> Verweile doch, du bist so schön!
> (Then to the moment I could say:
> Linger you now, you are so fair!)

In his edition of the poems of Pierre Louÿs, Yves le Dantec shows, in a masterly analysis, how the poem of Louÿs, *Pervigilium Mortis*, his finest lyrical creation, was of the grotesque Montmartre cabarets that set a fashion for these bohemian establishments lasting to the present day, is difficult to ascertain. But it is worth dwelling on this matter to see the background of one of the key relationships in his life, the attachment to Erik Satie. There is evidence that Debussy was at the Chat Noir shortly after its opening in December 1881, playing frivolous cabaret music at the back of a modest brasserie on the Boulevard Rochechouart. He was again there after his return from Rome when the commercial success of this enterprise, now respectably housed in an entire building in the rue Victor Massé, had become world famous.

The history of the Chat Noir has frequently been recounted. It was founded by the unsuccessful but shrewd-minded painter Rodolphe Salis who, with the help of the Latin Quarter rhymesters, painters, and chansonniers known as the *Club des Hydropathes-Hirsutes*, established Montmartre as a site for a harmless type of night-club having fake associations with Rabelais and François Villon, crossed with macabre parodies and a nostalgia for the gutter. A journal was issued in January 1882 publicizing its farcical activities, along with poems by Verlaine and cartoons by Forain, Steinlen, and Caran d'Ache. Though its reputation was established by the snobs and its *habitués* were café draughtsmen and songsters, the Chat Noir was visited over a period of about ten years from 1885 by prominent artists of this decade, including Banville, Verlaine, Maupassant, Huysmans, and Renan.

By no means a negligible venture, the Chat Noir produced an original artistic contribution. This was the coloured shadow plays, the *Ombres chinoises*, an impressionistic anticipation of the art of the cinema. They were the work of Henri Rivière, painter, poet, and mechanical inventor, assisted by a pianist, often Charles de Sivry whom Debussy had good reason to remember, and a reciter. Caran d'Ache was also closely associated with this venture. Through a form of magic lantern enamelled glasses were projected on to a miniature screen, producing an illusion of landscapes and scenes of daybreak and sunset of great colouristic subtlety.

The year of the opening of this miniature Chinese shadow theatre,

inspired by these lines of Goethe and also by the last sonnet of Keats. An analysis of the influence of Goethe on Gide is given in Jean Delay's *La Jeunesse d'André Gide*, from which it is clear that Debussy, closely associated with Louÿs and Gide at the time of the composition of the Quartet and *L'Après-midi d'un faune*, shared their ideas derived from these poets.

which functioned weekly on Friday evenings, is stated to have been 1891, but there is evidence that in some form it had been in existence earlier. The entry in Tchaikovsky's diaries for 5 March 1888 states that he had seen that evening what he calls the *Ombres françaises* in the company of Caran d'Ache with whom he had dined at the home of Monsieur and Madame Benardaky. Since Tchaikovsky refers to 'supper in a café' on this occasion one imagines that the café was the Chat Noir. It would thus just be possible for Debussy, six years after his second visit to Russia in the service of Madame von Meck, to have met at these impressionistic *séances* in the rue Victor Massé the beloved composer whom his misanthropic hostess had kept so mysteriously in the background.

Three of Debussy's friends were, with Salis, among the founders of the Chat Noir. They were Adolphe Willette, the draughtsman of charming Pierrots and Columbines who illustrated the first edition of Debussy's song *Mandoline*; the light poet and water-colourist Georges Lorin; and his inseparable friend Maurice Rollinat, a melancholy, intense figure, a sort of local Heine whose volume *Les Névroses* contains harrowing poems on Chopin and Poe and who set to music poems by Baudelaire sung by Yvette Guilbert. The other founders, Edmond Haraucourt, who in 1882 created a scandal with his 'Poèmes hystériques', *La Légende des sexes*, and the *Hydropathe* novelist Emile Goudeau, who was to reflect the vogue in Paris of Tchaikovsky by introducing a description into his novels of *None but the lonely heart*, were also known to Debussy at this time.

At the original Chat Noir musicians and poets performed at the back of a brasserie between two rows of tables and benches. Looking like a blonde Juno, Madame Salis surveyed the proceedings from a raised platform behind a bar with an upright piano at her feet. Here Debussy took turns playing and singing with the Polish poetess and song-writer, Marie Krysinska;[1] with the well-known chansonniers, Georges Fragerolle and Paul Delmet; and with the macabre Maurice Rollinat, his face twisted into a horrifying grimace as he sang his gruesome songs, usually about the victim of a vampire woman. Later we have evidence that Debussy became the life of the party.

---

[1] A minor figure with only rudimentary poetic gifts, Marie Krysinska (died 1908) claimed, on the strength of her prose poems published in the Chat Noir Journal, to have been one of the originators of the *vers libre*. 'Où sont-elles les nouveautés?' Verlaine asks of the technique of the *vers libre* poets. 'Est-ce que Rimbaud n'a pas fait tout cela avant eux? Et même Krysinska?'

Moreover, the reliable memoirs of Henri Büsser disclose an impor-
...t sequel to these early studies. Speaking of the period about 1890
...sser writes: 'Among the *auditeurs* in the class of Ernest Guiraud
...ten saw a mysterious person, aged between twenty-five and
...nty-eight, whom Debussy had introduced to our master with
...y strong recommendation. His name was Erik Satie and he
...d his living by playing the piano in a night-club. He seemed
...very little gifted and toiled enormously to produce a simple
...r-subject for a fugue, the sort of thing we were normally
...d to produce on the spot.'

...episode suggests that Debussy, struck by Satie's original
...generously urged Guiraud, his former master, to take this
...usician under his wing. 'Satie had already published some
...ces with odd and even ridiculous titles,' Büsser continues,
...ay he brought to play in class his *Pièces en forme de poire*
...duet) which he performed with César Galéotti, a student
...treat Satie maliciously. Our assistant master, André
...s furious with Satie for this unforgettable display and
...s so unpleasant for the unfortunate young man that he
...t in the Conservatoire again.'

...e incident places the Debussy-Satie relationship in a
...light. We see in the first place that the *Trois Morceaux*
..., Satie's most successfully ironic set of piano pieces,
...e been a caustic reply to Debussy's criticism of the
...is music, were written some thirteen years earlier
...ibuted to them in the published edition. More to
...he significance of the word *poire* (a mug or a dupe)
...e quaint parodies of scholastic exercises mingled
...t tunes. The *poire* was neither Satie himself nor
...y case would hardly have criticized the music
...end for its formlessness, but the kind-hearted
...good faith, must have offered his strange,
...ce of friendly advice. In the manner of a well-
...robably advised the young Satie to develop
...ich Satie's impertinent reply was the *Trois*
...oire. Possibly out of respect for Debussy,
...was clearly meant by Satie to be a gross
...allowed Satie's inadmissible breach of
...by his assistant, Gédalge.

[146]

Pierre Louÿs and Henri de Régnier
by Jacques-Emile Blanche

Gabriel Mourey in 1905

The playwright Maurice Donnay describes ar
company sang the song *Le Café* by Ben-T
line *Balzac n'a pas cessé d'en boire!*, 'the
conducting our wild chorus throughout

These were remote, youthful adventur
in later years, sharpened the dividir
between genuine artistic endeavour
efforts. When the feverish bohemia
Debussy had succeeded, or almost su
rescue. This was the innocent, tim
musical child and also a musical
least three of the Montmartre cal
refuge in the frivolities of M
that Toulouse-Lautrec had l

A mystery has hitherto su
his adolescent years, conc
and the nature of their
the Paris Conservatoire
eight years, in the ele
solfège class of Alber
and the harmony cl
an untalented pup
piano and his pi

The archives
statements. Th
vatoire for f
piano class,

¹ Frédéric
extended to
² The C
the comp
the prod
Ile Sai
Les Pl
Prou

Paul Verlaine in 1869

Catulle Mendès

M
ta
Bi
I o
twe
a ve
earne
to be
count
expecte

This
gifts, ha
unruly n
piano pie
'
and one
(for piano
inclined to
Gédalge, wa
made matter
never set foo

This strang
rather different
en forme de poir
believed to hav
formlessness of
than the date att
the point, we see t
in the title of thes
with vulgar cabare
Debussy, who in a
of his ingenuous fri
Guiraud who, in all
eccentric student a pie
meaning teacher, he p
a sense of form; to w
Morceaux en forme de F
Guiraud ignored what
insult to his master an
manners to be dealt with

The episode could only have taken place in 1890, since this was the one year that Büsser was a member of Guiraud's class. It seems, therefore, that Debussy could not have discovered Satie as pianist of the Auberge du Clou in 1891, as Satie claimed. They must have met earlier, either at this particular cabaret, or at the Chat Noir, or, as is more likely, at the Conservatoire when they were contemporaries. This being so, what emerges from Büsser's disclosure is that Debussy had taken a protective, avuncular attitude towards his eccentric friend, which he maintained until the end of his life, despite Satie's numerous hostile provocations. The taunting of Guiraud, disastrous as it turned out to be, was the least spectacular of an unceasing flow of such incidents. Often most humorous, they show Satie, 'a gentle medieval musician lost in our century' as Debussy affectionately describes him, to have been a victim of mingled exhibitionism and self-torture. On Guiraud's death in 1892 his untutored pupil grotesquely applied for his coveted seat at the Academy. His extravagant exhibitionism, a root feature of his character, clearly reflected in his work, aroused curiosity, though often not much more than curiosity. In the end Satie had created a legend, hardly matched by his musical achievement.[1]

We are of course concerned with Satie's motives and compulsions only in so far as they illuminate his friendship with Debussy. We may readily believe that Debussy, who constantly extolled the freshness of the child vision, found in Satie a similarly uninhibited enthusiasm for the first, novel experience. 'The more one learns about Satie,' Roger Shattuck shrewdly observes, 'the more one comes to see him as a man who performed every contortion in order to keep sight of his childhood. Like a child who twists his body as he walks in order not to lose sight of his shadow, Satie made sure that the most treasured part of his past was always at his side.' Debussy had himself assessed the ordeals of maintaining the child vision in adult life, and the greater ordeals of Satie, almost infant-minded by comparison, must have aroused his compassion, the more so since, by his nature, this independent figure was doomed to court failure or disaster. Frustration was intolerable to him not only in his work, often reduced, in defiance of frustration, to an expression of impotence, but in normal human intercourse.

[1] Further facts relating to the personal and artistic relationship between Satie and Debussy are incorporated in *Erik Satie: his Studies, Notebooks and Critics*, a Ph.D. thesis by W. P. Gowers (Cambridge, 1966).

Hence the uneasiness and the suspicion at the core of Satie's relationship with Debussy, the violent outbursts of temper and, in the form of self-punishment, the humiliations which Satie hankered after and inflicted upon himself. How else can we interpret the fact that, as a regular visitor to Debussy's home in later years, Satie was accustomed to accept an inferior brand of wine, set aside for him, while his host enjoyed a finer bottle? Hence, too, the unbreakable bond between them, a mother-child relationship of a kind, in which each reluctantly played his part, but to which they were pledged by their common determination to maintain in their working lives the child's instinctive and ingenuous vision. Hence, finally, the unpredictable manifestations of envy and greed that appear throughout each of their lives. Satie's sense of inferiority drove him to exhibitionism and something like megalomania; Debussy's refusal to submit to material or emotional frustration brought frequent suicidal broodings and sudden kleptomaniac expressions. Poverty, too, marked their lives, material poverty and, in a sense, spiritual poverty since child instincts cannot always be nourished with impunity. Debussy and Satie were united here with Verlaine, who freely recognized poverty as the price eventually to be paid by all who have attempted to uphold in maturity the child's pristine innocence and candour:

L'homme pauvre du coeur est-il si rare, en somme?
Non. Et je suis cet homme et vous êtes cet homme,
Et tous les hommes sont cet homme ou furent lui.

Debussy soon came to deplore the fashion for cabaret music established by the Chat Noir. Writing to Pierre Louÿs in 1898, he mercilessly condemns the current standards of taste degraded by the chansonniers, Paul Delmet and Georges Fragerolle, adding in this category the charming and inoffensive Reynaldo Hahn. He also deplores the popularization in the Montmartre cabarets of Baudelaire and Verlaine. Since much of the music of Satie remained close to cabaret vulgarity, Debussy could only have tolerated this streak in his friend because he recognized that Satie lacked both the skill and the maturity of mind to subject these ordinary, sentimental tunes to an effective ironic treatment.[1]

[1] Satie had sent to Chabrier one of his compositions beautifully copied out in red ink and Gothic script. No acknowledgement was received. It is possible that Satie would have become a very different composer had he obtained the encouragement from Chabrier so readily given to him by Debussy.

It was, however, a mark of Debussy's underlying respect for Satie that he orchestrated two of his short pieces. Towards the end of 1896 Satie and Debussy were accustomed to meet on Monday evenings at the home in the Avenue Beaucourt of the Swiss conductor Gustave Doret, together with the rising composers of the day, Charles Bordes, Guy Ropartz, and Paul Dukas. At one of these gatherings Satie played to Doret his *Trois Gymnopédies* which, though technically extremely simple, seemed beyond his powers. Debussy offered to play them for him, and it was at Doret's suggestion that they were orchestrated by Debussy and conducted by Doret at a concert of the Société Nationale on 20 February 1897. Fourteen years later, on 25 March 1911, when the vogue for Satie was such that entire concerts were being devoted to his works, Debussy himself conducted his orchestrations of the *Gymnopédies*, following a performance of some of Satie's piano pieces by Ravel.

Reciprocal influences of one kind or another must surely have existed in this long and strange relationship, but what were they? The *Gymnopédies* revive a medieval spirit, greatly cherished by Debussy. The frequently mentioned influence, on the other hand, of Satie's *Sarabande* of 1887 on Debussy's *Sarabande*, written seven years later, is difficult to establish. Both composers were drawn to the child-like innocence of the characters of Maeterlinck, though Jean Cocteau's contention that Satie had discovered Maeterlinck before Debussy is without foundation. It was Debussy who was the first of the many composers to be inspired by Maeterlinck, having approached the author on the subject of *La Princesse Maleine* at the time of its publication and having, according to one source, actually written the music.[1] 'Dieubussy!' declared Satie in abject admiration. Yet something of Satie's candour of spirit affected Debussy too. Perhaps in the end we may see Satie's most lasting influence in *Pelléas et Mélisande*, in the wonderful characterization of the child Yniold, possibly also in the innocence of the characters of Pelléas and Mélisande themselves, offsprings of Satie's self-denying poverty of spirit and of his primitive child-like wonder.

[1] 'Hitherto no theatre has extended hospitality to M. Debussy who has in his portfolio a score composed for Maeterlinck's *Princesse Maleine*.' (Alfred Bruneau, 'The Young French Composers of To-day' in *The Musician*, London, 23 June 1897.)

14
Mallarmé

... vain and monotonous as all art is when contrasted with
the immediacy and necessity of experience.

Wallace Fowlie

At midnight on the day of the first performance of the *Prélude à
l'Après-midi d'un faune*, 22 December 1894, Pierre Louÿs wrote to
Debussy, comparing it to the sensuous quivering of leaves moving
in a breeze: 'Your prelude is delightful. I am just home and wish to
tell you immediately. A more charming paraphrase of the poem we
both love can't be imagined. There's constantly a breeze among the
leaves, and with so much variety and fantasy. You've given me real
joy—not for the first time, as you know.' In October of the following year Debussy sent Louÿs a copy of the orchestral score of
L'Après-midi with the dedication, alluding to his work on poems of
Louÿs, 'Quelques airs de flûte pour charmer Bilitis'.

Both admirers of Mallarmé, Louÿs and Debussy were frequently
at the famous Tuesday evenings at which Mallarmé presided in the
rue de Rome. It has hitherto been held that Debussy was only an
occasional visitor at these gatherings, but recently published works
show that he belonged to the inner circle of Mallarmé's friends.
About 1892 he knew Mallarmé sufficiently well to invite his friend
Prince André Poniatowski[1] to one of the 'Mardis', and at about the
same time he took Mallarmé to hear Gregorian chant sung at the
Eglise Saint-Gervais. They heard Wagner at concerts at the Cirque

[1] Poniatowski makes a charming reference to the astonishment which, as a wealthy
business man, he expected to create among the poets and painters at the rue de Rome:
'How did Debussy get to know this club-man?' he writes, anticipating a rebuff. 'And
knowing him, why bring him here?' The Prince, who was a friend of Degas, as well as
of Debussy, was immediately welcomed and became closely associated with Mallarmé,
through whom he met other friends of Debussy, Georges Rodenbach, Whistler, and

d'Eté, in 1893 they were together at the first Paris performance of *Die Walküre* and a few days later, at the memorable first performance of Maeterlinck's *Pelléas et Mélisande* at the Théâtre des Bouffes-Parisiens. Four years later, on 2 February 1897, Debussy was one of a small group, including the American-born Francis Viélé-Griffin, who had published two of Debussy's poems, and Rodin, who offered a dinner to Mallarmé to celebrate the publication of his *Divagations*. At the restaurant Père Lathuile a bouquet in the form of a lyre was placed on the table and Mallarmé, seated between Léon Dierx, the last of the Parnassian poets, and Rodin, made a short speech, in a rather awkward manner according to Debussy, thanking his young friends for their gesture and regretting the absence of Debussy's principal collaborators, Maeterlinck and Louÿs.[1] When Mallarmé died the following year Paul Valéry, the poet's nearest disciple, felt that Louÿs and Debussy should be the first to be informed. 'I'm completely overcome, Mallarmé died yesterday morning,' he wrote to Louÿs. 'Tell Debussy.'

It was thus natural that Debussy was attracted by one of Mallarmé's principal works. *L'Après-midi d'un faune*, begun in 1892 and completed in September 1894, was announced in Paris and Brussels in the course of its composition as *Prélude, Interludes et Paraphrase finale pour l'Après-midi d'un faune*. From this description it is clear that the work was originally intended as an accompaniment for Mallarmé's poem, as a *glose* for a dramatic presentation. Vallas, who incorrectly refers to the second section in the singular, as an *Interlude*,

Huysmans. A copy of *L'Après-midi d'un faune*, addressed by Mallarmé to the Princess Poniatowska, bears the dedication:

> Faune
> avec ton chant s'il brusqua
> Le cours de l'heure qui s'éloigne
> Retiens près du Bois de Boulogne
> La Princesse Poniatowska.

[1] In his description of this banquet, in a letter to Pierre Louÿs of 9 February 1897, Debussy mentions the presence of other guests: the revered and influential Parnassian poet José-Maria de Hérédia, whose daughter Louÿs was to marry two years later, and Ernest La Jeunesse, the gifted homosexual critic, unfortunately deformed, and whose appearance was pathetically said to resemble a body-louse. The previous year La Jeunesse had had a spectacular success with his *Les Nuits, les ennuis et les âmes de nos plus notoires contemporains*, consisting of brilliant parodies of Maeterlinck, Huysmans, Anatole France and others. Debussy writes: 'Tu dois savoir tout ce qu'il faut savoir du banquet Mallarmé? Je m'y suis prodigieusement ennuyé; Mallarmé semblait partager mon avis, et a dit, d'une voix de polichinelle mélancolique, un petit discours froidement gêné. Francis Viélé-Griffin avait l'air d'un policeman et le petit La Jeunesse d'une maladie; j'ai fait là la connaissance de M. José-Maria de Hérédia, ça fait quelqu'un de plus à saluer et ça ne m'a donné aucune émotion.'

maintained that this and the *Paraphrase finale* had only been barely sketched out and that the whole work was ultimately compressed into the *Prélude*. We must await the publication of further correspondence of Debussy at this period to see his original conception of *L'Après-midi d'un faune*. In the meantime we may note that not only was Mallarmé's eclogue originally conceived for the stage, but that in 1891, fifteen years after the first edition, a list of his works which appeared in the Paris journal *Pages* refers to *L'Après-midi d'un faune* as a poem 'for reading or for the stage'. Clearly, Mallarmé never abandoned his dramatic conception of the work. Moreover, Debussy's original plan, for a score of incidental music, must necessarily have been undertaken with Mallarmé's approval.

The several early forms of Mallarmé's eclogue are worth dwelling upon. Originally conceived as an *Intermède héroïque*, it is first mentioned in a letter of March 1865, from Mallarmé to Henri Cazalis. This letter anticipates the very problem which, twenty years later, disturbed Debussy when writing *Diane au bois*. Seeking a means of recording fleeting impressions, Debussy had been anxious in this work to 'sacrifice dramatic action to an expression of the long exploration of inner feelings'. Mallarmé was likewise concerned with recording the acuteness of the momentary sensation. 'I have found an intimate and peculiar manner of depicting and setting down very fugitive impressions,' he writes of his early *Intermède*. 'What is frightening is that all these impressions are required to be woven together as in a symphony, and that I often spend whole days wondering whether one idea can be associated with another, what the relationship between them may be and what effect they will create.' Later *L'Après-midi* is said by Mallarmé to be 'definitely theatrical; it is not a work that may conceivably be given in the theatre; it demands the theatre'. At the suggestion of Théodore de Banville it was planned to be given at the Théâtre Français as a one-act piece in verse, in the style, in fact, of Banville's own *Diane au bois*. In the summer of 1865 Mallarmé read to Banville and Constant Coquelin a draft of the poem, now entitled *Monologue du Faune*, in the form of a theatrical scene for a narrator and actors performing in mime. The central theme of a faun dreaming of the conquest of nymphs is that of the final version, but the episodes are more sharply exteriorized, the transition from the dream world to the waking world is less ambiguous, and the imagery is both more boldly erotic and less subtle. Reasonably enough, Banville and Coquelin declared that the *Monologue* was simply not cast in a dramatic form. It is likely, however, that this version, with its many stage directions, was known to Debussy since Mallarmé's manuscript of the *Monologue* eventually became the property of Ernest Chausson with whom Debussy, at the time he was writing *L'Après-midi*, was on intimate terms. Without knowing the date of Chausson's acquisition of Mallarmé's manuscript we can hardly take our investigation further. We must be content to say that the works of Mallarmé and Debussy both originated as dramatic conceptions and that they had both strong affinities with the earlier work of Banville.

In his setting of *Diane au bois* Debussy chose the scene of the conquest of Diana by Eros. A flute solo plays a symbolical role in this early score, but its character is conventional. *L'Après-midi d'un faune* has a much more sophisticated theme: the faun's dual attraction to two nymphs and the fantasies of lesbianism, expressed in the final line, 'Couple adieu! Je vais voir l'ombre que tu devins', arising from his failure to seduce them. The character in *Diane au bois* that attracted Mallarmé was the satyr Gniphon who similarly expresses a dual attraction. In illustration of this point Dr. Mondor quotes these lines of Gniphon, 'the tireless satyr', as he subtly describes him, 'obsessed with symmetry':

> Enfin tout est par deux; moi, j'aurai deux amantes
> Lyre et Syrinx, duo rare et mélodieux
> Vous bercerez mes jours dorés. Merci, mes dieux!
> L'une par sa douceur calmera mon martyre
> L'autre le causera; l'une me fera rire
> Et l'autre me fera pleurer. . . .

Other sources of Mallarmé's *L'Après-midi d'un faune* include a contemporary trial, at Carpentras in Provence, of a shepherd for the rape of a young girl; Baudelaire's poem *Lesbos* from the *Fleurs du Mal*; and, most plausibly, the myth of Pan pursuing the nymph Syrinx who, with her sisters, is changed by Diana into rushes. As Pan embraces the rushes his breath becomes sweet music. Hidden in this myth is the theory, re-stated by Mallarmé, that a function of the dream is to allow love to be sublimated into music.

It would be absurd to seek in Debussy's *Prélude* a close illustration of the dark symbolism of Mallarmé's poem. The music, Debussy insisted, is to be regarded only as 'a very free illustration and in no way as a synthesis of the poem'. Nevertheless, since this is music clearly fertilized by poetic symbolism, there was a marriage of minds of some kind and certain interpretations that have been made of Mallarmé's aesthetic also illuminate the inspiration of Debussy.

Mallarmé's poem goes far beyond its theme of abduction. Buried in its abstruse language is a philosophical treatise on the life of the senses and the psychology of sublimation. It is also an exploration of the borderlands between the conscious and the half-conscious, the waking state and the state of reverie. In his *Introduction à la Psychanalyse de Mallarmé* Charles Mauron observes the deliberate confusion in *L'Après-midi* between these various degrees of consciousness and unconsciousness. The faun emerges from a dream, plays like a child with the fantasies of his dreams, but satisfies his desires only by plunging back into sleep. The poet's art consists of never allowing us to be quite sure if the faun is dreaming (*Aimai-je un rêve?*) or whether, when awake, he is aware of the distinction between primitive desire and the sublimated artistic vision. Another critic, Wallace Fowlie, similarly draws attention to a duality of meanings in the poem. The dual meaning of the opening line, 'Ces nymphes, je les veux perpétuer', this critic suggests, represents a condensation of the entire work. 'Copulation,' he explains, 'may well be one significance of the afternoon's quest; and—the word "perpetuate" is of a refined elegance—preservation by means of art may be the other.' Indeed, duality of one kind or another is reflected throughout the poem. There are two nymphs, one chaste, living on illusion, the other experienced, sighing for love; and there are in reality two fauns, both the lascivious faun and the aloof, objective faun watching himself wrestling with desire. The faun actually addresses himself as another person. The desires of neither are fulfilled; nor can they be since in the faun's quest for the nymphs, as in his flute-playing, there is a constant interplay between action and indolence. In the end Venus herself is possessed, this being the wildest of fantasies, which can only signify that the faun is about to take his final refuge in sleep.

There is a difference between the dreams of sleep and the musings of reverie. The latter are considered by Mallarmé to be adolescent and even impotent. And from one viewpoint the faun, too, is the adolescent artist anxious to make amorous conquests but remaining more truly a poet. Here Mr. Fowlie emphasizes that *L'Après-midi* is 'Mallarmé's most significant inquest into the perplexing but omnipresent relationship between the sexual dream world of the poet and his creative life as a practising poet'. The imagery in the description of the faun as an 'ingenuous lily', playing with blown-up grape skins, his passion bursting like the purple pomegranate, is clearly shot through with erotic associations ('Cet admirable poème cochon,' said Verlaine). Yet the heart of the poem is in a definition of sublimation. Mallarmé attempts to trace the process in which desire first vanishes into the dream and is then transformed into music:

> Et de faire, aussi haut que l'amour se module
> Evanouir du songe ordinaire de dos
> Ou de flancs purs suivis avec nos regards clos
> Une sonore, vaine et monotone ligne.

I think we may see in the last line the origin of the flute solo at the opening of Debussy's score. In the preceding lines the faun's flute-playing is actually described as 'a long solo':

> Qui, détournant à soi le trouble de la joue,
> Rêve, dans un solo long, que nous amusions
> La beauté d'alentour par des confusions
> Fausses entre elle-même et notre chant crédule.

These four lines, which bring us to the heart of Debussy's inspiration, are interpreted by Mr. Fowlie thus: 'In the high notes of the flute the entire experience of love may be reduced into a single melodic line, vain and monotonous as all art is when contrasted with the immediacy and necessity of experience. As he plays thus on his instrument, the faun is master of himself and his feelings. He is able to follow inwardly the dream of having seen the nudity of a nymph, her back and side, and to sing of such a vision without experiencing the need of acting upon it.' In the end *L'Après-midi* is seen to be a poem about how a poem, or indeed, music, is written.

Several of Mallarmé's opinions of Debussy's score have been recorded, not all of them in agreement. Since the poem aims at an entirely sonorous ideal it is not surprising that Mallarmé was said by René Peter to have declared: 'I thought I had myself set it to music;

it is a transposition du *même au même*.'[1] Poniatowski, on the other hand, speaks of 'long meditations in the course of which the musician received from the poet his conception of the role of music'.[2] Mallarmé attended the first performance of Debussy's work at which he scribbled down a few lines, later transcribed in the form of a dedication to the composer. He had been invited to attend in a letter from Debussy of 21 December 1894, amusingly written in imitation of Mallarmé's labyrinthine manner. He wished Mallarmé to encourage the arabesques which, possibly from vanity, he felt to have been dictated by the faun's flute:

Cher Maître

Ai-je besoin de vous dire la joie que j'aurai si vous voulez bien encourager de votre présence les arabesques qu'un peut-être coupable orgueil m'a fait croire être dictées par la flûte de votre Faune?

Votre respectueusement dévoué

Claude Debussy

Earlier Debussy had played over the score to Mallarmé. In a letter of 25 March 1910 to G. Jean-Aubry, Debussy states that this took place at his home in the rue de Londres where the wallpaper, consisting of pictures of Monsieur Carnot surrounded by little birds, made one never want to be at home.[3] His letter continues: 'Mallarmé

[1] Suzanne Bernard questions the authenticity of this statement of Mallarmé. It was amazingly attributed, by Laurent Tailhade in his *Fantômes de Jadis*, to Renan on learning that there was question of setting to music his *Vie de Jésus*.

[2] There had been an earlier work, *Glose à l'Après-midi d'un faune* by V. Emm. C. Lombardi, described in *La Revue Indépendante* of January 1888 as consisting of 'ten pages of music for piano showing some slight charm but lack of experience'. Lombardi was an Italian musician, admired by Massenet, and also an obscure member of the extravagant 'Instrumentalist' school of symbolist poets led by René Ghil. In Ghil's *Traité du Verbe* (1885) an arbitrary poetic system is described in which each of the vowels in the spoken or written language is required to evoke a specific colouristic or sonorous equivalent. Though at first sympathetic to Ghil, Mallarmé, who wrote a preface for the *Traité du Verbe*, became severely critical of him, particularly as Ghil had declared in *La Wallonie* (December 1887) that Lombardi's *Glose* for *L'Après-midi* had provided what was lacking in Mallarmé's poem. From the description given by Suzanne Bernard of Lombardi's privately printed piano piece (a copy of which was in the possession of Henri Mondor), it seems to have been a rather amateurish effort. Containing extracts from the poem written above the stave, it purports to illustrate the abstruse poem line by line, having a central section consisting of variations on a *grand leitmotiv du Midi*.

[3] Debussy's memory was apparently at fault here; he was living at this time at 10 rue Gustave Doré. But the allusion to Sadi Carnot, President of the Republic, may not be insignificant: his assassination shortly before the first performance of *L'Après-midi*, in July 1894, was an unforgettable blow to French prestige.

[156]

came in with his prophetic air and his Scotch plaid around him. After listening he remained silent for a long time; then said: "I didn't expect anything like this. It is music that brings out the feeling of my poem, providing it with a warmer background than colour."' Elsewhere, in an undated letter to Debussy, Mallarmé speaks of 'your illustration of *L'Après-midi d'un faune* which presents no dissonance with my text; rather does it go further into the nostalgia and light with subtlety, malaise and richness'.

A copy of the poem was to be presented to Debussy, but there was apparently some delay. Characteristically, Mallarmé wrote: 'I hadn't put aside the *Faune* which you quite rightly sent someone to fetch. But suddenly, yesterday, when I saw the water running I thought of it. Why should this be?' The copy was eventually received, containing illustrations by Manet and the dedication in the form of an exquisite conceit by Mallarmé in which the senses of sight and sound are mated and intermingled:

> Sylvain d'haleine première
> Si ta flûte a réussi
> Ouïs toute la lumière
> Qu'y soufflera Debussy.[1]

The performance at the Salle d'Harcourt in the rue Rochechouart was given under Gustave Doret, a young Swiss conductor who had spent long hours with Debussy studying the score 'already covered with corrections'. Until the last moment Debussy 'was constantly modifying one effect or another'. Alterations were tried out and compared at rehearsals. What the tenuous work sounded like on this first occasion may be judged from a remark of Louÿs: 'The horns were appalling and the rest of the orchestra were hardly much better.' Yet from the first the work was a triumph and, though given towards the end of a long and varied programme, had to be repeated.[2]

Debussy's paraphrase of *L'Après-midi d'un faune*, which was as daring and also as esoteric when it first appeared as Mallarmé's poem,

---

[1] Among other artists in Debussy's circle to whom Mallarmé dedicated poems were Ernest Chausson, Pierre Louÿs, José-Maria de Hérédia, Catulle Mendès, Georges Rodenbach, Henri de Régnier, Francis Viélé-Griffin, and Augusta Holmès.

[2] Other works in this programme were Glazounov's *La Forêt*, J. Bordier's *Suite serbe*, Henri Duparc's *La Vague et la Cloche*, Bourgault-Ducoudray's *L'Enterrement d'Ophélie*, Saint-Saëns's Third Violin Concerto, Guy Ropartz's *Prière*, and César Franck's *Redemption*.

has since become his most popular work. *Faune y soit qui mal y pense*, wrote the music critic Willy of an early performance. It later served as music for several ballets and it has had the sardonic fate in recent times of having been transformed into a jazz number. Yet something had happened in *L'Après-midi* from which there was no going back. Something had snapped, and something had also disintegrated. For the first time in modern music themes are not developed. No sooner are they announced than they become merged with other themes, modulate, change their character or disappear in fragments. Over the length of a mere 108 bars there is a constant tonal ambiguity. It is true that coherence is achieved by maintaining an underlying tonal centre, but the fluid sense of harmony is such that the maximum freedom is allowed in the movement of each part. A wonderful stroke occurs when the work concludes not with a re-statement of the opening arabesque, but with a mere fragment of it, now in a new harmonic perspective, creating the illusion of incompleteness.[1]

In 1905 Debussy was described in the *Mercure de France* as 'aspiring to the heritage of Mallarmé'. Eight years later there appeared the first of the complete editions of Mallarmé's poems. As if to mark the occasion three of them were set by Debussy, *Soupir*, *Placet futile*, and *Eventail*, which he dedicated to the memory of Mallarmé and to his daughter Geneviève, the faithful, unobtrusive server of punch at the 'Mardis' in the rue de Rome.[2] With the exception of the *Nöel des enfants* they were his last songs. The choice of these three poems from the 1913 edition, the first two of which were also set in this year by Ravel, was not haphazard. In *Placet futile* as in *Apparition*, set by Debussy thirty years earlier, he was drawn to the aphrodisiac

[1] In 1944 Mallarmé's *Hérodiade*, the sister poem of *L'Après-midi d'un faune*, was set in the form of an 'orchestral recitation' by Hindemith. *Hérodiade* is also a philosophical discourse, written from the conviction that beauty is in the end cold, forbidding, and inaccessible. The times had moved against the sensuous view of Mallarmé and it was in keeping with the defiant outlook of the 1940s that Hindemith, half a century after Mallarmé's death, was attracted to the wintry, almost metallic figure of *Hérodiade*.

In his *Lettres à quelques-uns* (1952) Paul Valéry states that Mallarmé had been staunchly adverse to settings of his poems and that even Debussy had encountered difficulties. Yet his influence later persisted in many spheres. Apart from his appeal to Pierre Boulez, it is significant that both Mallarmé's *Hérodiade* and *L'Après-midi d'un faune* were abundantly drawn upon by James Joyce in *Finnegans Wake*, a work close to the heart of several contemporary composers.

[2] In Camille Mauclair's *Le Soleil des Morts*, consisting of a series of life-like portraits of Mallarmé and his circle, Geneviève Mallarmé (Sylvaine) successively attracts Paul Adam, Debussy, and Pierre Louÿs. But none of them dares to declare his love for her and they are resigned to remain friends. Geneviève is likened in this perspicacious work to 'Morella, the Morella of Edgar Allan Poe; she re-experiences, in a living form, her father's exteriorized ideas and feelings' (see Appendix F).

symbolism of a woman's hair. *Soupir*, addressed to Mallarmé's wife, is shot through with memories of Poe (the 'dead water' and the 'calm sister'). But it is the choice of *Eventail* that is most significant. In 1913 Debussy was facing a severe material and artistic crisis. *Eventail* is a poem spoken by a fan (actually the fan of Geneviève Mallarmé), and for this strange poem Debussy wrote music inspired for the last time by the dream—not the dream of sleep, but the dream of the waking state, plunging into pure imagination. Half tauntingly half consolingly the fan, opening and closing before a woman's eyes, both reveals and obscures the object of desire, and in the end stoically urges the onlooker to refuse life and to lie to reality.

15
Pierre Louÿs

Happiness is not in the intellect or the fancy—but in the wife, the heart, the bed, the table, the saddle, the fireside, the country.

Melville

The first musician for me would be he who knew only the sorrow of the profoundest happiness and no other sorrow: there has not hitherto been such a musician.

Nietzsche

'Among my friends you are certainly the one I have loved the most,' Debussy wrote to Pierre Louÿs in 1903. Not only Debussy, but Gide, Valéry, and Mallarmé were drawn to this underrated poet, critic, and connoisseur of the arts. 'Who among his friends was not greatly indebted to him?' asks Valéry. 'The most illustrious of them, Claude Debussy, found in Louÿs support, guidance, and a mind that was able to open up new literary visions. In every way and at all times Louÿs was of the greatest help to Debussy throughout his career.' Earlier writers have been reluctant to accept this judgement of Valéry. This was partly because the nature of their relationship has long remained obscure, but it was also because in the popular view Louÿs had acquired an unfortunate reputation based, like the popular view of D. H. Lawrence, on a pornographic interpretation of his novels, particularly *L'Homme de Pourpre*, *Une Volupté nouvelle*, and *Aphrodite*. Valéry, it was felt, had exaggerated the benevolent role played by Louÿs in Debussy's life, and attempts were made to belittle Debussy's long and intimate relationship with a writer who, it was believed, flourished only in the salacious backwaters of the Symbolist movement. An important series of unpublished letters from Louÿs to Debussy, as well as a closer study of the published correspondence between them, suggests that there were sentimental

[160]

or prudish motives here. In fact, Valéry was well placed to assess their relationship: he had himself been inspired by Louÿs and his assessment of Louÿs's influence on Debussy was the simple truth.[1]

Eight years younger than Debussy, Louÿs, at the beginning of their friendship in 1893, was an adventurous young poet of twenty-three, living on a comfortable private income, cultivated, gifted, and ambitious. 'There was an exquisite youthfulness about him,' writes André Gide, his class-mate at the Ecole Alsacienne. 'It was as though a sort of boiling agitation inside him were shaking the lid of his reserve in a kind of passionate stammer. I thought it the most charming thing in the world.' With Debussy there were no barriers of any kind. It was a full relationship embracing not only their common musical and literary interests but practical matters and also their emotional attitudes to women and money. They planned at one time to live together 'in a large house at Neuilly at the end of an alley of trees, as in Lamartine', and although they ultimately decided against this romantic project they were constantly together, relishing food, women, books, and music in large and eager satisfaction. Money was an important consideration, but not in a conventional sense. In Debussy's mind, ready to grasp at remote symbols, the very name of his friend, pronounced not as it is usually heard today but without sounding the final 's', was identical with that of the twenty-franc gold piece. Psychological theories that would attribute the intimacy of their relationship to this casual fact are not exaggerated.[2] Louÿs was generous and unstinting; Debussy was impecunious and dependent. Yet money seems never to have been a subject of dispute or ill-feeling. Nor is there any sign that Louÿs used his friend's financial dependence to exert a selfish power in their relationship. Money was shared, and so were confidences of their amorous lives. No secrets were kept from each other on the fluctuations of their

[1] 'The friendship of Pierre Louÿs was a capital episode in my life,' Valéry wrote shortly after the death of Louÿs in 1925. 'It was by sheer chance that I met him and as a result my life was completely changed.' About 1894 Debussy, Louÿs, Valéry, and Gide appear all to have been on close terms with each other. 'I dined with André Gide and Valéry,' Debussy wrote on 27 July 1894 to Louÿs, then in Algeria. 'We spoke a great deal about you, not the least delightful moments of this evening.'

[2] Several references in the correspondence with Louÿs and the memoirs of René Peter show that Debussy was conscious of this association. A letter of about 1895 to Louÿs reads: 'On est dans la purée noire, comme qui dirait en fa dièse mineur, verte, multicolore et jusqu'au cou! Claude vient demander à son petit ami le service d'un LOUIS! ! ! pour lequel il lui adresse un merci reconnaissant, pour Pierre, qu'il reçoive son amitié dévouée.'

hearts.[1] Only marriage appears to have reduced the intensity of their friendship, though even here they each acted in response to a similar unconscious motive. One must imagine a high degree of sensibility in these artists that drove them to choose wives because of the euphony of their names. On 24 June 1899 Pierre Louÿs married Louise de Hérédia, daughter of the poet José-Maria de Hérédia. The event is announced to Debussy thus: 'Par un amour de la rime riche qui lui vient sans doute de son père, Mademoiselle Louise de Hérédia échange son nom contre celui de Louise Louÿs qui est plus symétrique et plus équilibré.' Five months later, on 19 October, Debussy married a model, employed at the Soeurs Callot, Lilly (diminutive of Rosalie) Texier. 'Mademoiselle Lilly Texier,' we read in a letter to Godet, 'a changé son nom inharmonique pour celui de Lilly Debussy—bien plus euphonique, tout le monde en conviendra.'[2]

If ever the complete correspondence of Debussy and Louÿs is assembled and published, the indications are that it will reveal a relationship similar to that of Verlaine and Rimbaud. I am not suggesting that Debussy and Louÿs were drawn together by an overt homosexual attraction. Nor were there sudden hostile collisions between them. But as with Verlaine and Rimbaud there were frequent identifications of artistic and physical values. In artists where buried conflicts rise easily to the surface music is a woman, her hair, the look in her eyes, the movements of her body.[3] In his *Pervigilium Mortis*, rated by Yves le Dantec

---

[1] Recounting the attempt at suicide of his mistress Gabrielle Dupont, Debussy wrote to Louÿs in 1897: 'Jamais je ne t'ai oublié; j'ai beaucoup pensé à toi et même causé avec toi. . . . J'ai été tout de même bouleversé et, encore une fois, attristé de te sentir si loin, si irréfutablement loin. . . . Les paroles que l'on dit les yeux dans les yeux amis ne se remplacent pas par de l'écriture.'

[2] 'Names are everything,' says Lord Henry in Wilde's *Picture of Dorian Gray*. In his *Psychanalyse de Mallarmé* Charles Mauron notes that Mallarmé's sister Maria, whom he calls 'Miss Mary', died in adolescence, that Mallarmé married Marie Gerhardt and that his mistress of the later years was Méry Laurent. D'Annunzio was similarly obsessed by euphonious names, choosing as companions on a sailing cruise two young men for the sheer sound of their beautiful names, Ippolito Santilozzo and Valente Valori. The names were hardly qualifications for seamanship, Mr. Anthony Rhodes points out, 'for Santilozzo was unable to handle a sail, and Valori was a martyr to sea-sickness'.

[3] Of a performance of the *Ballade* for piano and orchestra by Gabriel Fauré Debussy wrote: 'The *Ballade* is almost as lovely as Mme Hasselmans, the pianist. With a charming gesture she readjusted a shoulder-strap which slipped down at every lively passage. Somehow an association of ideas was established in my mind between the charm of the aforementioned gesture and the music of Fauré. It is a fact, however, that the play of the graceful, fleeting lines described by Fauré's music may be compared to the gesture of a beautiful woman without either suffering from the comparison.'

as one of the greatest French love poems, Louÿs has lines such as

Le battement du sein palpitait dans son vers

or

Ferme sur toute moi, sur moi, ton bras qui tremble!

in which the poet not only adores a woman, he is the woman.

Hardly any of Debussy's friends, not even Godet or Mourey, were able to measure, as Louÿs seems to have done, the complex feelings aroused in Debussy by Wagner. A letter written by Louÿs on 29 October 1896 is worth quoting in full for the light it throws on their fervent Wagnerian discussions:

My dear Claude,

We recently had on the subject of Richard Wagner a most serious conversation. If we were not so intelligent, you and I, I should not suggest taking it any further, but since neither of us imagines that he will be ultimately convincing I think we may enjoy this skirmish in which you bring to bear the heavy guns of your musical knowledge against my vain, slender arguments.

Now how you exaggerate! On Monday you said things of which you simply don't believe nine-tenths [. . .] I, on the other hand, in a serious discussion of this sort, wouldn't dare go to such lengths. I merely said that Wagner was the greatest man who had ever existed, and nothing more. I didn't say he was great God himself, though in fact I was inclined to say something of this sort. I merely pronounced judgements with which everyone would agree.

After thinking over all this during the past week, and having had during this time many an imaginary conversation with you, I now want to set out my feelings which I have no intention of changing before the end of the century: (1) Not only do I admit, but I fully believe, that certain composers, Bizet for instance, and even more Moussorgsky perhaps, are superior to Wagner in expressing simple feelings of which they find a vocal equivalent. (2) I am absolutely convinced—and I am not giving you a point; I am ready to say this to everyone—that in no opera of Wagner or anyone else, in none of the vocal works of Schumann, the Russians or any composer you may name is such harmony to be found between the written and the sung words as in *Pelléas*.

But if this were *all* in *Pelléas*, it would merely be a second-rate work. Why? Because, set against an orchestra of a hundred and twenty instrumentalists, the singer is of no more significance than the piccolo. Music which should transcend drama is thus reduced to the level of the spoken word. Mademoiselle Bartet can be heard every evening declaiming phrases as beautiful as those of Mozart or Schumann, and the fury of Golaud (as his part is *sung*) is precisely the fury of Mounet-Sully[1] which is indeed remarkably fine.

Music is the breathing in your Prelude to the Faun, it is the sudden breath of air as Pelléas emerges from the subterranean vaults. It is the wind from the sea in the first act. It is the funereal monotony of the fifth act.

In situations such as these Wagner was really himself. More than anyone, since the beginning of art, Wagner has understood and expressed *movement* of all kinds, from its absence to a state of paroxysm. He even wrote a work, *Lohengrin*, on this very subject. 'Lohengrin is a character who comes and goes,' said Mallarmé, 'and there can be nothing more dramatic.' The Venusberg Music (even before the ballet of 1861), the arrival of Lohengrin, the Rhine-maidens' Scene, the flight of Sieglinde and Siegmund, the Ride of the Valkyries and the arrival of Wotan—these are things which had never before been conceived, written, painted nor played. And when we come to the great episodes: the departure of Siegfried after Scene i of *Siegfried*; the scene of the Anvil and the Fire Music; the delirium of Tristan, the arrival of Isolda and the death of Tristan; the third act of *Götterdämmerung*, from the shattering of the spear; Act II, Scene i and Act III, Scene i of *Parsifal*, including the Prelude and the second transformation scene—here I believe that no one will ever compare with Wagner.

Movement in this sense may seem to be a minor matter. But this is not so at all. Movement is life; and movement as it is made to express the passion of Tristan is not less real or wonderful than that of the wooden horses at a roundabout, or movement, as we may imagine it, inhabiting the danseuses at the Opéra as they masturbate in imaginary intercourse with Wotan.

If we cannot agree on this essential matter let us not worry

[1] Julia Bartet (1854–1941) and Jean Sully Mounet, known as Mounet-Sully (1841–1916) were the most celebrated tragic actors of their time who often appeared together at the Comédie Française in Greek dramas and plays of Shakespeare, Racine, and Victor Hugo.

overmuch. You used to come round to my view and there is no reason to suppose that I might not eventually agree with you, given the time for such a radical change.

Your

Pierrelouÿs.[1]

If there is any doubt of the moral support Debussy received from Louÿs, their correspondence from the spring of 1898 shows that Louÿs was perhaps alone at this time in assessing Debussy's true stature. He was well placed to do so, having heard the whole of *Pelléas* played at the piano by Debussy as early as 1895, and indeed, as we may judge from both the preceding and the following letters, Louys's opinion of *Pelléas* at this time was remarkably prophetic. In April 1898 Debussy wrote to Louÿs, then travelling in Egypt and Italy:

I really do need your affection, I feel so lonely and helpless. Nothing has changed in the black background of my life and I hardly know where I am going if it is not towards suicide—a senseless ending to something that might have turned out better. I've got into this state of mind from continually fighting against silly and despicable impossibilities. You know me better than anyone and you alone can take it upon yourself to tell me that I am not altogether an old fool. . . .

In a letter dated 5 May 1898, Louÿs replied urgently and with deep concern:

I have just returned from Rome where I saw your portrait near that of M. Ingres and delightfully placed.[2] I assure you that I was most moved seeing you there, not a great likeness perhaps, but

[1] This is not the only example of Louÿs's insistence that his friends should share his superlative feelings. Writing seven years earlier, on 14 August 1889, to André Gide, he declared that Victor Hugo was 'le plus profondément vibrant de tous les hommes! Il a tout senti. Il a tout exprimé, et d'une manière définitive. . . . Tu me réponds: "Mais je l'admire autant que toi!" Oui, mais tu ne l'aimes pas et je l'aime plus encore que je ne l'admire. Swinburne l'a dit admirablement:

"Praised above all be thou
Praised and beloved."

And beloved, entends-tu? Et dire que, malgré mes quatre pages tu ne l'en aimeras pas pour un sou de plus.'

[2] Debussy's portrait painted by Marcel Baschet is at the Villa Medici in Rome.

there you were in that glorious dining hall. I immediately felt that
of those three hundred portraits three or four figures may survive
and that you will be one of them. I can hardly tell you, therefore,
how absurd I find your letter, which I have only received today
and which was sent on to Cairo the day I arrived in Naples. I had
feelings of that kind myself four years ago, but at that time no one
had ever praised my work sincerely, and I wondered whether I
wasn't mistaken, whether I really did have any contribution to
make to literature. The day when I saw myself ruined, without a
sou to my name, without a contract with any publisher or theatre,
I had my hand on a revolver, and I would *certainly* have used it
had it not been for my brother.[1] And what I would have done
would have been a very stupid thing. (I'm telling you what
happened on the evening of December 24, 1894. You can imagine
that I haven't forgotten.)

Now you, my dear chap, you haven't the shadow of an excuse
for nightmares of this kind—because YOU ARE A GREAT MAN.
Do you understand the meaning of this? You have been given to
understand as much. But I am telling you this. And you will
perhaps believe me when I add that I have never said this to anyone.
Whatever troubles you may have, this thought must dominate
everything. You must continue with your work, and you must
get it known, two matters from which you wish to be relieved,
but which must represent everything for you. It's not by giving
music lessons that you will be assured of a livelihood, it's by doing
everything to get *Pelléas* performed. You think of practical
negotiations as beneath you but I think you may be mistaken, for
the main point is that you should be able to work and you will not
be able to work without having the wherewithal in your home.

Think over this. All that you say concerns me deeply. If you
think I can be of any use tell me how. I will do everything I can on
my own without mentioning it to you. To begin with you will
have *Cendrelune*,[2] but you won't be able to do much with that;

---

[1] In 1891, at the age of twenty-one, Louÿs had inherited 300,000 francs. In March of
that year he was afflicted with tuberculosis and was warned that he might have only
three years to live unless he led an abstemious existence. He determined, however, to
spend 100,000 francs each year, bringing himself to ruin on Christmas Eve 1894. Until
the success of his novel *Aphrodite* two years later Louÿs was supported by his brother.
[2] This was the scenario of a Christmas story by Louÿs, originally conceived for
production at the Opéra-Comique with music by Debussy. Several sketches for the
work, originally entitled *Geneviève* and later *Psyché* and *Kundrynette*, were made by

you need something that will assure you of twenty louis in your pocket before seeking new harmonies; nothing can be so inspiring. (Between ourselves I am hoping that my wretched reputation might enable you to find a second Hartmann—or the same one—when you have the libretto. But I am not certain.)

We must talk over all this. I returned to Paris the day before yesterday and I am leaving tomorrow for the provinces, not far away. Write me a note which I shall receive on Sunday evening telling me if I may bring a little lunch to your place, Monday at one o'clock.

Your friend,

Pierre.

The mention here of Hartmann allows us to investigate Debussy's means of support during these years. The reference is to Georges Hartmann, a generous and farsighted publisher whom Debussy met about 1890. Hartmann, who was the representative of the Wagner family in France, played an important part in French musical life, having co-operated with Alfred Ernest in the French translation of *The Ring* and having founded, in 1873, the Concerts de l'Odéon which later became the Concerts Colonne. Among the composers he adopted were Bizet, Franck, and Saint-Saëns. To Debussy, the last of his discoveries, he was particularly generous, providing him from about 1894 onwards with a yearly income of 6,000 francs. The early works of Debussy, appearing under the imprint Fromont, were in fact all published by Hartmann with whom Fromont was associated. 'He was sent to me by Providence,' Debussy wrote to Louÿs, 'and he played his part with a grace and charm rather rare among philanthropists.'

If ever it were possible to assemble Debussy's correspondence

Louÿs with variants suggested by Debussy and Hartmann. The subject was apparently inspired by *Parsifal*. In correspondence with Louÿs Debussy remarks, 'Cendrelune est tout de même trop petite pour jouer les Parsifal', and elsewhere, 'Tu veux donc que je demande à André Gide de finir *Cendrelune*.' Gide's assistance was proposed since symbolical elements, suggested by Debussy and deriving from *Parsifal* and the Art Nouveau, had discouraged Louÿs. 'Ecris toi-même *Cendrelune*,' he writes to Debussy. 'Tu en es parfaitement capable. A force de faire des changements à ce petit livret, il m'est devenu complètement étranger. Tel qu'il est, je ne pourrais plus le développer. Cette religiosité, ce triomphe du lys sur la rose et de la pudeur sur l'amour,—c'est de l'hébreu pour moi.' The project was abandoned before any music was written. A version of the story is published in *Poëtique* (Paris, 1930), part of the *Oeuvres complètes* of Louÿs.

with Hartmann, extending until the benevolent publisher's death in the spring of 1900, a study might be written on the lines of the studies on the material existence of Verlaine and Baudelaire entitled *De quoi vivaient-ils?*[1] It is certain that whatever funds Debussy received from Hartmann, Louÿs, and others he remained impecunious, unable to meet his mounting debts and living in almost abject poverty. The single room in which he lived at 42 rue de Londres is vividly described by Vital Hocquet, a humble plumber much interested in music who was one of Debussy's friends at the Chat Noir. It was 'a kind of attic in which, in great disorder, were a rickety table, three straw-bottomed chairs, something resembling a bed and, on loan, a splendid Pleyel piano'.[2]

Before the appearance of *L'Après-midi d'un faune* and the Quartet Prince Poniatowski had been moved by Debussy's financial plight to approach his American friends, the conductors Anton Seidl and Walter Damrosch, with a view to organizing a concert of Debussy's works in New York. 'His only means of support were piano lessons at five francs an hour,' Poniatowski comments, 'and he was getting into an exasperated, almost neurasthenic state of mind as I clearly gathered from his letters.' Poniatowski's idea, to which Seidl was sympathetic, was that Debussy should introduce in New York his *Fantaisie* for piano and orchestra and other works, and that if the concert was successful he would approach Andrew Carnegie for support for Debussy over a period of two or three years. In a letter to Poniatowski of 9 September 1892, Debussy writes in detail of this American project:

As you quite rightly tell me, I perhaps owe the best things I have done to the desperate life I have led up till now, and perhaps hard times do bring things out of one more effectively than a carefree, spineless existence and a sense of security lulling the mind into a state of indolence. But besides being a fellow normally glued

[1] The bulk of Debussy's correspondence with Hartmann, consisting of seventy letters, was dispersed and sold in separate lots at the Hôtel Drouot, 28 April 1958.

[2] Debussy apparently possessed no scores or anything approaching a personal library at this time. Nor did Verlaine or Rimbaud. Something is apparent here of Debussy's creation, Monsieur Croche, based on Valéry's Monsieur Teste, who says 'I haven't had any books for twenty years. I've burnt my papers too ... I can remember what I want.' Writing of a visit he paid to Debussy at an unspecified time 'in an apartment near the Boulevard Péreire', Pierre Lasserre, under the pseudonym Jean Darnaudat, states: 'The only musical creation which he did not disdain to possess was his piano.'

to his table, watching the butterflies at the bottom of his
inkwell, I am also ready for adventure, ready to put my dreams
into action so long as this doesn't mean being brought down to
earth to find them reduced to nothing by the wretched facts of
reality.

But we must now appraise objectively my commercial value for
the Americans. You mention names such as Rubinstein and
Tchaikovsky. But these are people who are already known and
who, if you will allow me to say so, are an advertisement for
themselves. My case is much more difficult, partly because I am
completely unknown, but also because my art is rather obscure,
requiring from the listener an effort on his part, for I have never
attempted to court the public and for very good reasons. I should
have your influence behind me there of course, and I gather from
what you tell me that it is easy to give oneself airs. Perhaps,
however, it's not so easy to get on without a practical aim in
view.

There is no point in hiding from you that if I were to leave for
America I should require to be *completely* set up. For a long time
now I've looked upon all such people as tailors and shirtmakers as
characters in a fairy tale. I tell you this for I shouldn't want you to
undertake such a great responsibility without seeing some chance
of a return. I will certainly do exactly as you tell me, but it's my
duty to inform you of these things even though my burning
desire is to go straight ahead.

The three works suggested for this New York concert were the
Scènes au crépuscule (the original form of the *Nocturnes*), the *Fantaisie*,
and 'un petit oratorio dans une note mystique et un peu païenne'
which can only be *La Damoiselle élue*. Seidl's programmes had,
however, been settled and the venture to establish Debussy's
reputation in the United States at this early period came to nothing.
Debussy and the Prince remained, however, on excellent terms, and
in February 1893 Debussy sent his patron the longest letter he is
known to have written. Spontaneously setting out ideas running
through his mind at this time on his conception of love, which he
equates with desire, musical naturalism, which is whole-heartedly
deplored, and the difficulties of his career, this letter is one of the
most revealing documents we possess on Debussy's development at

this period. Confiding family difficulties to the Prince and the disappointment of his parents at his failure to establish himself, he says:

In writing about one's troubles, however genuine they may be, they immediately become melodramatic and unnatural. Anyhow we needn't be surprised at our worries. They develop what might be called the Cult of Desire, and at heart Desire is everything: one has a mad craving, almost a positive need for a work of art (a Velasquez, a vase of Satsouma or a new kind of tie). The moment it is possessed what joy!—this is truly love. By the end of a week this feeling has gone. Five or six days may go by without your even noticing this possession. True, the feeling may return if you have been away from it for some months—just as sunshine is wonderful when you see it for the first time on an April morning but which then begins to pall throughout the long summer months. I think what we can say about Desire is that ultimately everything derives from and is bound to it—which turns out, however, to be a rather pleasant illusion. The desire for happiness is more or less the same thing. One can only be relatively happy, to a limited extent, some people by possessing millions, others by having children whom they expect to follow in their glorious footsteps. I don't know if, like myself, you are 'a maniac for happiness', that is to say wanting to achieve happiness in a certain way, by altogether individual methods and for a decidedly lofty aim, which, however, often makes one appear a scoundrel or an unfortunate idiot. [The allusion is to the lines in Jules Laforgue's poem *Solo de Lune*: 'Maniaques de bonheur, Donc, que ferons-nous?'] You do well to be concerned with railways, to live in a world of figures without being troubled, as are those who love art, by the sorry sight of the would-be artists of today. We have had *Werther*, for instance, by Massenet in which this composer showed himself to be a master in the art of pandering to stupid ideas and amateur standards. Everything in this work is pretty second-hand, and what is deplorable is the way a fine genuine subject is turned into a sentimental mockery of itself. The same thing happened to *Faust*, massacred by Gounod, and *Hamlet*, most unfortunately dealt with by M. Ambroise Thomas. When you come to think of it, the law convicts people who go to great pains to forge bank notes but not forgers such as these who are motivated by the same lucrative aim. I should approve of a warning printed in certain publications: 'The setting of any of this text to music is prohibited.'

A rising star on the musical horizon is one Gustave Charpentier who seems destined to be renowned for both his fertility and his unbeautiful music. He is a follower of Berlioz, a tremendous humbug, I believe, who managed to believe in his own hoaxes. Charpentier lacks Berlioz's rather aristocratic nature. He is downright vulgar to the point of writing an opera to be called *Marie* [eventually *Louise*] to take place in Montmartre. His admiration for the masses has been inspired by a book called *La Vie du Poète*. This antiquated romantic title tells us quite a lot, but what you can't imagine is its utter lack of taste, the triumph of beer-hall music in the opera house. It's full of tricks and is altogether out of place ['Ça sent la pipe et il y a comme les cheveux sur la musique']. A small example is the closing scene at the Moulin Rouge where of course the poet finally ends up. Here there is even a prostitute screaming out in ecstasy.

Our poor music! How it has been dragged into the mud! Needless to say, all the little snobs, afraid to be taken for nincompoops, proclaim it a masterpiece—it's unbearable! Good Lord! music is a dream from which the veils have been drawn! It's not even the expression of a feeling—it *is* the feeling itself. And they want to make it tell cheap stories when, in fact, we have newspapers to do this job perfectly well. It's hard, I can tell you, to see such things going on; it's as if a beautiful, adored woman were at your arm and some hooligan came along and grabbed her. I really feel this to be almost a personal insult. I'm not saying that I'm more talented than these people, but I do declare that I genuinely love music, which I fancy must be rather unusual since this disrespectful treatment seems to be perfectly natural.

By way of consolation I recently had a most rewarding musical experience. This was at Saint-Gervais, a church where an intelligent priest[1] has the idea of reviving some beautiful ancient religious music. An unaccompanied mass of Palestrina was a

[1] The 'Bottin' of 1893 gives the name de Bussy as the curé of Saint-Gervais. He is not known to be a relative. It is likely that this was the 'Debussy' whose visit to Solesmes on 6 August 1893 or 1894 is described in a letter from Dr. Beckett Gibbs published in *Les Modes grégoriens dans l'oeuvre de Debussy* by Julia d'Almendra (Paris, 1947). There is no evidence to support the suggestion that Claude Debussy visited Solesmes on this date. See E. Lockspeiser, 'New Literature on Debussy' in *Music and Letters* (April 1959).

marvel. Written in a very severe style, this music is extremely pure; its feeling is not conveyed by shrieks of any kind but by melodic arabesques. What you hear are the shape, the outline and the intertwining arabesques which combine to produce unique melodic harmonies. When you pass through Paris I promise to take you to hear this music for no prose could possibly describe it. I also heard a mass of Vittoria, a Spanish primitive. This has a fierce ascetic mysticism, expressed as is the music of Palestrina, by very simple means.

When one hears such music one wonders how it came about that this beautiful art developed in such an unfortunate manner. Undermined at its roots, it led to the development of the opera. Very few musicians were there of course; at any rate they had the sense to know they would be out of place and that they would be revolted by their own small-mindedness. The audience consisted rather of literary people, of poets and people who care about the integrity of their art. Others were fashionable people annoyed at having to get up so early. All of which gives one courage to go on living in one's own dream, to go on seeking the inexpressible which is the aim of all art.

In a post scriptum Debussy adds: 'I think I am under an obligation to you for a golden visit which has given me a little peace of mind.' Since the American project had failed Poniatowski had undertaken to offer support in order to provide Debussy, as he says, 'if not with comfort at any rate with the possibility of working for a year or two in peace.'

16
Gide and Wilde

Je vois dans le Mal un plaisir esthétique . . . et c'est un grand
progrès.

Pierre Louÿs (A André Gide)

Following his early association with Debussy, Mallarmé, and Louÿs, Prince Poniatowski travelled widely abroad. Debussy's friendship with him continued, however, possibly until 1900 when the Prince, anxious to show his gratitude for Debussy's introduction to Mallarmé, deposited funds with Henri de Régnier and Louÿs for the publication of Mallarmé's complete works. In the meantime many projects were toyed with and sometimes pursued by Debussy for works in collaboration with Louÿs. They include, besides *Cendrelune* with its *Parsifal* associations, a ballet on Louÿs's novel *Aphrodite*, planned to be given at the music-hall L'Olympia, and a symphonic suite on *Le Voyage du Roi Pausole*. No music was written for either *Aphrodite* or *Le Roi Pausole* though Debussy was clearly attracted to the latter. It was in this satirical novel that Louÿs caricatured, in the figure of Taxis, the puritanism of his Huguenot friend Gide, 'Ci-Gide' as he was derisively known. 'You can imagine how delighted I am with *Le Roi Pausole*', Debussy declared to Louÿs in June 1901. 'In fact I should like to thank you in a more lyrical fashion.' The friendship between Gide on the one hand and Debussy and Louÿs on the other had seriously foundered. A certain hypocritical streak was detected in Gide, a sensualist and a staunch Protestant. On 23 June 1901, Debussy sent Louÿs a letter (reproduced in the illustration facing page 193) in the form of a short piece of music poking fun at Gide by quoting the Chorale of Luther together with a Mazurka of Chopin both of which Gide adored.

[173]

A free translation of the text written above the music in this letter runs:

My dear Pierre,

On the matter of André Gide (Chorale of Luther followed by Mazurka of Chopin Op. 3745 and repeat of Chorale), I saw him the other day at the home of J. C. Mardrus [an orientalist who had made a bold translation of *The Arabian Nights*]. (Musical portrayal of conversation between Mardrus, his wife and Gide.) J. C. Mardrus in good humour and Lucie Delarue Mardrus speaking through her nose. Long live Gide the country gentleman at Cuverville and Gide the writer in Paris (*Vive à jamais André et même Gide*). He's still alive. But he's going to potter about in the country (literally, 'he is going to give himself up to growing chickweed.'). (The voices of the spheres.)

Good night,

C.D.

For his marriage at Saint-Philippe-du-Roule in June 1899 Louÿs had asked Debussy to write a wedding march to be played by the organist. 'I intend to suggest to him,' Louÿs writes, 'un petit programme sébastienbachique' (J. S. Bach was greatly admired by Louÿs) to be preceded by 'la célèbre et inédite *Hochzeitmarsch* by Debussy'. Debussy, who dearly wished to comply with this request, was prevented from doing so only by a temporary indisposition.[1]

In 1894 Louÿs stayed at Biskra in Algeria with Gide and had wanted Debussy to join them there.[2] In his *Journal* Gide gives many remarkable descriptions of the Arabic music he heard at Biskra and one cannot help regretting that Debussy was denied this first-hand

[1] Shortly before his marriage, at the end of May 1899, Louÿs sent Debussy the inkwell which he had used when writing all his earlier works. 'Tu m'as beaucoup ému en me le demandant,' he confesses, 'je suis très heureux de te le donner, et de t'embrasser. Ton amitié a rempli toute ma vie de garçon.' Four years later Debussy sent Louÿs as a Christmas present a short *Noël*, the text of which ('Oh! ta bouche! En voilà des chichis, Qu'on fasse venir Liane de Pougy') refers to a celebrated courtesan.

[2] Louÿs had originally intended to go to Bayreuth in the summer of 1894, but on his way, at Geneva, changed his mind. Debussy comments: 'Au fond Bayreuth est un mauvais enseignement, et c'est un univers un peu borné. . . . Combien mieux, Biskra doit nous apprendre de combinaisons nouvelles.

Mais, dans cette affaire,
Que devient Wagner?
Et qu'est-ce qui . . . Biskra?
C'est Cosima. . . .'

The third line contains a play on the word *bisquer*, to annoy or vex.

contact with Oriental music.[1] Elsewhere, in *Si le grain ne meurt* (known in the English translation by Dorothy Bussy as *If it die*) Gide gives an alluring sketch of Meriem ben Atala who inspired Louÿs's well-known prose poems, the *Chansons de Bilitis*:

> Meriem was amber-skinned, firm-fleshed. Her figure was round but still almost childish for she was barely sixteen. I can only compare her to a bacchante—the one on the Gaeta vase, for instance—because of her tinkling bracelets too, which she was continually shaking. . . . Her cousin En Barka was dancing there too. They danced in the antique fashion of the Oulad, their heads straight and erect, their busts motionless, their hands agile, their whole bodies shaken by the rhythmic beating of their feet. How much I liked this 'Mahommedan music' with its steady, obstinate, incessant flow; it went to my head, stupefied me like an opiate, drowsily and voluptuously benumbed my thoughts.[2]

The *Chansons de Bilitis* were published in 1895 and dedicated to Gide 'in memory of Meriem ben Atala'. Three of these prose poems were set by Debussy: the second of the series, *La Chevelure*, appeared in the journal *L'Image* (October 1897) with designs by Van Dongen, and the remaining two, *La Flûte de Pan* and *Le Tombeau des Naïades*, were completed by September 1898. A copy of the score of the three songs bears the following dedication: 'Pour Pierre Louÿs à cause du 19 Octobre 1899', the date of Debussy's marriage to Rosalie Texier. It is impossible not to be impressed by the numerous cross-identifications associated with this work, as if Gide, Louÿs, and Debussy, together with their mistresses or partners, were enmeshed in triangular situations of an almost impenetrable complexity.

A work of pure sensuous charm, its finely moulded recitatives

[1] Nineteen years later, in June 1913, Bartók visited Biskra and the neighbouring towns of Sidi-Okba, El Kantara, and Constantine. In his study 'Die Volksmusik der Araber von Biskra und Umgebung', published in the *Zeitschrift für Musikwissenschaft* (Leipzig, June 1920) Bartók gives numerous examples of Arabic music, describing its scales and rhythmic features, the instruments used and the ceremonies with which the music he heard was associated.

[2] Gide adds, rather enigmatically, that Louÿs 'persuaded himself he owed it to me as a friend to make Meriem his mistress'. Following their journey to Algeria, Gide and Louÿs met in March 1895 at Algiers where they quarrelled bitterly on issues arising from the trial of Oscar Wilde. Louÿs returned to Paris in April 1896 with Zohra, the sister of Meriem, with whom he lived until the end of the year. She was well known to Debussy, and in the photograph with him taken by Louÿs (facing page 97) appears in Moorish costume against a background of wall-paper in huge Art Nouveau designs.

resembling those in *Pelléas et Mélisande*, the *Chansons de Bilitis* were not publicly performed until 17 March 1900 when they were sung at the Société Nationale by Blanche Marot accompanied by Debussy. Six months later Louÿs was approached by Fernand Samuel, director of the Théâtre des Variétés,[1] for a version of the *Chansons de Bilitis* to be recited and mimed. Debussy was begged to write a short score to accompany this scene. He eventually provided a score for two harps, two flutes, and celesta to accompany the recitation and mime of the *Chansons de Bilitis* given not at the Théâtre des Variétés but at the Salle des Fêtes of *Le Journal* on 7 February 1901.[2] Hurriedly written, the score was forgotten until 1914 when, anxious to supply his publisher with a new work, Debussy arranged six of these pieces under the title *Six Epigraphes Antiques* for both piano duet and piano solo.[3]

Other projects of Debussy and Louÿs must be assessed against the background of the friendship between Louÿs and Oscar Wilde. The two writers, both committed to the full life, met in Paris in November 1891 and the following year in London where Wilde invited Louÿs to a performance of *Lady Windermere's Fan*. Their early correspondence shows Wilde greatly delighted with his new friend. 'French

[1] A curious sidelight on the prevalent anti-Semitism in France arising from the Dreyfus affair is provided by the fact that Fernand Samuel was a Jewish pseudonym. The real name of this well known director of the Théâtre des Variétés was Théodore Louveau. His pseudonym was adopted to enable him to compete more successfully with the many prominent Jewish directors.

[2] Louÿs writes to his brother of the rehearsals for this spectacle: 'Je passe cette semaine toutes mes après-midi avec des femmes nues. C'est du joli. Il s'agit de modèles qui vont représenter onze *Chansons de Bilitis* sur la scène du *Journal*, tantôt avec des voiles drapés, tantôt en robes de kôs, tantôt sans rien du tout que leurs deux mains ou leur position, de trois-quarts en arrière. M. Béranger a fait appeler le directeur et l'a menacé de l'envoyer dans les *in-pace* de la République s'il donnait suite à son projet.'

[3] The original score, presented to Louÿs and described by Debussy as 'mince et rapide' was heard again in Paris at the Théâtre Marigny in 1954. The ten original pieces and the arrangements of the *Six Epigraphes Antiques* are entitled:

Chant Pastoral	Pour invoquer Pan, dieu du vent d'été	(i)
Les Comparaisons	Pour que la nuit soit propice	(iii)
Les Contes		
La Partie d'osselets		
Bilitis		
Le Tombeau sans nom	Pour un tombeau sans nom	(ii)
L'Eau pure du bassin		
Les Courtisanes égyptiennes	Pour l'Egyptienne	(v)
La Danseuse aux crotales	Pour la Danseuse aux crotales	(iv)
La Pluie au matin	Pour remercier la pluie au matin	(vi)

A most acceptable version of the *Epigraphes Antiques* for full orchestra was recently made by Ernest Ansermet.

Camille Claudel

Geneviève Mallarmé

Rosalie Texier-Debussy at Bichain, *circa* 1902

poetry has always been among my most adored mistresses,' he writes, 'and I should be very happy to think that among the poets of France I shall find some true friends.' A copy from the library of Louÿs of Wilde's *A House of Pomegranates*, which appeared in 1891, bears the inscription:

Au jeune homme qui adore la Beauté
Au jeune homme que la Beauté adore
Au jeune homme que j'adore
Oscar Wilde

Shortly after their meeting Wilde submitted to Louÿs the draft of his *Salomé*, eventually dedicated to Louÿs,[1] handsomely published in deep purple covers by the *Librairie de l'Art Indépendant* in 1893, in the same year as Debussy's *La Damoiselle élue*.

In February 1893 Debussy and Wilde met at a banquet at the home of Georges Louis, the poet's brother.[2] The company included many brilliant personalities of the time in the arts and sciences as well as prominent figures in the diplomatic service. Among the writers besides Wilde were Valéry, Gide, Régnier, and Hérédia. The painters included Antoine de la Rochefoucauld, associated with 'The Cult of Isis', Jacques-Emile Blanche, and Besnard, and sculpture was represented by Pierre de Coutouly. The diplomatic figures included the Marquis de Montebello, French Ambassador at St. Petersburg, who arranged the visit to France of Nicholas II, Léon Bourgeois, later a prominent figure in the League of Nations, Captain Walewski, grandson of Napoleon, and the French representatives in China, Egypt, and South America. 'Pas un juif', Louÿs notes with satisfaction, listing the names of his brother's guests. Alone Debussy represented music at this banquet.

We have dealt earlier with affinities between the work of Debussy and Wilde's *Portrait of Dorian Gray*. We may now see a reflection of Wilde's ideas in two of the many projects entertained between

[1] Richard Strauss first became acquainted with *Salomé* in the German translation of Hedwig Lachmann. Louÿs does not seem to have been present at the Paris performance of Strauss's *Salomé* in 1907. At that time Louÿs and Debussy were estranged and Louÿs was negotiating with Puccini for an opera libretto based on his *La Femme et le Pantin*. In a letter of 15 April 1907, to Sybil Seligman, Puccini writes: 'Inouï [i.e. Louÿs] has written me another idiotic letter claiming damages and indemnification for not having put his libretto to music.'

[2] In the account of this banquet in *Broutilles inédites* Louÿs omits to give the date on which it took place. Wilde was in Paris in February 1893 and April 1894. Judging from the presence of other guests the former date is more likely to be correct.

Louÿs and Debussy. In a letter to Debussy of 31 May 1894, Louÿs says, 'You know that we shall no longer be able to do *La Danseuse*.' This must refer to the poem of this title by Louÿs, dedicated to Wilde and opening with the lines:

> Elle tourne, elle est nue, elle est grave; ses flancs
> Ondulent d'ombre bleue et de sueur farouche.

The following year, on 27 November 1895, Louÿs mentions the subject of Daphnis and Chloe as a scenario for a ballet: 'Would you have the courage to write in twelve days a ballet in three scenes, thirty minutes' music on a libretto of myself, the title of which is *Daphnis et Khloé* (with a beautiful K)?' Louÿs seems to have derived the idea of this subject, based on the story of Longus, from Wilde. 'Oscar Wilde was so fond of the Greek story of Longus,' writes Guillot de Saix in his study of the origin of Wilde's tales, 'that one day, needing money, he thought of devising a scenario in collaboration with Lord Alfred Douglas for his friend Dalhousie Young. Under the title *Daphnis et Khloé* he gave a draft of the tale to Pierre Louÿs.' It was customary for Wilde to recount his tales verbally before committing them to paper. On 14 January 1896 Louÿs gives further details to Debussy of this scheme: 'Your wishes are fulfilled. The scheme is going so well that if it is ready your music will be heard in a fortnight . . . I am writing the scenario. . . . Here are some ideas of the characters: Chloe, a rather silly but sentimental creature; Daphnis, a flautist—a pastoral theme ardent but simple; Lykainon, a well informed but contemptuous figure. . . . The plan is (1) C. and D. are unspoilt; (2) L. teaches D.; (3) D. teaches C. Curtain. For the first scene we need a theme in the nature of the opening phrase of *Parsifal*. . . . The score begins with a flute theme. . . . To save time couldn't you pinch something from the *Faun's afternoon* [in English in the original] by a certain Debussy. . . . But hurry up. It will be played every day for a fortnight. And it will be paid in bank notes [in English in the original].'

No mention of the fact that the idea of this scenario derived from Wilde is made in this letter. It is signed, as a play on the name Houston Stewart Chamberlain, 'Houst! Ton Chamberlain!' (Hi! Your Chamberlain), probably as an allusion to Chamberlain's support of Wagner. 'Ask him to come with you tomorrow', Debussy amusingly replies. 'Is it to be for xylophone, banjo or

Russian bassoon? And just imagine that he is no further than Wagner and still believes in the recipes of this old poisoner!' The scenario was completed by Louÿs and some music was written by Debussy, but we have no trace of it.

The previous year, in 1895, Wilde's French friends were deeply moved by his notorious trial in London and organized a petition for the judgement to be reversed. From Holloway prison Wilde wrote to his friend in Paris Robert Sherard, asking him to convey his gratitude to Sarah Bernhardt, the Goncourt Brothers, and Louÿs. Since the projected performance of *Salomé* at the Palace Theatre in London in 1892, with Sarah Bernhardt in the principal part, had been banned, his play was given as a gesture of confidence in Wilde at the Théâtre de l'Oeuvre, in February 1896, by the same company that three years earlier had produced Maeterlinck's *Pelléas et Mélisande*. By this time the draft of Debussy's score for *Pelléas* was completed, and three months earlier, in December 1895, he had negotiated for its performance in the form of a chamber opera at the same theatre. If this had materialized Debussy's *Pelléas* and Wilde's *Salomé* would have been given at the Théâtre de l'Oeuvre within a few months of each other.

In prison Wilde was deeply in debt and sent a telegram to Sarah Bernhardt, asking her to buy *Salomé* from him and to advance him four hundred pounds. Debussy, too, was beginning to be crippled by debts. In June 1898, a year before his marriage, he wrote an agitated letter to Hartmann informing him that he was in the direst straits. He was about to be prosecuted and all his goods would be sold on account of a debt of fifty-five francs. On 13 June 1899, at the time of the marriage of Louÿs and only four months before his own marriage, he writes in similarly anxious terms to Louÿs, imploring him for a loan of fifty francs, adding with legitimate exaggeration, 'Je suis dans la purée la plus noire, sans parler de mes 300,000 francs de dettes.'

17

Gabrielle Dupont and Rosalie Texier

L'être le plus prostitué, c'est l'être par excellence, c'est Dieu.

Baudelaire

On 19 October 1899, at the time of an acute financial crisis, Debussy married Rosalie Texier and moved to a small apartment at 58 rue Cardinet. At the civil ceremony Pierre Louÿs was a witness, together with Erik Satie and Lucien Fontaine, a patron of the arts at whose country home, at Mercin, Debussy had stayed. A mannequin employed by the Soeurs Callot in the rue Taitbout, Rosalie Texier (called Lilly or Lily-Lilo) remains a shadowy figure. We have no body of correspondence or reliable memoirs which allow us to measure the personality of this simple Burgundian girl, the daughter of a railway employee (controller of telegraphs) at Montereau in the department of Yonne. Debussy writes of his marriage in a letter of 5 January 1900 to his old friend Robert Godet:

I must tell you straight away of what has happened. Two things: I've moved and I'm married. Yes, my dear friend, and please remain seated. Mlle Lilly Texier has changed her disharmonious name to Lilly Debussy, much more pleasant-sounding, as everyone will agree. She is unbelievably fair and pretty, like some character from an old legend. Also she is not in the least 'modern-style'. She has no taste for the music that Willy approves, but has a taste of her own. Her favourite song is a roundelay about a grenadier with a red face who wears his hat on one side like an old campaigner—not very provoking aesthetically.

Nor, apart from an account of Léon Vallas, have we any first-hand information on the circumstances which led to Debussy's marriage. Vallas, who was well acquainted with Rosalie Texier and to whom she confided many facts of her relationship with Debussy, categorically declared that he would never reveal them. We know from him, however, that they had lived together before their marriage and had separated. 'Then, suddenly, a violent love possessed Debussy and he wished to marry her within a few weeks. On the advice and experience of Gaby Lhéry [the assumed name of Gabrielle Dupont, Debussy's mistress from about 1889] who remained on friendly terms with the new lovers, she refused to resume their life together. Debussy threatened to commit suicide if she did not accept his offer of marriage. In 1927 Rosalie Texier allowed me to read the tragic letter Debussy sent her in 1899, a letter in a romantic style, ardent and tender and of moving beauty. As a result of Debussy's anxious insistence she agreed to resume their old relationship, but on a legal footing.'

Two facts emerge from this admittedly incomplete account. Debussy's marriage to Rosalie Texier closely followed the marriage of Louÿs to Louise de Hérédia, and the significant fact, already referred to, though it may seem trivial, that marriage offered an harmonious change of name, as indeed had the marriage of Louÿs. ('Mademoiselle Lilly Texier a changé son nom inharmonique pour celui de Lilly Debussy, bien plus euphonique.')

There was no religious ceremony for the reason, given by Rosalie Texier to Léon Vallas, that it would have involved a cost of eighty-five francs. On the morning of his marriage Debussy gave a piano lesson to his pupil Mademoiselle Worms de Romilly in order to be able to pay for their wedding breakfast. Paul Poujaud, who met the newly wedded couple in the evening on their way to the Brasserie Pousset, declared that their entire fortune consisted of six francs, the remainder of the fee from the morning's lesson. There are striking resemblances here on the matter of money and women between the psychology of Debussy and that of Verlaine and Baudelaire, and even more with the psychology of Poe. A prominent feminine element dictated the actions of these sensitive, mercurial artists who sought not to give protection in their relationships with women but to procure security. A single letter from Debussy to Lilly is known to us which hardly uncovers the nature of their attachment. It is in the Bibliothèque Doucet in Paris, dated 16 July 1902 from London where Debussy had gone with Mary Garden shortly after the production of *Pelléas*:

> My dear sweet wife,
> Your letter did me so much good. If only you knew how lonely I feel. Not hearing your commanding voice calling 'Mi-mi' I become as melancholy as a guitar. I was delighted with your lack of courage. It's all very well to be a fine strong woman, but there are times when the fine strong woman should also have weaknesses. . . . Would you believe it to be impossible to procure a decent cup of tea? Oh for my Rue Cardinet and my dear wife who, among other gifts, can make tea. In England there are no such women. Their women, with complexions like uncooked ham and primitive animal-like gestures, are for the horse-guards. Well, certain journeys are necessary if only to learn that one had better stay at home. Did I need this experience to show me that I really cannot get on without you? It may be logical but it is also a piece of quite useless moral surgery.

The intimate friendship with Louÿs was maintained in the early months of Debussy's marriage, but certain formalities creep in, as if these two unconventional figures were playing at living respectable bourgeois lives. Debussy now sends his greetings to 'Madame Pierre Louÿs'. They speak with a certain naïve pride of their homes as 'chez moi' and 'chez toi'. 'You can't imagine how sad and comic it seems to me', Debussy writes, 'to leave visiting cards at your home.' Six months after his marriage, in May 1900, Debussy's publisher Hartmann died and his modest income was cut off. Earlier he had begged Louÿs to remember 'ces pauvres petits Debussy qui traînent une vie où il y a certainement plus d'amour que de bifteck'. It was on the whole a black year. In August Lilly underwent an operation and signs of tuberculosis were declared. On 9 December the first performance was given under Camille Chevillard at the Concerts Lamoureux of the first two *Nocturnes*, *Nuages* and *Fêtes*. Debussy's debts were continuously mounting and he must have relied entirely on the generosity of Louÿs and other friends.

There had been at least two earlier plans for marriage, and indeed from 1894 onwards Debussy was frequently matrimonially inclined.

[182]

Before this time dates his friendship with the sculptress Camille Claudel, sister of Paul Claudel. Our only information on the nature of this episode is given by their mutual friend Robert Godet who lets it be known that this highly gifted and original artist was an object of rivalry between Debussy and Rodin. The younger sister of Claudel, who wrote a searching study of her work, Camille Claudel was an ethereal, beautiful woman. She walked with a slight limp, due to a dislocation of the hip, not perhaps insignificant in view of the fact that Debussy, like Poe, was drawn to younger women who were of inferior status or otherwise afflicted. Debussy and Camille Claudel were drawn together by their common admiration of Degas and Hokusai, among other artists, and by their preoccupation, in sculpture and music, with childhood and death. Much of Camille Claudel's work, influenced by Rodin, is highly symbolical and is remarkable for its expressive drapery, 'like a Wagnerian chant', says her brother. Debussy was greatly impressed, Godet tell us, by her gruesome portrayal of one of the Fates, *Clotho* (now in the Luxembourg Museum in Paris), spinning out the thread of life like the Norns in *Götterdämmerung*, and particularly by the wonderful élan in her sculpture entitled *La Valse*.[1]

In the early 1890s, we cannot be sure of the period, Debussy proposed to Catherine Stevens, daughter of the Anglo-Belgian painter Alfred Stevens.[2] Later, in February 1894, he was officially engaged to the singer Thérèse Roger who was to accompany him on 1 March of that year to Brussels for the concert of his works at the exhibition of Impressionist paintings at La Libre Esthétique. This engagement had been announced by Debussy to his friends in an anxious and rather surprisingly formal manner.[3] A mystery

[1] Both of these works of Camille Claudel date from 1893. *La Valse*, described by her brother as 'toute roulée dans l'étoffe de la musique', was presented by Camille Claudel to Debussy and was said by Godet to have been an inspiration to him until his death. Though in later years it was always on his mantelpiece, it mysteriously disappeared after his death. In the study by Claudel of his sister's work, published in 1913, Debussy's name is not mentioned. Enigmatically, a reproduction of *La Valse* bears the caption: 'Bronze, exemplaire unique, appartenant à M. X.'

[2] A letter from Catherine Stevens to René Peter states: 'Despite the current opinion of him and although he was said to be so covetous, he gave me proof during an acute crisis in our family, of such disinterested love that I would certainly have married him had I not known Henry.' The reference is to a successful doctor who was able to assure Catherine Stevens of material security.

[3] A letter of February 1894 from Debussy to Pierre de Bréville states: 'Before leaving for Brussels I wish to inform you myself of my engagement to Mademoiselle Thérèse Roger. Please see in these hastily written lines proof of my friendship for you. I wish I had been able to give you further proof.'

surrounds the dramatic breaking off of this engagement on which some light is thrown by a letter of 22 March 1894, from Pierre Louÿs to a well-known hostess of the period, Madame de Saint-Marceaux. This is an extraordinary document, illuminating also Debussy's relationship with Gabrielle Dupont, to be dealt with presently, and setting out in a frank and genuine manner the facts of an acute emotional crisis in Debussy's life. His actions had apparently aroused violent hostility. In spontaneous, heartfelt terms Louÿs writes:

Madame,

The unfortunate telegram which brought about the rupture from which my poor friend is so greatly suffering has been widely misunderstood. But I admit that Debussy would appear to be condemned by the external facts, and I am not surprised at the scandal these have caused.

Perhaps you will allow me to add, however, that a young man cannot dismiss as a servant a mistress who has lived with him for two years, who has shared his hard life without complaint and against whom he has no reproach except that he may be tired of her and wishes to marry. Normally a matter such as this is settled by means of a few bank-notes. It is not a very delicate procedure, but it is a practical one. You know that Debussy was not even able to avail himself of this means. He had to approach the matter tactfully. He had to consider her feelings, to be discreet, for had he employed more brutal methods she would have been justified in taking revenge. Time was necessary. If his engagement had not been so hastily announced Debussy would have had the time to abandon his relationship so that by the time he was engaged he would have been completely free of his former attachment. This he was unable to do, or if you prefer, he did not see his way to go about it. And he has been cruelly punished.

As for the rumours which you have heard of his earlier life I can assure you that they are monstrous slanders. I believe that the honour of a man (I am not speaking of the artist with which we are not concerned) cannot be affected by anonymous letters, usually written by a liar and in any case by a coward.

[184]

I know personally that Debussy is incapable of having lived in the way that he is said to have lived. I know this also from two people who have known Debussy for twelve years and are as revolted as I am by the dark intrigue of which he is the centre. I am able, moreover, to tell you their names: they are MM. Raymond Bonheur and Etienne Dupin. M. Lerolle and M. Chausson will tell you what their evidence is worth.[1]

I am writing to you in profound grief and in a spontaneous manner which I must ask you, Madame, to forgive. I know of nothing more distressing than to see a man thus dishonoured in a single week, a man whom one loves and for whom one has the greatest regard, who, over a period of fifteen years, has had an unfortunate existence and who sees all doors closed against him at the very moment when it is realised that he is a man of genius.

Believe me, Madame, to be

Yours respectfully,

Pierre Louÿs.

The mistress referred to was Gabrielle Dupont. A large amount of vulgar literature has been written on the subject of Debussy's relationship with her, based on no reliable evidence, with no psychological insight into the delicate problems involved and seeking only to arouse the baser responses. We may disclose a few relevant facts, gleaned from two articles on her by an old family friend, Henri Pellerin, published in a local journal at Lisieux, *Le Pays d'Auge*. Gabrielle Dupont was born at Lisieux in Normandy on 11 June 1866, daughter of a dressmaker. At the age of twenty-one she left for Paris, where she lived a free life.[2] She is said to have stated that she spent ten years of her life with Debussy, so that her liaison with him must date from 1889. She was known during this time under the pseudonym Gaby Lhéry. Monsieur Pellerin records that she was 'a woman with a strong dominating personality incapable of playing a passive role'. Among her physical attractions were her green or

---

[1] The friendship of these very people seems in fact to have been tried. See note 1 on page 126 for the opinion of Madame Lerolle-Chausson.

[2] Monsieur Pellerin writes: 'Jolie comme un cœur, bien tournée, ne manquant pas d'audace, elle fut vite remarquée, d'abord sur les trottoirs, et ensuite dans certains cafés, où elle passait le plus clair de son temps libre à fumer des cigarettes devant une chope de bière. . . . Vers 1887, elle était devenue la maîtresse d'un jeune aristocrate, en mal de romantisme, le comte de Villeneuve.'

blue-green eyes[1] and her dyed blonde hair, giving her the appearance of 'a woman who might have come out of a picture by Toulouse-Lautrec'.

Questioned in later years on her life with Debussy, this forceful, independent woman replied: 'We had painful scenes due to the lack of money.' Since she subsequently lived a life of luxury, as the mistress of an aristocrat, one imagines that there must have been idealistic as well as physical motives that compelled her to share the life of Debussy in the rue de Londres and the rue Gustave Doré. Her later life was not, however, roses all the way. Alfred Cortot, visiting a theatre at Rouen, recognized her as an elderly usherette, possessing at that time several valuable manuscripts of Debussy, including the score of *Rodrigue et Chimène* and a version of *L'Après-midi d'un faune*. Three years after his separation from her, in June 1902, Debussy sent her a copy of *Pelléas et Mélisande* with the inscription: 'A Gaby, princesse du mystérieux royaume d'Alle-monde. Son vieux dévoué Claude Debussy.' She died during the last war, on 12 May 1945, aged seventy-nine, at the Château de Familly in Normandy where she had been evacuated from a home for the aged at Orbec. Monsieur Pellerin gives a moving picture of this important figure in Debussy's life during her last days: 'Addicted to cigarettes, she begged everyone for them but the generosity of her friends and relatives was insufficient. At night, in an old coat and knitted woollen hat, she would prowl along the edge of the pavements, indifferent to anyone who might recognize her, searching for cigarette ends.'[2] In her younger days she was the subject of several remarkable photographs taken by Pierre Louÿs who had an original conception of the camera's pictorial possibilities. His photographs of Debussy and Gaby (facing pages 80 and 96) suggest the opulent décor of a Vuillard. The two photographs of Gaby mysteriously draped (facing page 81) were obviously inspired by the spirit of the Art Nouveau.

[1] Women with green eyes had a particular appeal for contemporary artists, notably Baudelaire in his poem *Le Poison* ('Tout cela ne vaut pas le poison qui découle De tes yeux, de tes yeux verts'), Barbey d'Aurevilly, and Albert Samain. In *Le Bonheur dans le crime* Barbey d'Aurevilly describes the hypnotizing effect of a powerful woman whose eyes are 'two green stars': 'Chose étrange! dans le rapprochement de ce beau couple, c'était la femme qui avait les muscles, et l'homme qui avait les nerfs.'

[2] Her sister Blanche Dupont lived at Orbec. Monsieur Pellerin states that Gaby and Debussy paid several visits to her there and that on one occasion Debussy was inspired to write *Jardins sous la pluie* by the sight in this town of the formal French garden of the Hôtel de Croisy.

Debussy's personal and sentimental life, like that of the heroes of Poe, several times bordered on the *crime passionnel*.[1] After the upheaval caused by his engagement to Thérèse Roger, life with Gaby was resumed but three years later she was to become the victim of another melodramatic episode, this time with the result that she took her revenge by an attempt at suicide. Debussy writes to Louÿs on 7 February 1897:

I've had some troublesome business in which Bourget seems to have joined forces with Xavier de Montépin[2]—which may not be altogether impossible. Gaby, with her steely eyes, found a letter in my pocket which left no doubt as to the advanced state of a love affair with all the romantic trappings to move the most hardened heart. Whereupon—tears, drama, a real revolver and a report in the *Petit Journal*. Ah! my dear fellow, why weren't you here to help me out of this nasty mess? It was all barbarous, useless and will change absolutely nothing. Kisses and caresses can't be effaced with an india-rubber. They might perhaps think of something to do this and call it The Adulterer's India-Rubber!

On top of it all poor little Gaby lost her father[3]—an occurrence which for the time being has straightened things out.

I was, all the same, very upset and again very sad to feel you so far away, so hopelessly far away that I hadn't the strength to pick up my pen and write to you. I didn't think I could give you the right feeling of the thing. For writing is not the same as looking into the face of a friend. You will think perhaps: 'It's his own fault.' Well, there you are. I am sometimes as sentimental as a *modiste* who might have been Chopin's mistress. I must say that my heart is still capable of fluttering instead of getting on quietly with its own business. . . . Now don't let us speak of this any more, and believe me to be still your fine strong Claude.[4]

[1] It is difficult not to suspect some terrifying experience in his early childhood, the pattern of which was relentlessly repeated. 'A small house set in a great garden where one was afraid when young, that's what I should like to have', he wrote to André Caplet in 1911. In later life he felt a particular sympathy with the elements of fear and terror in the memories of Roderick Usher.

[2] Xavier de Montépin (1826–1902), popular author of serial stories and melodramas.

[3] Auguste-Edmond Dupont died on 7 February 1897.

[4] No trace has been found in the press at this time of this episode, the account of which was probably exaggerated since in a letter to Louÿs of only a month later, 9 March 1897, there is the post scriptum: 'Gaby te remercie et t'envoie son meilleur sourire.' We can hardly trust, therefore, the statement in a biography of Ysaÿe by

Nor was this all. Seven years later, in 1904, very much the same pattern was repeated with an attempted suicide by Lilly Texier. The external cause was the abandonment of Lilly for Emma Bardac, to whom Debussy's daughter, Claude-Emma, was born in 1905 and whom, after divorce from Lilly, he was able to marry on 20 January 1908.[1] Suicide is an inverted form of aggression, and one must imagine both Gaby and Lilly to have been headstrong, violent women, though skilful enough to avoid death in their attempts at suicide. It is possible that they were also inspired by strong histrionic motives. The revolver was freely resorted to in affairs of the heart and other violent conflicts at this period. It symbolized a gesture of masculine defiance and it was also the symbol of a sadistic explosion. The renowned courtesan, Liane de Pougy, had at about this time made a spectacular attempt on her life in front of the home of her lover, but she also made an equally spectacular recovery in time to marry the Roumanian prince Georges Ghika.[2]

The revolver was also very nearly used by Maeterlinck in his quarrel with Debussy. Maeterlinck had challenged Debussy to a duel as a result of the choice of Mary Garden as Mélisande in the place of his mistress, Georgette Leblanc. In the memoirs of Lucie Delarue-Mardrus we read that Maeterlinck took this matter seriously to the extent of practising shooting. 'One morning, taking as a moving target his black cat who was walking towards him in his garden, purring, he fired at her and killed her on the spot.'

Antoine Ysaÿe and Bertram Ratcliffe (London, 1947): 'Gaby, after coming out of hospital—for she attempted suicide—went to stay at first with Madame Chausson and afterwards with Madame Ysaÿe in Brussels.' The liaison, obviously severely disturbed though apparently indissoluble, was to last a further two years and was broken off only at the time of the marriage of Louÿs, followed shortly by Debussy's own marriage.

[1] A report of Lilly's attempted suicide, which had taken place on 13 October 1904, was published in Le Figaro, 4 November, under the heading, A Parisian drama: 'Mme. D . . . a beautiful young woman married to a distinguished composer, considered the leader of the young school and of whom a work recently obtained great success at one of the subsidized theatres, has, in these last days, attempted to commit suicide by shooting herself twice in the groin. She has been taken to a nursing home in the rue Blomet and her state is now hopeful.' A statement in Le Figaro of 3 January 1905, that she had attempted suicide a second time, as a result of which she was in a grave state, is without foundation.

[2] Frustrated in a love affair, Prince Ghika had also attempted suicide. A well-known demi-mondaine, Polaire, 'something between a fox and a woman', as she is described by André Germain in Les Fous de 1900, 'présenta l'un à l'autre les deux révolvérisés.'

18
Pelléas et Mélisande

Et tous ces souvenirs, c'est comme si j'emportais un peu
d'eau dans un sac de mousseline.

Maeterlinck

Regardez-moi, regardez ce que le souvenir a fait de moi. . . .
Debussy after E. A. Poe

Debussy's great conquest in the years of his maturity was the transformation of opera into poetry. The Symbolists had attempted
unsuccessfully to invade the theatre, beginning, as we have seen,
with Mallarmé's original conception of *L'Après-midi d'un faune*. The
first truly Symbolist play, Maeterlinck's one-act drama *L'Intruse*, was
given together with a short play by Verlaine at the Théâtre d'Art in
Paris on 21 May 1891. Significantly these plays, given as a benefit
performance for both Verlaine and Gauguin, were preceded by
recitations of poems by Edgar Allan Poe. *L'Intruse* was a *drame
d'attente*, the theme of which is that man is unknowing, lost, and can
rely only on occasional flashes of intuitive perception.

On 17 May 1893, five days after the first Paris performance of the
mythological opera, *Die Walküre*, Maeterlinck's *Pelléas et Mélisande*
was given a single performance at a matinée at the Théâtre des
Bouffes-Parisiens. The essential plot of this symbolical drama has an
affinity with the legend of *Tristan*. The tender, guileless Mélisande
is tricked by her innocence into marriage with Golaud. Fading into
the gloom of his ancient castle, her life is suddenly illuminated by
her love for Golaud's half-brother, Pelléas, with the result that the
ingenuous lovers are annihilated in an incestuous feud. Funds were
raised for this performance from several wealthy people, including
Henri de Régnier and Tchaikovsky's friend, the Princess Meshcherskaya, who presented the company with the scenery. The production
at the small theatre of the Bouffes-Parisiens was by Lugné-Poe,

[189]

director of the Théâtre de l'Oeuvre and known for his productions of Ibsen,[1] aided by Camille Mauclair. Lugné-Poe himself took the part of Golaud, the part of Mélisande was taken by Mlle Meuris, who had earlier played the leading role in Ibsen's *The Wild Duck*, and the part of Pelléas was also taken by a woman, Marie Aubry. The costumes were the work of Paul Vogler, based on the portraits of Memling and also on the Pre-Raphaelite pictures of Walter Crane. Grey tones and shadows were cast from lighting overhead, and a thin gauze curtain separated the audience from the stage. In the audience were Henri de Régnier, Whistler, Mallarmé, and Debussy. The curtain fell no less than eighteen times between the scenes of the five acts, prompting the critic of the *Annales du Théâtre* to suggest a performance by marionettes at the Chat Noir.

Almost alone with Debussy, Mallarmé responded to the philosophy of *Pelléas*, accepting death, in the entangled rivalries of love, as the only certain factor, indeed the only certainty of life.[2] Drawing a comparison between *Pelléas* and Maeterlinck's earlier poems, *Serres chaudes*, set as a song-cycle by Chausson, W. D. Halls maintains that *Pelléas* brings to the surface an underlying streak of sadism. This, he says, 'expresses itself as a desire to inflict cruelty upon innocence'. And he goes on: 'Maeterlinck himself associates sadism with pity, and certainly the dramatic use of brutality to emphasize the wrong suffered by beauty and virginity heightens the effect of compassion. But this persecution of the innocent may be more than a mere literary device, and represent a state of morbid pathology in the psychology of the poet, whose *Serres chaudes* had betrayed a mind at the end of its tether and, in the wildness of its imaginings, near to dementia.' If we bear in mind the fascination for Debussy of the tales of Poe, particularly *The Fall of the House of Usher*, of Villiers de l'Isle Adam's *Axel*, and of Wagner's *Parsifal* we see the immediate appeal which *Pelléas*, illustrating in a similar manner the psychology of innocence and cruelty, was bound to make.

Debussy must have begun work immediately on the score, for

---

[1] Two years later, in 1895, Lugné-Poe with the Théâtre de l'Oeuvre gave a season of Maeterlinck and Ibsen in London, the repertory including *Pelléas* and *The Master Builder*. It was on this occasion that Maeterlinck met Bernard Shaw and W. B. Yeats. The costumes for *Pelléas* had been left behind and at the eleventh hour Lugné-Poe is said to have procured a costume for Pelléas from a Scotch boy he had come across in the street, clad in kilt, sporran, and glengarry.

[2] Following Debussy, a whole generation of musicians was to be inspired by *Pelléas et Mélisande*. They include Schoenberg, Sibelius, Puccini, Fauré and Cyril Scott. Mallarmé's remarkable study of *Pelléas* appears in Appendix E.

on 6 September 1893, less than four months after Lugné-Poe's production, Debussy wrote to Chausson that one scene was finished ('A Fountain in the Park', Act IV, Scene iv). The following month, on 2 October, he expresses disappointment with these first efforts: 'The ghost of old Klingsor, alias Richard Wagner, appeared at a turning of one of the bars so I tore the whole thing up and struck off on a new line with a little compound of phrases [*une petite chimie de phrases*] I thought more characteristic. I have tried to be both Pelléas and Mélisande [*Je me suis efforcé d'être aussi Pelléas que Mélisande*].' He speaks also in this letter of using a novel means of expression—silence, 'perhaps the only means of throwing into relief the emotional value of a phrase'.[1]

Towards the end of 1893 work on *Pelléas* must have been considerably advanced. Both Camille Mauclair and Henri de Régnier had approached Maeterlinck on Debussy's behalf for permission to use his play as a libretto for an opera, and as a result Debussy, together with Pierre Louÿs, paid a visit to Maeterlinck at Ghent. In an undated letter of 1893 to Chausson Debussy gives his impression of this memorable visit:

I saw Maeterlinck, with whom I spent a day in Ghent. At first he assumed the airs of a young girl being introduced to her future husband, but after some time he thawed and was charming. When he spoke of the theatre he seemed a very remarkable man. As for *Pelléas*, he authorized me to make any cuts I like and even suggested some very important and useful ones himself.[2] He says he knows nothing about music and when he comes to a Beethoven symphony he is like a blind man in a museum. But really he is a very fine man and speaks of extraordinary things in a delightfully simple way. When I thanked him for entrusting me with *Pelléas* he insisted that it was he who should be grateful to me for setting

[1] In view of the use of the modes in *Pelléas*, particularly in the scene of the letter read by Geneviève, it is significant that at this very time Debussy was pursuing his studies of the Renaissance masters which he had begun in Rome at the suggestion of Liszt. In the same letter he speaks of the Mass of Vittoria which he was to hear the following Sunday, 8 December 1893, at Saint-Gervais and of which he gave an impressive account to Prince Poniatowski.

[2] Four scenes are cut from the original version of the play (Act I, Scene i; Act II, Scene iv; Act III, Scene i; and Act V, Scene i). In addition short passages are omitted and a few lines altered. All these omissions and changes were made to relieve the libretto of ideas that were too naïvely symbolical and merely hold up the action. Such a scene is also the second scene of Act IV in which Yniold, son of Golaud, is alarmed by a flock of lost sheep, and which was later cut from the opera at Debussy's wish.

it to music. As my opinion was the very opposite I had to use
what little diplomacy I am endowed with.[1]

Several memoirs and letters provide us with impressions of *Pelléas*
in the early stages of its composition. From the several manuscripts
known to us of the work[2] the rough sketch must have been drafted
at fever pitch and great speed. The text is omitted and the notation
frequently consists of notes without tails. Less than two years after
the first sketches were made the work was announced by Debussy
as finished: it was at any rate complete in his mind. He writes to
Henri Lerolle on 17 August 1895:

I have found myself sadly obliged to finish *Pelléas* while you
are so far from me. Moreover, that has not been done without
some foot-stamping; the scene between Golaud and Mélisande,
above all! For it is there that one begins to have a premonition of
catastrophes, there where Mélisande begins to lie to Golaud and
to become enlightened about herself, aided therein by this Golaud,
a fine man all the same, who shows that it is not necessary to be
entirely frank, even with little girls! I believe that the scene before
the grotto will please you. It tries to be all the mysteriousness of
the night, where amid so much silence, a blade of grass stirred from
its sleep makes a really disquieting noise; then, it is the near-by sea
which sings its sorrows to the moon, and it is Pelléas and Mélisande
who are a little afraid to speak amid so much mystery. . . .

Now, all my worry is beginning; how will the world get along
with these two poor little beings? (I hate crowds, universal suffrage
and tricoloured phrases! . . .) Wait, there is Hartmann, who is
certainly a representative of a good, medium intelligence. Ah
well! the death of Mélisande, such as it is, does not move him
more than a trifle. On him, it has no effect. For the rest, in France,
every time a woman dies in the theatre, it must be like the *Dame
aux Camélias*; it suffices to replace the camellias with other flowers
and the woman with a princess in a bazaar! People cannot concede

---

[1] A rather different account of this meeting is given by Louÿs who, though of French
parentage, was born at Ghent. In a letter to his brother Georges of 20 April 1914, he
writes: 'I have only been back there once, in 1892 or 1893, on a famous visit when I
accompanied Debussy to seek Maeterlinck's permission to set *Pelléas* to music. I had
to speak for him because he was too shy to say anything himself. And as Maeterlinck
was even more shy and didn't say anything either I had to reply for Maeterlinck as
well. It's a scene that I shall never forget.'
[2] See Appendix E.

Théodore de Banville

Stéphane Mallarmé

Letter from Debussy to Pierre Louÿs

that one leaves discreetly, like one who has had enough of this planet, the Earth, and is going away where the flowers of tranquillity blossom! . . .

A later letter to Lerolle, of 28 August 1895, is of particular interest for we see that Debussy was developing ideas, common to Mallarmé and Swinburne, on the symbolism of a woman's hair ('Gardez vos rêves pour mes cheveux') and on the identification of the sea with a mother figure ('Notre bonne mère la mer'). He writes:

Pelléas and Mélisande began to sulk and no longer wanted to come down from their tapestry. I have therefore been obliged to play with other ideas. Then, a little jealous, they returned to bend over me, and Mélisande, with the soft, silky voice which you know she has, said to me: 'Drop these little follies, the longing favourites of the cosmopolitan public, and keep your dreams for my hair; you know well that no other tenderness is like yours.'

And the scene in the underground caverns was done, filled with subtle terror and mysterious enough to give vertigo to the best inured souls! And also the scene on leaving those same caverns, filled with sunlight, but with sunlight bathed by our good mother the sea. . . .

I have also completed the scene with the little sheep, in which I have tried to put something of the compassion of a child to whom one of the sheep first gives the conception of the game in which he cannot take part; and also of the pity which people eager to be comfortable no longer feel. Now I am working on the scene between the father and son, and I am afraid, I must have such profound and sure things at my command! There is a 'little father' ('Petit père') in it that gives me nightmares.[1]

Not only nightmares[2] were caused by the symbolism of Pelléas, but tears were almost provoked. Earlier, in an undated letter of 1894, he had written to Chausson:

It's Mélisande's fault—so will you forgive us both? I have spent days in pursuit of those fancies of which she is made. I had no

---

[1] The translation of these two letters is by Oscar Thompson (Debussy: Man and Artist, New York, 1940).
[2] In a letter to Hartmann of 23 July 1898, Debussy describes a nightmare he has had in which Golaud appears as a bailiff.

courage to tell you of it all—besides, you know what such struggles are. I don't know if you have ever gone to bed, as I have, with a strange desire to cry, feeling as if you had not been able to see during the day some greatly loved friend. Just now I am worried about Arkel. He is from the other side of the grave and has that fond love, disinterested and far-seeing, of those who will soon disappear—all of which has to be said with doh re mi fah soh la si doh. *Quel métier!*

The opera was essentially completed, though not orchestrated, by August 1895. Of the various known manuscripts the most important, following the first rough draft, is the complete piano and vocal score at the New England Conservatory of Music at Boston. This, like other manuscripts of single scenes or sections, shows that Debussy was mainly concerned, after the first draft, to eliminate time gaps in the recitative. Where needless rests occurred over unchanging harmonies in the unfolding of the text whole passages are shifted backwards sometimes as much as a bar, thus accentuating the tension. Less often, when the poetic sense demands emphasis, phrases are expanded. In the Boston manuscript there are several places where the emphasis on a particular note has apparently caused much heart-searching, two or three variants being discernible. Apart from these matters of relative tension the score that was conceived between 1893 and 1895 is substantially the same as that which was performed in 1902. Only the interludes were expanded at the last moment, during the rehearsals, to allow time for the change of scenes. The full score was written only after the work was accepted in May 1901 for performance at the Opéra-Comique.[1]

The conception of opera as a poetic as well as a musical genre was so foreign to the tradition of any opera house that any kind of conventional production seemed quite unpractical, as in fact it still is. Jokingly, but in despair at ever seeing his work presented to a sympathetic public, Debussy said he hoped for a production in Japan, that is to say a production as far removed as possible from

---

[1] An excellent study of the variants in many of the manuscripts of *Pelléas* was made by Oswald d'Estrade-Guerra in 1957. In regard to the manuscript of the full score, used for the early Paris performances and now at the Bibliothèque du Conservatoire, Monsieur d'Estrade-Guerra draws attention to several changes in the orchestration that were made in this score during the rehearsals and also later. These do not appear in the published version. The form sanctioned at any one period by the composer was therefore known only to the conductors at the time.

any suggestion of stylized operatic rhetoric. At least four abortive schemes for the performance of *Pelléas* were proposed before it eventually reached the Opéra-Comique. In December 1895 a chamber version was proposed at the Théâtre de l'Oeuvre, directed by Lugné-Poe, during a season including plays by Ibsen and Wilde. An undated letter to Camille Mauclair states that Debussy was hoping for two private performances at the Pavillon des Muses, a sumptuous mansion belonging to the wealthy friend of Marcel Proust, Robert de Montesquiou. In 1895 Debussy had been approached to provide a symphonic suite on *Pelléas* to be performed in London. This must surely have been in connexion with the production that year of Maeterlinck's play by Lugné-Poe at the 'Independent Theatre' in the Strand.[1] Debussy was radically opposed to any such adaptation of his work. The following year he similarly forbad Eugène Ysaÿe, who had attempted to get the work produced at the Théâtre de la Monnaie at Brussels, to give it in concert form. He writes to Ysaÿe on 13 October 1896:

If this work has any merit, it is in the connexion between the drama and the music. It is quite obvious that at a concert performance this connexion would disappear and no one could be blamed for seeing nothing in those eloquent 'silences' with which this work is starred. Moreover, as the simplicity of the work only gains significance on the stage, at a concert performance they would throw in my face the American wealth of Wagner and I'd be like some poor fellow who couldn't afford to pay for contra-bass tubas.

The underlying inspiration of *Pelléas*, both the drama of Maeterlinck and the opera of Debussy, derived from Edgar Allan Poe and in particular *The Fall of the House of Usher*. The wide influence of

[1] In his letter to Debussy of 27 November 1895 proposing the ballet *Daphnis et Chloé*, Louÿs writes: 'Why do you refuse to do a symphonic suite on *Pelléas* for London? It's nothing to do with me, but do you think it's such a bad idea? Obviously if you do not do it yourself you have the right to forbid anyone else from doing it, but if I were you I shouldn't care.' It must have been with the consent of Debussy, who possessed the musical rights in the play from Maeterlinck, that Fauré wrote his well-known suite *Pelléas et Mélisande*, originally in the form of incidental music for the first production in English of the play at the Prince of Wales's Theatre in London in 1898. On this occasion a remarkably fine cast ensured its first true success. Forbes-Robertson, the producer, took the part of Golaud, Martin Harvey played the part of Pelléas, and Mrs. Patrick Campbell was the Mélisande. In Pre-Raphaelite style, some of the costumes were designed by Burne-Jones.

Poe in France—he was in a sense a creation of the French—has been
the subject of several studies, but it is in *Pelléas* that this influence was
most noticeably absorbed. In a letter to Léon Lemonnier of 22 June
1928 Maeterlinck declared: 'Edgar Poe has exerted over my work,
as over that of all others of my generation, a great, profound and
lasting influence. I owe to him the birth in my work of a sense of
mystery and the passion for the beyond.'[1] In *Pelléas* the old castle in
the imaginary kingdom of Allemonde, lugubrious and haunting its
inhabitants with painful memories, is a counterpart of the crumbling
House of Usher. The character of Pelléas himself, 'so pale and feeble
and overcome by destiny', is a reflection of Usher, the quintessential
man of an over-refined civilization. Mélisande, too, has an affinity
with Poe's characters: she largely re-creates the affecting charm of
such typical women in Poe's tales as Ligeia or Morella, destined to
die of some unknown and unfathomable illness. As so often in Poe,
the love of Pelléas for Mélisande is aroused by his sense of her
approaching death: 'Tu es étrangement belle quand je t'embrasse
ainsi. Tu es si belle qu'on dirait que tu vas mourir.'

Poe's works, in the translation of Baudelaire, were known to
Debussy at an early period. At the beginning of 1890, three years
before work was begun on *Pelléas*, he was engaged on an orchestral
work based on *The Fall of the House of Usher* and described as 'a
symphony on psychologically developed themes'.[2] We have no
knowledge of this early project, but there is evidence that Poe's tale
was prominently in Debussy's mind when writing *Pelléas*. In his
letter to Chausson of 6 September 1893, the month the opera was
begun, he goes so far as to quote the very words used by Baudelaire
in his translation of *Usher* to describe his state of mind.[3] We have
further evidence of his attraction to Poe at this time in his reference,

[1] In Jules Huret's interview with Maeterlinck in 1892, published in his *Enquête sur
l'Evolution Littéraire*, Maeterlinck stated that the works of Poe he particularly admired
were the poems and, among the tales, *The Fall of the House of Usher*.

[2] This information is contained in a letter of André Suarès to Romain Rolland of
14 January 1890. Following a perspicacious account of Debussy's development at this
time ('Since *La Damoiselle élue* he is the black sheep at the Academy, a serpent suckled
at the breast of Gounod') Suarès states: 'Ce musicien . . . travaille à une symphonie sur
thèmes psychologiquement déroulés dont l'idée serait maint conte de Poe, en particulier *La Chute de la Maison Usher*.'

[3] The opening sentence of Baudelaire's translation reads: 'Pendant toute une
journée d'automne, journée fuligineuse, sombre et muette, où les nuages pesaient lourds
et bas dans le ciel, j'avais traversé seul et à cheval une étendue de pays singulièrement
lugubre.' Debussy's letter opens: 'J'ai beau faire, je n'arrive pas à dérider la tristesse de
mon paysage: parfois mes journées sont fuligineuses, sombres et muettes *comme celle
d'un héro d'Edgar Allan Poe*, et mon âme romanesque ainsi qu'une Ballade de Chopin.'

apropos of the visit in 1893 to Maeterlinck at Ghent, to André Gide's *Le Voyage d'Urien*: 'Enfin vous voyez que ce fut un voyage plus profitable que celui d'Urien.' This first novel of Gide describes in the form of an allegory a journey across a deserted ocean of self-discovery, ending in complete disillusionment, in the manner of Poe's *The Narrative of Arthur Gordon Pym*.[1]

Another project of the period of *Pelléas* must be mentioned before we assess the opera from a musical standpoint. This was a libretto that he intended to write on the story *La Grande Bretèche* of Balzac. In this grim tale of jealousy, having much in common with Poe's *Usher* and Maeterlinck's *Pelléas*, an enraged husband buries alive his wife's Spanish lover. The sight of the unfortunate Spaniard, it has been suggested, is described in terms which might almost apply to Debussy himself: 'Une figure d'homme sombre et brune, des cheveux noirs, un regard de feu.' Debussy confesses to having been 'disturbed' by this tale which takes place in a mysterious abode recalling the house of Usher or the castle of Allemonde. The project dates from September 1895, when the first draft of *Pelléas* had been completed. It was abandoned, though not before Debussy had set out ideas of an opera on this subject which he hoped to have performed abroad.

At first sight the score of *Pelléas* resembles no other opera in that it appears to consist of fugitive impressions, intertwined associations, and varied changes of mood none of which are ever sharply exteriorized. The tone of the five acts, playing for no more than two and a half hours, is kept consistently to that of a sombre, voluptuous dream. For this reason it would appear to defy analysis in terms of any of the conventional techniques. The opera, however, is based on a highly original technique of its own, evolved instinctively and which has been minutely investigated by Maurice Emmanuel. Broadly speaking, this technique, designed to convey the *état d'âme* of the characters and the maze of unconscious conflicts between them, is based on a novel interplay of rhythm and harmony, on a vocal style alternating between song and recitative, on the use of motives with psychological associations, and on a conception of the

---

[1] Debussy's knowledge of these works of Poe and Gide is discussed in my *Debussy et Edgar Poe* (1962). When writing to Chausson in January 1894 Debussy was obviously thinking of a passage strongly reminiscent of Poe in *Le Voyage d'Urien*. The passage of Gide describes a horrifying site of bats in a grotto causing Urien to doubt his very identity. Debussy writes: 'J'ai en ce moment l'âme gris-fer et de tristes chauve-souris tournent au clocher de mes rêves! Je n'ai plus d'espoir qu'en *Pelléas et Mélisande* et Dieu seul sait si cet espoir n'est pas que de la fumée!'

orchestra as a vast chamber ensemble fully participating in the drama.

Aspiring to an ideal of harmony that should 'drown tonality', many of the harmonic progressions have either an ambiguous or a symbolical purpose. Here Monsieur Emmanuel's close scrutiny of Debussy's harmonic ideas has not been surpassed. In Act II, Scene i the tonal ambiguity of a progression of chords of the seventh, ninth, and eleventh is designed to illustrate the hopeless loss of Mélisande's ring ('Elle est perdue, elle est perdue'), and this progression is followed by a sequence of four chords in four different tonalities (C major, B major, A major, and F minor) immediately evoking the widening circle of water in the mysterious well ('Il n'y a plus qu'un grand cercle d'eau'). Elsewhere profundity is expressed by simple, primitive chords, and anxiety by chords kept deliberately incomplete. The pathetic question of the dying Mélisande in Act v, 'Est-ce vous, Golaud? Je ne vous reconnaissais plus', achieves its full searching force by means of mere common chords, while the terrifying sight of the beggars in the grotto scene (Act II, Scene iii, 'Ce sont trois vieux pauvres qui se sont endormis') is wonderfully suggested by bare seconds, fourths, and fifths. One has to watch for details of great subtlety. Occasionally a single note, entirely foreign to the harmony, is introduced with striking effect, as in Golaud's threat to the child Yniold in Act III, Scene iv ('Je suis ici comme un nouveau-né perdu dans la forêt, — et vous . . .').

No less varied and resourceful is the rhythmic structure of *Pelléas*. The prelude to Act I, consisting of no more than twenty-two bars, makes use of eight different rhythmic figures. It is in fact a miniature overture of intensely concentrated expression. It would be wrong, however, to suppose that melodic ideas are not developed in symphonic fashion. Where the scenic action is continuous or the mood consistent symphonic development is obviously demanded and the rhythmic basis of a theme is then expanded on a broad scale. Examples are the chorus towards the end of Act I, the scene before the castle in Act III in which Golaud compels Yniold to spy on Mélisande, and the terrible scene of cruelty (Act IV, Scene ii) in which the enraged Golaud drags Mélisande by her hair. Such passages, introduced to mark emphasis or continuity, offer a dramatic contrast to the freely drawn recitative.

Much has been written on Debussy's departure from Wagnerian

methods, but in fact the musical and psychological unity of *Pelléas* is ensured by a consistent use of the *Leitmotiv*. Identifying recurrent themes in the work, Maurice Emmanuel lists thirteen which occur in this order: Remoteness, Golaud, Mélisande, Destiny, Pelléas, The Fountain, The Ring, Yniold, Love's Awakening, Death, Love's Fulfilment, The Child, and The Pardon. Though they are not in any way obtrusive, largely because of the tenuous texture of the orchestration, they are used with great imaginative resource and in fundamentally the same manner as the *Leitmotive* in *Tristan* or *Parsifal*. In the Prelude to Act I and towards the end of the act ('C'est le navire qui m'a menée ici') the themes of Golaud and Mélisande are combined. Among other such symbolical associations the themes of Pelléas and Mélisande are intertwined in the interlude before Act II, Scene ii, and at the opening of Act IV there is a contrapuntal combination of the themes of Golaud, Pelléas, and The Fountain. By means of all these associative ideas a much deeper perspective is added to the play.

The role of the orchestra similarly follows the Wagnerian conception, that is to say it is predominantly symphonic. But the texture, in which there is seldom any doubling, is infinitely lighter. The composition of the orchestra is the same as that of *Tristan* except for the absence in *Pelléas* of a bass clarinet. The strings are frequently divided, sometimes into as many as twelve parts, and there are seldom any extended *tutti*. The chamber-music conception of the symphonic orchestra gives the impression that each instrument is treated as a soloist. An independent part is often given to the double basses, the bassoons are treated melodically, and there are extraordinary lugubrious rolls for the timpani. Flutes, harps, and clarinets are marvellously used in the lighter textures. Muted horns and trumpets, such as we find in the *Nocturnes* and *La Mer*, are used to depict terror. Trombones are used sparingly, underlining Golaud's blind rage with powerful dramatic effect. The orchestra of *Pelléas* is richer than that of *L'Après-midi d'un faune* or the *Nocturnes*, though it is more subdued than that of *La Mer* or the orchestral *Images*. It has an ethereal, poetic beauty entirely of its own, bearing a family resemblance to the orchestra of *Parsifal*, in which Debussy admired the effects 'illuminated as from behind', but more affecting in detail and subtlety.

There remains the variety of vocal styles drawn upon or explored.

Before the first performance Debussy gathered together the cast and implored them to forget that they were singers. They were to expect no formal arias nor anything in the nature of a developed vocal scene. By a curious anticipation Jean-Jacques Rousseau, who was a foresighted theorist, though, to judge by *Le Devin du Village*, a poor composer, had defined a type of recitative peculiar to the French language. His theories had been discussed at the Conservatoire during Debussy's student years, in the courses of Bourgault-Ducoudray. Rousseau declared that 'le meilleur récitatif est celui où l'on chante le moins . . . il doit rouler entre de fort petits intervalles, n'élever ni n'abaisser beaucoup la voix. Peu de sons soutenus; jamais d'éclats, encore moins de cris, rien qui ressemble au chant, peu d'inégalité dans la durée ou valeur des notes, ainsi que dans leurs degrés.' Indeed, repeated notes and small intervals can easily be found extremely monotonous, as in fact they certainly seemed to Richard Strauss when he heard *Pelléas* at the Opéra-Comique in the company of Romain Rolland. It is the great art of the vocal writing in *Pelléas* that it avoids monotony. This is achieved partly by the imaginative orchestration and partly because the recitative is frequently varied by lyrical developments. In the love scene between Pelléas and Mélisande (Act III, Scene i) the recitative of Pelléas suddenly develops into a passionate outburst encompassing the whole tenor range. Much of Act IV is consistently lyrical, and by contrast the almost spoken climax of this act ('Je t'aime . . . Je t'aime aussi') is thrown into prominent relief. Debussy follows no set conception of a vocal style in *Pelléas*. He was concerned, as the sketches clearly show, constantly to economize rests between the phrases, thus maintaining a taut but flexible continuity, and at the same time to allow the maximum lyrical expansion when the occasion demanded.

As an opera *Pelléas* was the realization of Mallarmé's ideal of a stage work, namely a work which, though exteriorized, should explore all the hidden conflicts buried in the pages of books.

In May 1901 *Pelléas* was formally accepted for production at the Opéra-Comique. Albert Carré, the director, encouraged by André Messager to consider a series of private performances for the unconventional opera, as yet unscored, decided to risk a repertory performance. The dress rehearsal took place on 28 April 1902 in the afternoon and the first performance on 30 April. In the meantime a violent quarrel broke out between Maeterlinck and Debussy, the reason for which has so far remained mysterious. In her memoirs Maeterlinck's mistress, Georgette Leblanc, alleges that it had been understood that the part of Mélisande was to be sung by herself, but that four months before the production Debussy had substituted a singer of his own choice, Mary Garden. As a result the two architects of *Pelléas*, whose timidity had almost made it impossible for them to communicate with each other, collided in a series of brutal scenes. Outwardly shy, Maeterlinck angrily exploded in a stormy protest, followed by a challenge to a duel and the threat of a beating with his walking-stick. Since Maeterlinck was an accomplished swordsman for whom Debussy could hope to be no match Albert Carré had volunteered to take his place. Maeterlinck appears to have relished the prospect and even to have rehearsed his act. 'Put yourself there, in the place of Carré', he declared to Lugné-Poe, standing him against his garden wall and thrusting a sword in his hand. Possibly because even at the time of the quarrel the inflamed author never really believed in his case, the duel did not take place. Nor was there any sequel to the threat of a 'thrashing' which, we are told by Georgette Leblanc, was made by Maeterlinck in Debussy's home in the rue Cardinet. Debussy, according to this account, had collapsed weakly, calling for smelling salts, and the aggressor generously retired.[1]

Later evidence published by W. D. Halls and Mary Garden, as well as the correspondence of Debussy and Maeterlinck, compels us to look further into this episode. In the first place Georgette Leblanc had a wretched reputation as a singer, and whatever assurances were given her, possibly out of consideration for Maeterlinck, dominated by his ambitious mistress, it is clear that both Carré and Debussy were agreed on the choice of Mary Garden for the part of Mélisande from the start. There could be no reason for any underhand action on the part of Debussy who was concerned merely to support the singer best suited for the part. Bewildered by Maeterlinck's violent outbursts, he several times refers to his behaviour as 'pathological'. It is certain that Maeterlinck did his best to undermine the

[1] Writing about 1925 to the impresario Henry Russell on the subject of this episode Maeterlinck says: 'L'histoire de Debussy est à peu près exacte; mais si j'avais un gros bâton, ce n'était que ma canne habituelle. Du reste, je n'ai pas eu à menacer d'en faire usage, car Debussy qui me voyait d'assez méchante humeur, pour se débarrasser de moi, s'empressa de me promettre tout ce que je voulais.'

production, writing a letter to *Le Figaro*, two weeks before the first performance, expressing the wish that the opera would be a resounding failure. It is possible also that he lent his support to the publication of an official programme, sold outside the theatre, in which the plot of the opera, his own work, was ironically and even obscenely parodied.

It is probably true, as Debussy himself stated, that Maeterlinck had no feeling for music whatever ('When it comes to music he is like a blind man in a museum'), though it is doubtful whether he could have been indifferent to the enormously heightened significance of his play which Debussy's music provided. There must have been a deeper explanation for the suddenness of Maeterlinck's outburst than the trumped-up rivalry of two singers. Two years after Debussy's death, in 1920, Maeterlinck heard Debussy's opera for the first time. On 28 June he wrote to Mary Garden, who had taken the part of Mélisande at the Metropolitan Opera: 'I had sworn to myself never to see the lyric drama *Pelléas et Mélisande*. Yesterday I violated my vow and I am a happy man. For the first time I have entirely understood my own play, and because of you.' This can only be read as an admission of some hidden motive in Maeterlinck's actions. Referring to his quarrel with Debussy in a statement to Henry Russell about 1925, he says: 'Today I find that I was completely wrong in this matter and that he was a thousand times right.'

The hidden motive must surely be that Maeterlinck had become aware, perhaps only half consciously, that his rival in *Pelléas et Mélisande* was Debussy. *Pelléas* as a play is in fact an opera libretto in search of a composer. Without the music the play has certainly a period significance, though nothing of the symbolism that is made to reverberate so disturbingly in Debussy's score. Hence the catcalls, the chuckling and the fighting between supporters and adversaries at the first performance of *Pelléas*. Harmonically far less adventurous than *Parsifal*, it could not possibly have been so provocative on purely musical grounds. The explanation of the violent hostility it aroused is surely in the fact that the realities of the dream were brought to the surface in this unique opera of poetry, rather too overwhelmingly, rather too alarmingly to be faced with comfort.

THE VON MECK FAMILY

Family tree compiled by Nadezhda von Meck's grandchildren, Count George Bennigsen and Madame Galina von Meck, showing Debussy's friends and associates in this family and, in the marriage of Nicholas von Meck and Anna Davydov, the relationship of the von Meck and Tchaikovsky families.

Karl Otto Georg von Meck (22 June 1821–26 January 1876) married on 14 January 1848
Nadezhda Filaretovna Fralovskaya (29 January 1831–14 January 1894)

Elisabeth (1848–1903) m. Alexander Yolshin	Alexandra (1850–1921) m. Count Paul Bennigsen	Valdemar (1852–1892) m. Elisabeth Popov	Julia (1853–1915) m. Ladislas Pachulsky (Violinist with Debussy in Mme von Meck's trio)	Lydia (1855–1910) m. Friedrich Loewis of Menar	Nicholas (1861–1929) m. Anna Davydov (niece of Tchaikovsky)	Alexander (1862–1911) m. Annie France in 1885 (from Glenelly, Scotland)	Sophie (Sonia) (1867–1936) m. (1) Alexis Rimsky-Korsakov (2) Prince Dmitri Galitzin	Maximilian (1869–1950) m. Olga Kiriakov	Michael (1870–1883)	Ludmilla (1872–193–) m. Prince Andrey Shirinsky-Shykhmatov
One daughter	Four sons (Emmanuel, George, Leony and Adam); three daughters	Vladimir m. Barbara Karpov (author of *Beloved Friend*)		Four sons; seven daughters	Three sons (Andrey, Marc, Attal); three daughters (Kyra, Galina, Lucella)	Two sons (George, Michael)	From first marriage 3 sons (Boris, Dmitri, Georgy); 1 daughter	1 son		2 sons 3 daughters

APPENDIX B

CONVERSATIONS WITH ERNEST GUIRAUD

The following record of the conversations between Debussy and Ernest Guiraud was made by Maurice Emmanuel under curious circumstances. Whilst still a student at the Conservatoire, Emmanuel was attracted to the medieval modes and planned to introduce them in his compositions. This met with the stern disapproval of his master Léo Delibes, with the result that Emmanuel sought the support of the more broad-minded Guiraud with whom he was able to pursue his studies unofficially. Debussy had maintained a friendly relationship with his former master Guiraud, and in 1889 and 1890, after his visits to Bayreuth, often discussed aesthetic problems with him. These discussions were inspiring to Emmanuel to the extent that he jotted down some of the main points. Though they are set out in a haphazard fashion they light up a corner of the mind of Debussy at a time when Wagner was still a revolutionary and when the young Debussy was beginning to discover his way.

GUIRAUD: You say that the cor anglais solo in the third act of *Tristan* is a classical aria, an 'exercise'? It doesn't in any way suggest Beethoven.

DEBUSSY: Because you don't hear the harmony beneath it. But let us look further. Berlioz is much further removed from Bach and Mozart than Wagner. He is less tonal than Wagner, though Wagner is more accomplished in transitions from major to minor.

GUIRAUD: How harsh; it's constantly chromatic. You can't call that classical.

DEBUSSY: Classical signifies major and minor.

In the classical style chords are resolved. The classical style implies near modulations (a closed circle).

Romantic: a label that to my mind has no significance. The language of Schumann, Berlioz, and Liszt is the classical language. I hear in them all the same kind of music.

GUIRAUD: But this insipid, continuous music. No scenes, no cuts. You can't say it is anything like Mozart!

DEBUSSY: I shouldn't say it is the opposite of Mozart. It's a later development. No square-cut phrases, nevertheless Wagner develops in the classical manner. Wagner merely abandoned the perpetual perfect cadence and the hateful six-four chord. Supposing Mozart had had the idea of writing an act in one continuous movement, do you think he would have been able to achieve it? His was the convention of separate arias and four-bar phrases. Wagner develops in the classical manner. In the place of the architectural themes of a symphony, occurring at specified points, he has themes representing things and people, but he develops these themes in a symphonic manner. He derives from Bach and Beethoven, as we see in *Tristan* and *Meistersinger*—not to speak of his orchestra which is a development and enlargement of the classical orchestra.

GUIRAUD: But what about his treatment of the voices?

DEBUSSY: Yes, there we find a difference, but not a musical difference. Is it new? It may seem to resemble the spoken language; and it doesn't follow the four-bar phrase. There are no recitatives in the Italian manner and no lyrical arias. The words are subordinated to the orchestral accompaniment, but not sufficiently. It is music that sings too continuously. Singing should be reserved for certain points.

GUIRAUD: What kind of poet would you yourself have in mind?

DEBUSSY: One who only hints at what is to be said (*celui des choses dites à demi*). The ideal would be two associated dreams. No place, nor time. No big scene. No compulsion on the musician, who must complete and give body to the work of the poet. Music in opera is far too predominant. Too much singing and the musical settings are too cumbersome. The blossoming of the voice into true singing should occur only when required. A painting executed in grey is the ideal. No developments merely for the sake of developments. A prolonged development does not fit, cannot fit, the words. My idea is of a short libretto with mobile scenes. I have no use at all for the three unities. A variety of scenes in regard to place and character. No discussion or arguments between the characters whom I see at the mercy of life or destiny.

THE DIVISION OF THE OCTAVE
(*Debussy seated at the piano*)

DEBUSSY: 24 semitones=36 tones in the octave with 18 different degrees. No faith in the supremacy of the C major scale. The tonal scale must be enriched by other scales.

I am not misled by equal temperament. Rhythms are stifling. Rhythms cannot be contained within bars. It is nonsense to speak of 'simple' and 'composed' time. There should be an interminable flow of them both without seeking to bury the rhythmic patterns. Relative keys are nonsense too. Music is neither major nor minor. Minor thirds and major thirds should be combined, modulation thus becoming more flexible. The mode is that which one happens to choose at the moment. It is inconstant. In *Tristan* the themes heard in the orchestra are themes of the action. They do no violence to the action. There must be a balance between musical demands and thematic evocation. Themes suggest their orchestral colouring.

GUIRAUD (*Debussy having played a series of intervals on the piano*): What's that?

DEBUSSY: Incomplete chords, floating. *Il faut noyer le ton.* One can travel where one wishes and leave by any door. Greater nuances.

GUIRAUD: But when I play this it has to resolve.

DEBUSSY: I don't see that it should. Why?

GUIRAUD: Well, do you find this lovely?

DEBUSSY: Yes, yes, yes!

GUIRAUD: But how would you get out of this?

I am not saying that what you do isn't beautiful, but it's theoretically absurd.

DEBUSSY: There is no theory. You have merely to listen. Pleasure is the law.

GUIRAUD: I would agree with you in regard to an exceptional person who has discovered a discipline for himself and who has an instinct which he is able to impose. But how would you teach music to others?

DEBUSSY: Music cannot be learnt.

GUIRAUD: Come now, you are forgetting that you yourself were ten years at the Conservatoire.

DEBUSSY (*He agrees to this and admits that there can nevertheless be a doctrine*): Yes, this is silly. Except that I can't reconcile all this. True enough, I feel free because I have been through the mill, and I don't write in the fugual style because I know it. (*He is astonishingly direct in discussion and never seeks to avoid a point with a joke.*)

(*I wanted to show him the* Complainte de Notre-Dame *and* V'là que l'alouette chante. *He took little notice of it though he found it 'pretty, amusing'.*

He has no faith in plain chant nor in the chanson. He has a horror of plain chant; says it is the drug of the priests. He doesn't know the Te Deum *nor the old* Credo. *I played him the* Inviolata. *He said: 'It's a canticle for old women and white-clothed girls.'*)

GUIRAUD: What impressed you most in Rome?

DEBUSSY: The loggia of Raphael (not the stanze!) and the Madonna of the Rosary of Sassoferrato at S. Sabina. St. Peter's is a hall for well-meaning but tasteless giants. I prefer S. Severina. I adore the Villa Pia, of no practical value, with its porticos, balustrades, and ornamental façades. At Orvieto the Resurrection of Signorelli (not because of the trumpets!).

GUIRAUD: I don't know it.

Debussy at the piano strikes these chords:

GUIRAUD: It's all very meandering.

DEBUSSY: Certainly not! Consider the scale which is doubly chromatic. Isn't this one of our tools? Counterpoint is not given to us for nothing. As the parts go forward we come across some splendid chords.

The symphony of Franck is amazing. I could do with less four-bar phrases. But what splendid ideas! I even prefer it to the Quintet which I used to find thrilling. He has upset them at the Institute!

Lakmé is sham, imitative Oriental bric-à-brac. Only the comic English characters are well presented.

I like the overture to *Phèdre*, about the only work of Massenet I admire and the work of a true musician.

Incomplete chords, ambiguous intervals. . . . What I love in *Tristan* are the themes, just the right emphasis to suggest the visual scene in the orchestra.

Gluck is sometimes very conventional. In his recitatives he was unable to progress beyond the accepted style. And in his arias what threadbare ideas! *J'ai perdu mon Eurydice* is a piece of humbug. And for a musician who declares that he didn't wish to interrupt the dramatic action, what have you to say to his ballets in the middle of an act? Gluck took the rise out of the French. He was a thorough-going Italian.

APPENDIX C

THE HOAXES OF ANDRÉ DE TERNANT

In 1924 André de Ternant, said to have been born in London of French parentage and to have been an assistant to Francis Hueffer on *The Times*, published three articles in *The Musical Times*: 'Debussy and Brahms' (July 1924), 'Debussy and some Italian musicians' (September 1924), 'Debussy and some others on Sullivan' (December 1924). These articles, widely quoted and the subject of much controversy, gave details of supposed journeys of Debussy in Italy, Austria, and England as well as conversations he was reported to have had with many eminent musicians of his time, including Brahms, Verdi, Boito, and Sullivan. Ternant claimed that these details had been confided to him on an early journey Debussy made to England and that he had been pledged to keep them secret until after Debussy's death. To earlier writers, when knowledge of the bare biographical facts was limited, the facts disclosed by Ternant seemed plausible. Moreover, their authenticity appeared to be ensured in the course of correspondence carried on with Ternant by both Léon Vallas and myself. In his correspondence with Vallas, Ternant enlarged on a supposed early visit of Debussy to London, where he was said to have gone to negotiate the rights of Rossetti's *Blessed Damozel* or to find an English publisher for his setting of this work. As a result of this correspondence, in the course of which, states Vallas, Ternant supplied him with 'exact references', a picture emerged of Debussy's associations with certain Pre-Raphaelite figures in England which appeared both credible and illuminating.

Accepting Ternant's evidence in all good faith Vallas wrote in the first edition of his *Claude Debussy et son temps* that in 1887 Debussy had gone to London with a letter of introduction to the critic of *The Times*, Francis Hueffer, married to a daughter of the painter, Ford Madox Brown, and a close friend of Rossetti. Having tried to find him a publisher, Hueffer, according to this account, secured the interest of Novello's, but to no avail. Other statements emanating from Ternant maintain that in his early youth Debussy stayed at Belsize Park in London and that, on a visit to London of three weeks in 1895, he was introduced by Saint-Saëns to Sir Hubert Parry at the Royal College of Music.

All this was extremely ingenious on the part of Ternant, ready to add to his mystifications at the slightest provocation. Following a letter published by Léon Vallas in *Music and Letters* (October 1947) and further enquiries regarding the supposed English journeys of César Franck in a subsequent article of Ternant, in *The Choir* (February 1927), it was established that Ternant was a fraud and that these four articles were a hoax.

In the first place Ternant was not, as he let it be known, an accredited critic of *The Times*. At most he may have written odd notices as an assistant to Hueffer. In reply to his request for employment, *The Times* wrote to him in February 1893 stating that nothing could be offered to him. Ternant's name appears nowhere in Debussy's correspondence, nor was he known to any of Debussy's friends. Though it may have been permissible to earlier writers to take on its face value Ternant's invention of a journey made by Debussy to Vienna, today this account, showing so little knowledge of Debussy's character and containing reports of conversations in an oddly familiar style, reads like a grotesque caricature. After leaving the Villa Medici, our imaginative reporter writes, Debussy 'made up his mind to become personally acquainted with as many eminent foreign composers as possible and his greatest capture was Johannes Brahms. It was no easy task to approach the lion in his den. "Are you the Frenchman who wrote to me and called twice at my house?" Debussy bowed graciously. "Well, I will forgive you this time but don't do it again."'[1]

Elsewhere Debussy is said to have met Sullivan at a reception given by Augusta Holmès and to have admired him as a society gentleman. The composer of *The Pirates of Penzance* was held by this witty diabolist to be 'the greatest English wit in Parisian salons since Horace Walpole. . . . The brilliance of his conversation recalled the maxims of La Rochefoucauld.' Ternant's masterpiece, however, was his article on the severe figure of César Franck in *The Choir*. He sends Franck to Bayreuth, to Rome to be blessed by the Pope, and we find this dreamy, remote composer in unexpected high spirits, cracking jokes for the amusement of his dull English friends in several well-known London taverns. This was Ternant's most daring fantasy and his last. It was proved that Franck had never set foot in England.

[1] Sir Charles Stanford's reference to Brahms's knowledge of *La Damoiselle élue* in a letter to W. S. Hannam of 21 October 1909, which I had been inclined to offer in support of Ternant, is still puzzling though it is likely to have been a slip on Stanford's part. Possibly Stanford was confusing Brahms with Joachim.

APPENDIX D

SWINBURNE AND POE IN FRANCE

Although Debussy's sketches for operas on the tales of Poe, *The Fall of the House of Usher* and *The Devil in the Belfry*, belong to the latter part of his life and will be dealt with in the subsequent volume, his knowledge of the works of Poe dates from his youth and there is much evidence showing that his development was greatly influenced by the many translations of Poe's works that appeared in his youth, notably the translations of Poe's poems by his friend Gabriel Mourey. Several studies have evaluated the French interpretations of Poe from those of Baudelaire onwards. The most important are *Edgar Poe et les poètes français* by Léon Lemonnier (1932) and *Edgar Poe: Etude psychanalytique* by Marie Bonaparte (1933) with a preface by Freud (translated by John Rodker, *The Life and Works of Edgar Allan Poe*, London, 1949). The available sketches, manuscripts, and other unpublished documents of Debussy relating to his operas on tales of Poe are assembled and discussed in my study *Debussy et Edgar Poe* (1962).

It is clear that Debussy's life-long attraction to Poe forms part of the movement inspired by the French discovery of this writer, but during the earlier part of his life he was similarly attracted to another Anglo-Saxon writer, Swinburne, with whom in the French mind Poe was strangely associated. We have evidence of Debussy's knowledge of Swinburne from a letter of about 1890 to René Peter in which he says: 'There is still not a complete translation of Swinburne but you may find some of his poems translated in *Les Poètes modernes de l'Angleterre* by Gabriel Sarrazin and in *La Revue Indépendante* of May, 1888 and June, 1889.' These publications contain extracts from Swinburne's play *Chastelard*, many of the *Poems and Ballads*, *Laus Veneris*, and a study of Swinburne by Gabriel Mourey. 'Between Swinburne and Debussy,' René Peter comments in publishing this letter, 'the threads of Symbolism were drawn together in a way that foreshadows the whole series of his songs.' I think that this is reading too much into the influence of Swinburne. But it is significant in any view of the new sensibility brought into music by Debussy that before he set poems from Baudelaire's *Fleurs du Mal* and with

[211]

memories of *Tristan*, heard at Bayreuth, still ringing in his head, he had read Swinburne's *Anactoria*:

> I would find grievous ways to have thee slain,
> Intense device and superflux of pain;
> Vex thee with amorous agonies, and shake
> Life at thy lips, and leave it there to ache.

Several of Debussy's friends were aesthetically and personally associated with Swinburne. In her study 'Swinburne et sa légende en France' (*Revue de Littérature comparée*, July–September 1951) Dr. Souffrin-Le Breton published the correspondence between Swinburne and Pierre Louÿs from which it appears that the two poets were aware of a deep aesthetic affinity. Debussy must surely have been aware of this affinity and probably shared it. In 1891 Louÿs asked Swinburne to write a poem which he published in his review *La Conque* and on the death of Swinburne in 1909 we find Louÿs writing a moving letter to Robert Sherard, the friend of Oscar Wilde:

> With the death of Swinburne this year you have suffered in England an appalling loss. He was the greatest living poet. When I remember that he wrote to me when I was nineteen, that he contributed to my first review and that over a period of twenty years I never even went to see him I can't forgive myself. Only a fortnight before his death, not knowing that he was ill, I had suggested to the greatest French poets that a tribute should be paid to him in the form of a protest at his not having received the Nobel Prize. I had in mind an anthology to appear under the simple title, 'Poems for Swinburne'. Just as replies to my request were coming in we received the news that Swinburne had died.

Verlaine was similarly drawn to Swinburne, and on his first journey to England, in 1872, he declared that his great ambition was to see him. Indeed his main reason for learning English was to be able to read Swinburne, in the manner, it has been suggested, that Mallarmé learnt English in order to read Poe. In 1891 Gabriel Mourey published a translation of Swinburne's *Poems and Ballads* and some years later paid a memorable visit to the poet at Putney Hill. Paul Bourget, Mallarmé, and Henri de Régnier were other friends of Debussy who were influenced by Swinburne's sensuous lyricism.

There was also a personal aspect of Swinburne's attraction for the French: his physical appearance suggested a character from Edgar Allan Poe. When Swinburne visited Paris in 1882 to take part in the celebrations marking the eightieth birthday of Victor Hugo a pen-portrait of him appeared in *Le Figaro* by René Maizeroy suggesting 'a figure who had escaped from some fantastic tale of Poe'. His whole bearing struck this observer as most astonishing: 'His nervous shudders, the strange dreamy look in his eyes, his mobile features, his pale lips, high forehead, and his fair reddish hair gave the impression that Charles Swinburne was a highly refined artist, one of those poets haunted by the macabre and by death.' Maupassant wrote that he created 'l'effet d'une sorte d'Edgar Poe idéaliste et sensuel . . . une âme d'écrivain plus exaltée, plus dépravée . . . plus curieuse et évocatrice des raffinements subtils et antinaturels de la vie . . . un Edgar Poe fin-de-siècle'. It is interesting to see that this description corresponds fairly closely with Debussy's description of the character of Roderick Usher in his libretto based on Poe's *The Fall of the House of Usher*: 'La figure ravagée par l'angoisse, il ressemble un peu à E. A. Poe. Il regarde fixement devant lui, et pourtant ses yeux semblant ne pas voir. Ses gestes sont brusques et saccadés, sa voix rauque.' Swinburne also apparently inspired the character 'Charles Redburne, critique d'art anglais' in Debussy's unpublished play, *F.E.A.* (*Frères en Art*), 'a priest who upheld the cult of beauty'.

Several references in Debussy's early correspondence to characters or works of Poe show that following his early attempt to set *The Fall of the House of Usher* in the form of a 'symphony on psychologically developed themes' he remained a persistent reader of Poe. At a time when Poe was more widely appreciated earlier critics of Debussy in England and America, notably Arthur Symons and James Huneker, wrote of his music as evoking the atmosphere of Poe's tales. This aspect of his work is nowadays less readily seen. Yet we may truly see his work as the child of Roderick Usher himself, the prototype of the new artist embracing poetry, painting and music. Usher was a poet whose verse 'had an undercurrent of meaning'; he was a painter whose 'pure abstractions on the canvas grew touch by touch into vagueness'; and he was a musician whose 'wild improvisations on the guitar were the result of a morbid condition of the auditory nerve'. Other works of Poe known to Debussy include *The Narrative of Arthur Gordon Pym* with its extraordinary descriptions of the sea which he would not have forgotten when writing *La Mer*.

Though published much later, the psychoanalytic study of Poe by Marie Bonaparte strongly suggests that the explorations of the unconscious at the basis of the work of Freud formed part of a wide movement in the arts, as well as in psychological medicine, of which Poe was seen by his French admirers to be a precursor. We see from Madame Bonaparte's work how manifestations of the unconscious were progressively rising to the surface from *Parsifal* (1882) to Freud's *Interpretation of Dreams* and *Studies in Hysteria* (both of 1895) and to *Pelléas et Mélisande* (1902). Debussy frequently speaks of the 'hypersensibility' that united him to the figure of Usher. In 1911 he wrote of his works in terms that suggest that he had been reading Poe's *My heart laid bare* in his *Marginalia*, a French translation of which had recently been published. 'Combien il faut d'abord trouver,' Debussy writes, 'puis supprimer pour arriver à la chair nue de l'émotion.' Poe's notes, which had earlier inspired Baudelaire's *Mon coeur mis à nu* and which form an illuminating commentary on Debussy's achievement, read:

If any ambitious man have a fancy to revolutionise at one effort the universal word of human thought, human opinion, and human sentiment, the opportunity is his own—the road to immortal renown lies straight, open, and unencumbered before him. All that he has to do is to write and publish a very little book. Its title should be simple—a few plain words—'My Heart Laid Bare'. But—this little book must be *true to its title*.

Now, is it not very singular that, with the rabid thirst for notoriety which distinguishes so many of mankind—so many, too, who care not a fig what is thought of them after death, there should not be found one man having sufficient hardihood to write this little book? To *write*, I say. There are ten thousand men, who, if the book were once written, would laugh at the notion of being disturbed by its publication during their life, and who could not even conceive *why* they should object to its being published after their death. But to write it—*there* is the rub. No man dare write it. No man ever will dare write it. No man *could* write it, even if he dared. The paper would shrivel and blaze at every touch of the fiery pen.

[214]

APPENDIX E

MALLARMÉ ON *PELLÉAS*

At the time of the production of Maeterlinck's *Pelléas et Mélisande* Mallarmé was acting as dramatic critic for two papers, *Le Réveil Mensuel de Littérature* in Ghent and the *National Observer* in Edinburgh. He published an identical article on the play in French in both of these papers, in June and July respectively, 1893. Reproduced here, it appeared in a curtailed and amended form in the section *Crayonné au théâtre* in Mallarmé's *Divagations* (1897). This little-known original form of the article is interesting from several viewpoints. It sets out Mallarmé's ideas on the Symbolist theatre; it refers to contemporary criticism of Maeterlinck, notably by Octave Mirbeau, who had made excessive claims for *La Princesse Maleine*; and it reveals, rather surprisingly at first sight, that Mallarmé considered the static Symbolist play to be sufficient in itself. Though he was powerfully inspired by music, assembling words for their inherent associations almost regardless of their concrete meaning, Mallarmé was distrustful of musical settings of contemporary literature. Perhaps he felt his own unattainable ideal challenged; or he may have been envious of its realization. Time has not vindicated his theories. In fact, both *L'Après-midi d'un faune* and *Pelléas et Mélisande* live in the musical versions of Debussy. In regard to Debussy's version of the former Mallarmé was in two minds. The latter he did not live to hear.

In his study of Mallarmé's ideas[1] Jacques Scherer describes Mallarmé's conception of reading. Mallarmé held that the most important function of reading was to evoke in the reader's mind an imaginary theatre. The reader identifies himself with the scenes of a story or a novel, he interprets the characters in his own way, and he thus becomes not only a spectator at an imaginary theatre but also its producer. Mallarmé repeatedly uses the word *fêtes* to describe these imaginary scenes and Debussy's use of this word as the title of the second of his *Nocturnes* is perhaps no coincidence, particularly in view of the pageants Debussy had seen at the time of the Franco-Russian alliance. The function of the poet is similarly to awaken the producer of one's imagination ('le poète éveille par l'écrit

[1] *Le 'Livre' de Mallarmé* (1957).

[215]

l'ordonnateur de fêtes en chacun'). On another plane the associative experiences of music are aroused by poetry, and in this sense the reader is not only a listener but also a conductor. Mallarmé was less interested in music itself than in the effects produced by music. Above all he was inspired by the complexity of a musical texture. In contrapuntal music several ideas are expressed simultaneously. Even a single melodic line calls to mind an harmonic accompaniment. This depth of perspective cannot be achieved by words, though in the manner in which words may be juxtaposed Mallarmé did attempt an imaginative depth of this kind. A stone thrown in a lake creates ripples. The stone is lost and Mallarmé's words are the ripples. Contrariwise you may start with the outer ripples (the associations of words) narrowing down to the spot where the stone fell (the object), but of course it has disappeared, buried, as Mallarmé requires it to be, in the deeper layers of the unconscious. This approach explains Mallarmé's entirely novel and often bewildering conception of syntax and the fact that neither his verse nor his prose has a single meaning ('Il n'y a pas de vrai sens d'un texte', said Valéry); they have a variety of meanings.

The article on *Pelléas* is deliberately ambiguous in this manner. Characteristically, Mallarmé uses words or phrases of sumptuous associations ('triomphe du génie', 'splendeurs', 'idéale représentation', 'jouissance') and others that evoke desolation or poverty ('vacance aux gradins', 'le vide d'une salle', 'ingénue et étrange'). Negatives abound, and also superlatives. In his highly associative language there is constantly a play of ideas of bounty and of poverty.

Mallarmé argues that in *Die Walküre* the associations aroused by the rich orchestral texture, the scenery and the voices of mortals and gods suggest the poetic ideal of the Symbolists. Can the writer of traditional verse reach this ideal unaided by music? Yes, for the Symbolist play has the attributes of opera but without singing or accompaniment (in the form of the article in *Divagations*: 'Un opéra sans accompagnement ni chant, mais parlé'). The play in verse with its various themes deriving from the dream world suggests an imaginary theatre of the mind. The poet has musical ideas ('Un rhythme ou mouvement de pensée') and also visual ideas, such as his conception of woman who is a mermaid emerging from the foliage of baroque designs. These ideas buried in the artist's imagination find their expression in musical designs or a succession of chords, but they may also be expressed in affinities between poetic images. The dream has also a form. It has a symmetry as readily distinguishable as architectural symmetry. Faced with a creation of this kind, Mallarmé sees the writer of the Symbolist play, to be read alone, as Ludwig II, the patron of Wagner, listening to an opera in solitude.

Several attempts have been made to create a theatre of the mind in this manner, notably in the *Poèmes anciens et romanesques* of Henri de Régnier, the play in verse of Adolphe Retté, *Une belle dame passa*, the *mystère* of Ferdinand Hérold, *La joie de Maguelonne* and his poems *Chevaleries sentimentales* (mistakenly called by Mallarmé *Chevauchées sentimentales*), and *Swanhilde* by Francis Viélé-Griffin.

The theatre of Maeterlinck is an imaginative conception of this kind too, inspired, however, not by musical ideas but by the Shakespearean succession of scenes. Octave Mirbeau had audaciously written in 1890 of *La Princesse Maleine* that it was 'the work of this age comparable to what is most beautiful in Shakespeare'. Mallarmé argues that though Maeterlinck cannot really be compared to Shakespeare, there are perhaps mysterious aspects of Lear, Hamlet,[1] Cordelia, and Ophelia which the mind of Maeterlinck absorbed. His world is, however, closer to that of the Flemish primitives of Bruges and Ghent.

Pelléas et Mélisande was given a single performance before a public of the *élite*. There was no reason therefore to invite the critics who were nevertheless there. The series of short tableaux presented a sophisticated version of an old drama, an almost silent, abstract version reaching the true domain of music where, however, the introduction of musical sounds, even a meditative violin, would be out of place ('la partie d'un instrument même pensif, violon, détonnerait, par inutilité'). Maeterlinck's conception of the abstract and his manner of creating silence around his characters causes him to repeat his phrases in the form of an echo, thereby ensuring that they will sink into the listener's mind. In the end the poet will not need the vast resources of Wagner; he can touch upon as many associations and move his audience with them by the written word alone.

* * *

Tout, la polyphonie magnifique instrumentale, le vivant geste ou les voix de personnages et de dieux, au surplus un excès apporté à la

[1] Hamlet, 'le noir douteur', was a character with whom Mallarmé frequently identified himself, as did Debussy who saw Roderick Usher as a Hamlet-like figure.

décoration matérielle, nous le considérâmes, dans ce récent et tardif triomphe du génie ici, avec la *Walkyrie*; éblouïs par une telle cohésion de splendeurs en un art qui aujourd'hui devient la poésie: or va-t-il se faire que le traditionnel écrivain de vers, celui qui s'en tient aux artifices humbles et sacrés de la parole, tente, selon sa ressource, de rivaliser! Le bon livre versifié convie à une idéale représentation. Des motifs d'exaltation ou de songe s'y nouent entre eux et se détachent, d'après une ordonnance et leur individualité. Telle portion d'œuvre incline dans un rythme ou mouvement de pensée: à quoi s'oppose tel dessin contradictoire. L'un et l'autre, pour aboutir, et cessant, où interviendrait plus qu'à demi, comme sirènes confondues par la croupe avec le feuillage et les rinceaux d'une arabesque, la figure, que demeure notre seule idée. Ce théâtre, inhérent à l'esprit, quiconque d'un œil certain regarda la nature, le porte avec soi, résumé de types et d'accords: tels que les partage un tome, ouvrant des pages parallèles. Le précaire recueil d'inspiration diverse, sublime, c'en est fait; ainsi que du hasard, qui ne doit et pour sous-entendre le parti-pris, jamais qu'être simulé. Une symétrie comme elle règne en tout édifice, le plus vaporeux, de vision et de songes, prévaut, dans ce triomphe de la lecture. La jouissance vaine cherchée par feu le Rêveur-roi de Bavière dans une solitaire station aux déploiements scéniques, la voici, à l'écart d'un public encombrant moins que sa vacance aux gradins, atteinte, par le moyen ou restaurer le texte, nu, du spectacle. Volume en main, le véritable est fait de vers, je supplée, avec l'accompagnement de tout moi-même, au monde! ou j'y perçois le drame.

Cette moderne tendance marquée à quelque sceau d'absolu, soustraire à toutes contingences de la représentation, grossières ou même exquises selon le goût jusqu'à présent, l'œuvre par excellence ou poésie, a induit ici de très strictes intelligences, celle, en premier lieu, de Monsieur de Régnier ainsi que le suggère l'ensemble des *Poèmes Anciens et Romanesques*; ou guères plus tard qu'à l'instant, Monsieur Retté, avec sa suite diaprée, libre et large, nommée *Une Belle Dame Passa*. Installer, par une convergence de fragments harmoniques en leur centre, là même, une source de drame latente qui reflue à travers le poème, désigne ces jeunes maîtres et j'admire, autant, le jeu où insista Monsieur Ferdinand Hérold. *La Joie de Maguelonne*, notamment: *Chevauchées sentimentales* appartient au genre précité. Ouvertement et sans réticence, il nous octroie l'action je dirai dans

la plénitude, et faste entier : acteurs, le port noté par la déclamation,
puis le site, des chœurs, une multiple partition ; du fait de l'intègre
discours. Ou un tragique et chantant *Swanhilde*, de Monsieur Viélé-
Griffin, entr'ouvert le temps de le connaître tel. . . . Que dépouillé,
tout ici, de direct effet ou de mécanisme ! fondu, transportant l'invité
loin d'appréhensions.

Autre, l'art de Monsieur Maeterlinck qui, aussi, inséra le théâtre
au livre.

Non cela symphoniquement comme il vient d'être dit, mais avec
une expresse succession de scènes, à la Shakespeare ; il y a lieu, en
conséquence, de prononcer ce nom quoique ne se montre avec le
dieu aucun rapport, sauf de nécessaires. Un écrivain qui sauvegarde
l'honneur de la presse en faisant que toujours y ait été parlé ne fut-ce
qu'une fois, par lui, avec quel feu, de chaque œuvre d'exception,
Octave Mirbeau, à l'apparition, pour éveiller les milliers d'yeux
soudain, eut raison d'invoquer Shakespeare, comme un péremptoire
signe littéraire, énorme : puis il nuança son dire de sens délicats.

Lear, Hamlet lui-même et Cordélie, Ophélie, je cite des héros
reculés très avant dans la légende ou leur lointain spécial, agissent
en toute vie, tangibles, intenses : lus, ils froissent le papier, corporels,
pour surgir. Différente j'envisageai *La Princesse Maleine*, une après-
midi de lecture restée l'ingénue et étrange que je sache ; où domina
l'abandon, au contraire, d'un milieu à quoi, pour une cause, rien de
simplement humain ne convenait. Les murs, au massif arrêt de toute
réalité, basalte, en le vide d'une salle : les murs, plutôt de cette
épaisseur isolées, des tentures, vieillies en la raréfaction de l'endroit ;
pour que leurs hôtes déteints avant d'y devenir les trous, étirant, une
tragique fois, quelque membre de douleur habituel, et même
souriant, balbutiassent ou radotassent, seuls, la phrase de leur destin.
Tandis qu'au serment du spectateur vulgaire, il n'aurait existé personne ni rien ne se serait passé, sur les planches. Bruges, Gand,
terroir de primitifs ; désuétude . . . on est loin, par les fantômes, de
Shakespeare.

Les officiels juges de plusieurs grands journaux me paraissent, dans
une dernière aventure, improprement avoir joué de cette grande
allusion et pas sans quelque trouble dans la précipitation à malmener
une œuvre délicieuse et mystérieuse, jeune : attendu que restera
difficile à discerner si précisément ils reprochaient à l'auteur de
l'*Intruse*, des *Aveugles* et des *Sept Princesses* qu'il rappelât trop

Shakespeare ou de ne pas l'évoquer à leur gré suffisamment, distinction, du reste, important peu à mon constat, je crois comme au leur. Un pavé se trouvait à portée et plus carré, plus lourd, même que de la mauvaise foi. Ajoutons qu'il y avait raison, celle-ci, pourtant, à l'employer, uniment. Faire à un dramaturge étranger, nouveau, expier sa notoriété européenne issue d'un article fameux, à la place même d'où, excluant autre aide, elle s'était propagée presque en de la gloire. Tout une scission se fait, jusqu'à la colère, dans la littérature, par exemple entre les hommes contournant les soixante ans et maints qui émergent de leur trentaine, c'est question d'âge. Je m'amuse à considérer cet échange, et les poings; l'assaut: la défense unanime furieuse.

La pièce sauve du guet-apens, indiquait un choix sagace, *Pelléas et Mélisande*, de passion et d'inquiétude franchement. Montée avec perfection, par notre confrère Monsieur Mauclair, en toute simplicité; dite, souverainement. Ambigu décor et forêt comme appartements. Le costume dans le ton, très bien, de l'esprit et des rôles; prêtant cette significative coloration au geste. Une matinée seule. Elite. Le tort serait d'avoir dérangé, rien d'autre, en l'y convoquant, la grosse critique, chargée de formuler aux badauds tenus hors de cette solennité, l'opinion que tous sont incapables d'émettre parce qu'elle n'existe pas concurramment, du moins, au langage, ou se résoudrait par un bâillement. Aussi la bande argua, entre des griefs, très justement, d'ennui; mais cela demeure un malentendu, puisque ceux au nom de qui elle a le devoir d'exprimer ce sentiment devant une œuvre littéraire haute ou pure, manquaient.

L'ouvrage, imprimé à Bruxelles il y a un an environ, hier secoué sur notre scène (on pouvait, si privément et à l'abri d'intrusion) émane, de ses feuillets, un délice. Préciser? Ces tableaux, brefs, suprêmes. Tout a été rejeté de préparatoire et machinal, en vue que paraisse, extrait par enchantement, ce qui chez un spectateur se dégage d'une représentation, l'essentiel. Il semble que soit jouée une variation supérieure sur l'admirable vieux mélodrame. Silencieusement presque, comme les traits partent épurés, en l'abstention du déchet qui suffit d'ordinaire! silencieusement et abstraitement au point que dans cet art, lequel devient musique dans le sens propre, la partie d'un instrument même pensif, violon, détonnerait, par inutilité. Peut-être que si tacite atmosphère inspire, à l'angoisse qu'en ressent l'auteur, ce besoin souvent de proférer deux fois les choses, pour une certitude qu'elles l'aient été et leur assurer, à défaut de rien, la conscience de l'écho. Sortilège fréquent, autrement inexplicable, entre cent; qu'on nommerait à tort procédé.

Le poète, je reviens à mon début, hors d'entreprises prodigieuses comme Wagner, par exemple, ici n'a pas à s'ingénier d'autre chose que ce qui est son air respirable, l'âme seule et parfum de tout; qu'il s'adresse par l'intime écrit à l'ordonnateur de fêtes en chacun, ou communique avec une assistance comme l'occasion vient de se présenter avec charme.

THE MANUSCRIPTS OF *PELLÉAS*

The following lists set out the known manuscripts of *Pelléas et Mélisande* as a guide to the various stages of its composition between 1893 and 1902. With the exception of the full score in the Bibliothèque du Conservatoire all the manuscripts are piano and vocal scores.

HOLDERS

1. André Meyer (private collection)	June–July 1895
2. Robert Legouix (private collection)—(Act IV)	September–October 1893
3. Lucienne Bréval (Bibliothèque Nationale)—(Act IV)	September–October 1893 May 1895
4. Bibliothèque du Conservatoire	No date (? 1901–2)
5. New England Conservatory of Music, Boston: Act I	December 1893 January–February 1894
Act II	17 August 1895
Act III	No date
Act IV	September–October 1893 May 1895 January 1900 September 1901
Act V	No date

CHRONOLOGY

September–October 1893—Boston	Act IV
September–October 1893—Legouix	Act IV
September–October 1893—Bréval	Act IV
December 1893—Boston	Act I
January–February 1894—Boston	Act I
May 1895—Boston	Act IV
May 1895—Bréval	Act IV
June–July 1895—Meyer	Acts I, II, IV (in part), V
17 August 1895—Boston	Act II
January 1900—Boston	Act IV
September 1901—Boston	Act IV

SEQUENCE

Act I	Boston	December 1893
	Boston	January–February 1894
	Meyer	June–July 1895
Act II	Meyer	June–July 1895
	Boston	17 August 1895
Act III	Boston	No date
Act IV	Boston	September–October 1893
	Legouix	September–October 1893
	Bréval	September–October 1893
	Boston	May 1895
	Meyer (in part)	June–July 1895
	Boston	January 1900
	Boston	September 1901
Act V	Meyer	June–July 1895
	Boston	No date

APPENDIX F

LE SOLEIL DES MORTS

In 1898 a remarkable series of portraits was published of Mallarmé and his circle in the novel *Le Soleil des Morts* by Camille Mauclair. A young writer of twenty-five at the time, Camille Mauclair, whose real name was Séverin Faust, was one of the typical critics of the period, a prolific writer with highly developed psychological and descriptive gifts whose interests embraced music and painting as well as literature. His works on music include a valuable study of Schumann, a short history of music, and collections of essays entitled *La Religion de la Musique* and *Les Héros de l'Orchestre*, of much value in assessing the widening appeal of music in France as a result of the Wagnerian influence. His literary works include studies of Jules Laforgue, Baudelaire, and Poe, and his works on painting, for which he is best known, range from studies of Corot and Turner to Claude Monet and the Impressionists. 'L'âme de Camille Mauclair est une âme féminine', it was said, by which it was meant that he was able to absorb the main currents of contemporary thought. But he was also able to take an objective view of these currents, and his early novel, *Le Soleil des Morts*, is a *roman à clef* containing revealing portraits of the main personalities in the arts of his time. These portraits are deliberately romanticized but they are none the less authentic. The young author, plunged into a world of artists of feverish sensibility, boldly drew each character as he saw him. He believed with Carlyle that by his nature a great artist is incapable of judging his own stature. When the novel appeared in 1898,[1] and also when it was re-issued in 1924, it was widely held to offer a more penetrating view of the psychology of the Symbolists than many a critical study.[2] It is still a most valuable historical document deserving an up-to-date edition enlightened by a critical commentary.

Dedicated 'to my friend Ernest Chausson', the work also bears the inscription: 'Aux insatisfaits de l'époque . . . à ceux qui rêvent sans espérer, exaltant leurs âmes éperdues vers des soleils divers, liberté,

[1] It first appeared in serial form in *La Nouvelle Revue*, 15 February to 1 May 1898, and was published in book form later in the year.

[2] In the *Mercure de France*, 15 December 1924, J. Charpentier wrote of it as 'un document unique et qui vaut mieux pour nous aider à comprendre le symbolisme que la plus minutieuse étude critique.' A similar opinion was expressed by G. Jean-Aubry in his biography of Mauclair which appeared in 1905. An interesting study of the work also appeared in *Admirable 19ᵉ Siècle* by André Lebois (1958).

passion, ascéticisme ou gloire.' Apart from the unresolved conflict in the mind of André de Neuze (Mauclair himself) as a result of his attraction to the forceful character of Lucienne Lestrange (impersonating both Loïe Fuller and Georgette Leblanc) and to the shy, retiring figure of Sylvaine Armel (Geneviève Mallarmé, the poet's daughter), there is no central plot. The image of *le soleil des morts* recurs as a *Leitmotiv* symbolizing an illusory sense of liberty, the response of the senses, self-denial, or vanity. Though it is chiefly interesting for its study of the character of Mallarmé, who appears under the name Calixte Armel, the many subsidiary characters are also brilliantly sketched out, notably the arresting revolutionary composer Claude-Eric de Harmor, the aristocratic name which Mauclair invented for Debussy.[1]

The novel is divided into four main scenes: a scene at one of the legendary 'Mardis' at the home of Mallarmé in the rue de Rome in May 1891; a performance of *L'Après-midi d'un faune* at the Concerts Lamoureux; the funeral of Verlaine in 1896; and the dances of Loïe Fuller at the Folies-Bergères. The home of Mallarmé, frequently described in memoirs of the period, has probably never been so searchingly drawn. Under fictitious names Mauclair introduces Monet, the novelist Paul Adam, a figure who seems to be a cross between André Gide and Paul Valéry, and finally Debussy, 'le symphoniste ductile et bizarre' to whom he ascribes a work appropriately entitled *Motifs de Songe* but whose physical appearance, with monocle and ducal coronet, suggests not Debussy but Henri de Régnier. Apparently Mauclair wished to stress the seemingly aristocratic qualities of Debussy. He writes:

Through the blueish clouds of cigarette smoke shadowy figures and faces could just be distinguished. The soft, shaded lamp left the corners of the room in mystery. Sounds of voices rose, each

[1] Jean-Aubry states in his biography of Mauclair that the novel was submitted chapter by chapter to Mallarmé before its publication. An undated letter from Mallarmé to Mauclair expresses his unqualified approval: 'Votre groupement de types respire l'heure. ... Il assemble la légende d'un temps et, si près, le transporte haut.' Of the portrait of himself as Calixte Armel, so strongly attached to his daughter, he declares that while he is not able to see himself as others see him, Mauclair has certainly provided an extraordinary portrait. ('Toujours est-il que si l'aspect que dégage un homme à plusieurs ne lui demeure extérieur totalement vous êtes quelqu'un, Mauclair, qui m'aurez extraordinairement regardé.') Other characters who appear under fictitious names include Théodore de Banville, Catulle Mendès, Maurice Barrès, Verlaine, Zola, Willy, Pierre Louÿs, Whistler, Manet, Rodin, Toulouse-Lautrec, Ernest Chausson and Vincent d'Indy.

word carefully weighed. André de Neuze entered sympathetically into the scene and looked around him. The colour of gleaming gold shone out from the corner of a frame on the wall; it was a Manet. Engravings surrounded by white lacquer formed milky patches on the hanging tapestries. On the mantelpiece a transparent light struck the marble back of a mythological figure by Rodin. Luxuriously bound books were piled up on a console. De Neuze gazed at the severe Empire furniture and at the young people seated around the table on which were a glazed tobacco jar, Japanese ash-trays, and books. He knew the work of everyone there and was anxious to know them personally. Seated opposite was Germain Bussère, the Impressionist whose *Baignarde* with its tones of oranges and blues had created such a stir at the Salon, a dark powerful head, something of a bear or a curmudgeon with soft fawn-coloured eyes and a rather cruel mouth emerging from the thick growth of his black beard. His rough hands spread out over his knees were those of a workman. Nearby was the fair-headed Manuel Héricourt, author of ten brilliant novels, with long whiskers, sensitive nostrils, and clear blue eyes.... His shining pumps gave his feet a feminine appearance and he wore a dazzling diamond ring. . . . And there a three-quarter view, buttoned up in a frock-coat, of Elie Rochès, the Symbolist narrator and fantastic mathematician, the follower of Claude de Saint-Martin, of Edgar Allan Poe and of Villiers de l'Isle Adam. His angular yellowish face was unquestionably ugly and de Neuze became hypnotized by his almost inhuman watery grey eyes. Leaning a little to one side, he perceived the pale thin profile of Claude-Eric de Harmor, the impressionable, strange composer of the *Motifs de Songe* whose pieces had astonished all the musicians of Paris and whose recent preludes for orchestra provoked a battle at the Concerts Lamoureux. Disdainful, vague, his moustache drooping over his sensuous and abnormally large chin, he had bright eyes, a noble forehead and carried himself with the frigid elegance of a man of distinction. The grandson of a minister during the Restoration, he was a cousin of the Ducs de Hautfeuil who had quarrelled with his impoverished family. A tiny ducal coronet appeared on his cravat, the only point of relief on his dark clothes apart from a sparkling monocle which his finely shaped fingers allowed to drop from its thread.

[225]

Elsewhere Pierre Louÿs (Luc Deraines) invites de Neuze to hear
the 'Preludes' of Harmor at the Concerts Lamoureux. Calixte Armel
is there accompanied by his daughter, and so are figures impersonating Willy, Catulle Mendès, Octave Mirbeau, Manet, Whistler,
and Chausson (Méreuse). The concert takes place at the Cirque
d'Hiver and the work of Harmor is preceded by the 'Reformation'
Symphony of Mendelssohn. Armel is characteristically scribbling
his impressions in a notebook. Even the music of Mendelssohn,
prosaic as de Neuze finds it, has the effect of turning the circus ring
into a cathedral. The 'Preludes' open with a slow lament, amplified
then suddenly broken off and taken up again:

> The cry of a satyr is heard, suddenly stifled but later developed
> into a sobbing chant. . . . The writing is complex, strange and
> exquisite. 'Assez!' shouts a hoarse authoritative voice. . . . Is this
> music too refined and delicate for ordinary listeners? . . . The
> music is now lit up as if by the burning light of the sun and one
> hears the rhythm of the sea reproduced in primitive harmonies.
> Javanese flutes flash through the score, lingering on high notes or
> sparkling like running water, gongs are sounded, and the warm
> summer scene closes with a play of light in the form of an
> arpeggio figure. . . . The audience, applauding and hissing, is
> overcome by this audacious music. Wildly enthusiastic, de Neuze
> perceives the faces of his friends, pale or flushed with anger.
> 'Assez! Bravo! Vive Harmor! A bas, à bas! Bis!' In angry
> gestures women break their fans. 'It's even more insane than
> Wagner!' 'Go and play it abroad!' . . . Alone in the artist's room
> with Méreuse, Claude-Eric de Harmor was greeted by Armel
> who grasps his hand and presses it without saying a word.

After the performance de Neuze discovers Harmor in a café. 'Art
is an unfortunate illness,' Harmor explains. 'One is afflicted with art
as one might be afflicted with consumption, whereas the public
think of this slavery of the body and of one's dreams as one of the
liberal professions!'
Parts of Le Soleil des Morts are over-written and, like other documents of the period, allowances must be made for its verbal profusion and also for its pessimism. 'Il est certain que nous ne sommes pas
gais,' says de Neuze. 'Nous sommes nés au sein même de la mort.'

From another viewpoint it is a study of the collapse of the values of an *élite* and of the values of the new democratic public finding an almost religious satisfaction in music. The portrait of the vampire Lucienne Lestrange, with golden hair and green eyes, who enslaves first Harmor and then de Neuze, is possibly drawn from life. Despite his knowledge of Schopenhauer, Emerson, and Ibsen, Harmor is overcome by the attraction of Lucienne. In the end Mauclair distrusts the over-refined sensibility of his friends which merely paralyses action ('Vous en mourrez d'être trop sensibles!') and followed the publication of *Le Soleil des Morts* with *L'Ennemie des Rêves* (1899), the theme of which is a protest against egoism and vanity.

There is a remarkably fine analysis of the relationship between Mallarmé and his daughter and of her attraction to the members of his circle. Armel sees a reflection of himself in his daughter: 'Dans leurs tête-à-tête il oubliait son sexe, s'exaltait, devenait fiévreux, la poussait à l'extrême d'un raisonnement, rectifiait une erreur avec sa dureté de théoricien absolu.' But it was when music was played to them in the rue de Rome that father and daughter found themselves in intimate communion. Under the spell of music, 'Armel regardait haleter le démon de beauté dans le corps tiède et souple de Sylvaine.' Obviously some of Mallarmé's many friends must have been strongly attracted to Geneviève. In the novel we are told that both Harmor and Deraines were secretly in love with her but that, respecting her devotion to her father, they never attempted to go beyond friendship. Not for nothing did Mallarmé comment sympathetically on the 'extraordinary' portrait Mauclair had drawn of him. In his later years he was attracted to Geneviève, according to Mauclair, as was the hero in Poe's autobiographical tale *Morella* to his wife, that is to say excessively, and he was thus made to suffer the destiny of the father who too fondly loved his child. In Poe's tale the hero loves the child of Morella, bearing the same name, as he loved his wife. Drawing a daring parallel, Mauclair sees the ageing Mallarmé terrifyingly aware of a similar attachment to Geneviève ('Calixte Armel la contemplait avec une admiration effrayée'). She carries within her a terrible secret ('un secret plus profond encore que le sien') and personifies his own conscience:

'Sous l'intime communion de l'art, sous la nervosité de leurs épanchements subits, leurs psychologies subtiles ne s'affrontaient qu'avec des restrictions infinies. Mais Armel, en vieillissant, avait perdu un peu de ses défenses morales, cédait parfois: l'âme de Sylvaine, plus jeune, se gardait intacte. Et il y avait des heures où, se retrouvant en sa fille tel qu'il avait été durant son exil de jeunesse, Calixte Armel la contemplait avec une admiration effrayée, sentant la présence d'un secret plus profond encore que le sien. Selon le mot de Manuel Héricourt, Sylvaine Armel était Morella, la Morella d'Edgar Poe: elle revivait, vivante, la conscience de son père sortie de lui-même.'

APPENDIX G

OPINIONS OF DEBUSSY AND
MARCEL PROUST

From about 1885 to 1895 it was the custom for hostesses belonging to the more modest strata of Paris society to collect opinions from their visitors on artistic and social affairs. These opinions, given in answer to a printed questionnaire, were known as *Les Confidences du Salon*. We must not consider such opinions as forming more than a sophisticated drawing-room game. The answers were sometimes deliberately frivolous, or an impatient note would creep in, as when Proust, asked what was his present state of mind, replied, 'Annoyance at having to answer these questions.' Yet they provide occasional illuminating glimpses of the visitor's ideas and of the contemporary frame of mind. They are best appreciated by contrasting one questionnaire with another. It is interesting, for instance, to see that almost at the same time the twenty-six-year-old Debussy in 1889, and the twenty-year-old Proust in 1891, were both preoccupied with the ambivalence of Hamlet, as was Freud a few years later in his letters to Wilhelm Fliess. The questionnaire of Debussy, published in *Le Crapouillot*, December 1930, is reproduced below, followed by extracts from the questionnaire of Marcel Proust published in *A la recherche de Marcel Proust* by André Maurois, 1949. The reader will find it a simple matter to distinguish the light-hearted from the serious replies, and he will also find it instructive to compare the climate of ideas in which Debussy developed at the time of his visits to Bayreuth with that of Proust when he was writing his first book reviews for *Le Banquet*.

QUESTIONNAIRE OF DEBUSSY
(16 February 1889)

What is your favourite virtue? Pride.
What is the quality you most admire in a man? Will-power.
In a woman? Charm.
What is your favourite occupation? Reading while smoking complex tobaccos (*les tabacs compliqués*).
What is your distinctive feature? My hair.

What is your idea of happiness? To love.
Of unhappiness? Being too hot.
What is your favourite colour and flower? Violet.
If not yourself who would you be? A sailor.
Where would you like to live? Anywhere out of the world.[1]
Who are your favourite prose-writers? Flaubert, Edgar Poe.
Your favourite poets? Baudelaire.
Your favourite painters and composers? Botticelli, Gustave Moreau; Palestrina, Bach, Wagner.
Your favourite hero in life? Skobelev.[2]
Your favourite heroine in life? Madame de Beaumont.[3]
Your favourite hero in fiction? Hamlet.
Your favourite heroine in fiction? Rosalind.
Which is your favourite type of cooking and your favourite drink? Russian cooking; coffee.
What are your favourite names? It depends on who has them.
What is your particular aversion? Dilettantes; women who are too beautiful.
Which historical character do you loathe? Herod.
What is your present state of mind? Reflective and inquiring, except on 16 February 1889.
Which is the fault you are most easily able to accept? Faults in harmony.
What is your motto? Ever higher.

---

[1] 'N'importe où hors du monde.' The allusion, which also serves as a motto for a section of Gabriel Mourey's *L'Embarquement pour ailleurs*, which Debussy planned to set to music, is from Thomas Hood's *The Bridge of Sighs*:

> Mad from life's history,
> Glad to death's mystery,
> Swift to be hurl'd —
> Anywhere, anywhere,
> Out of the world!

[2] Mikhail Dimitrievitch Skobelev (1843–82), a Russian military figure known as 'The White General' who played an important part in the Russo–Turkish War. He made speeches in Paris in 1882 predicting the strife between Teuton and Slav and proclaiming a militant Panslavism. A 'Pantomime' entitled *Skobelev* was given in February 1889 in Paris at the Hippodrome.

[3] Possibly Marie Leprince de Beaumont (1711–80), a writer of children's books, generally illustrating a moral, who lived and worked in England as a governess.

QUESTIONNAIRE OF MARCEL PROUST
(about 1891)

What is your principal characteristic? The need to be loved and, more precisely, the need to be caressed and spoiled rather than the need to be admired.

What is the quality you require in a man? Feminine charm.

In a woman? A man's virtues and frankness in friendship.

What is your favourite occupation? Loving.

What is your ideal of happiness? Not, I am afraid, a very elevated one. I dare not say for I should be afraid of destroying it by putting it into words.

What would be your greatest misfortune? Not to have known my mother or my grandmother.

What is your favourite colour? Beauty is not in colour but in their harmonies.

In which country would you like to live? One where certain things I want would be realized as if by magic.

Who are your favourite prose-writers? Today, Anatole France and Pierre Loti.

Who are your favourite poets? Baudelaire and Alfred de Vigny.

Who is your favourite hero in fiction? Hamlet.

Who are your favourite heroines in fiction? Phèdre [crossed out by Proust] Bérénice.

Who are your favourite composers? Beethoven, Wagner, Shuhmann [*sic*].

Who are your favourite painters? Leonardo da Vinci, Rembrandt.

What are your favourite names? I have only one at a time.

What is it that you most dislike? My own bad qualities.

What is the fault you are most easily able to accept? Those that I understand.

What is your motto? I prefer not to say for it might bring me bad luck.

APPENDIX H

AUTOGRAPHS

The publication of Debussy's complete correspondence, desirable as it would be, can hardly be undertaken for many years. Too many letters are scattered in private collections, their significance often unknown to their possessors since they cannot have been correlated with other unpublished correspondence. Others have been withheld in deference to personal feelings or susceptibilities on aesthetic or moral matters. Nine slender volumes of Debussy's letters have so far [1962] been published, namely:

> *Lettres de Claude Debussy à son éditeur* (i.e. Jacques Durand), 1927.
> *Correspondance de Claude Debussy et Paul-Jean Toulet*, 1929.
> *La Jeunesse de Pelléas: Lettres de Claude Debussy à André Messager*, 1938.
> *Lettres de Claude Debussy à deux amis* (Robert Godet and G. Jean-Aubry), 1942.
> *Correspondance de Claude Debussy et Pierre Louÿs (1893–1904)*, edited by Henri Borgeaud, 1945.
> *Debussy et d'Annunzio: Correspondance inédite*, edited by Guy Tosi, 1948.
> *Lettres inédites à André Caplet (1904–14)*, edited by Edward Lockspeiser, 1957.
> *Lettres de Claude Debussy à sa femme Emma*, edited by Pasteur Vallery-Radot, 1957.
> *Tel était Claude Debussy* (Letters to Vallery-Radot), 1958.

We must not imagine that these publications contain the whole of Debussy's available letters to these correspondents. Not only are sentences suppressed, but important names are omitted and an unknown number of letters does not appear at all. Whatever the reason for such decisions they are to be regretted since a view is given of one aspect or another of the composer which is obviously falsified. An artist's correspondence is the most valuable source a biographer can hope to draw upon not only in regard to aesthetic or psychological matters, but for the verification of concrete facts.

Debussy's letters began to appear in sales catalogues quite early in his lifetime. The autograph letter of Debussy that appeared in the catalogue of Charavay, January 1902, caused him to exclaim that such cool courage on the part of the vendor 'certainly deserves the military medal'. The most important sale of Debussy's manuscripts took place in 1933 when the bulk of his legacy was dispersed. The catalogue of the sale organized by Georges Andrieux, 154 Boulevard Malesherbes, Paris (30 November–8 December 1933), lists this legacy under the headings: 'Souvenirs, notebooks, autographs; unpublished works in manuscript; scores with autograph corrections; books with dedications in the possession of Claude Debussy.' It may be too much to hope that all these possessions may one day be reassembled, but in the meantime I think it will be helpful to reproduce from this catalogue the names of Debussy's principal correspondents whose letters he kept. Among the musicians whose letters to Debussy were dispersed on this occasion and have remained unpublished are: André Caplet, Georges Charpentier, Edouard Colonne, Serge Diaghilev, Vincent d'Indy, Paul Dukas, Manuel de Falla, Gabriel Fauré, Charles Gounod, Serge Koussevitzky, Gabriel Pierné, Ildebrando Pizzetti, Nadezhda Rimsky-Korsakov, Igor Stravinsky, and Arturo Toscanini. Unpublished letters from literary figures to Debussy include those from André Gide, Maurice Maeterlinck, Stéphane Mallarmé, Camille Mauclair, Robert de Montesquiou, Sar Péladan, Henri de Régnier, Saint-Pol-Roux, and Paul Valéry. Publications dedicated to Debussy include works by Mallarmé, Stravinsky, Alfred Jarry, Charles Péguy, and Victor Segalen. Published works of Debussy containing his autograph annotations include: the String Quartet, *L'Après-midi d'un faune*, *Nocturnes*, *La Mer*, *Pelléas et Mélisande*, *Ibéria*, *Rondes de printemps*, and *Jeux*.

CHRONOLOGY

1835   Birth of Clémentine De Bussy (aunt).

1836   Birth of Manuel-Achille Debussy (father) at Montrouge, 10 May. Birth of Victorine Manoury (mother), Paris, 28 October.

1849   Birth of Jules-Alexandre de Bussy (paternal uncle), Paris, 11 December.

1854   Manuel Debussy enlists in the Marine Light Infantry.

1856   Voyage overseas of Manuel Debussy.

1859   Death of Louis-Amable Manoury (maternal grandfather) at a home for the insane, Clermont-de-l'Oise, 28 May.

1860   'Maison Debussy, Couture' opened by Clémentine De Bussy, 13 Boulevard des Capucines, Paris.

1861   Discharged from the Marines 11 July, Manuel lives with Victorine Manoury at Levallois; marries Victorine, 30 November, at Clichy and moves to Saint-Germain-en-Laye.

1862   Achille-Claude Debussy born at 38 rue au Pain, Saint-Germain-en-Laye, 22 August.

1863   Adèle-Clémentine (sister) born at Saint-Germain-en-Laye, September.

1864   Family leaves Saint-Germain-en-Laye. Liaison between Clémentine de Bussy and Achille Arosa. Baptism of Achille-Claude, 31 July, at Saint-Germain.

1867   Family settled in Paris, 11 rue de Vintimille. Manuel becomes a travelling salesman. Birth of Emmanuel Debussy (brother), 19 September.

1868   Jules-Alexandre serves in the Army. Manuel employed at the lithographic printing works of Paul-François Dupont.

1870   Birth of Alfred Debussy (brother) at Cannes, 16 February. First (?) visit of Achille-Claude to Cannes. Manuel, released from his employment with Dupont following the outbreak of the Franco-Prussian War, 15 July, is engaged as a clerk in the municipal service, December.

1871   Marriage of Clémentine de Bussy to Alfred Roustan at Cannes. Second (?) visit of Achille-Claude to Cannes; takes piano lessons at Cannes with Jean Cerutti. Manuel joins the

National Guard, March. Having subsequently become a communard and captain, 3 May, of the revolutionary troops, he takes part in the battle of Issy, 8 May. On the defeat of the Commune he is sentenced to four years' imprisonment, 11 December.

Achille and Victorine Debussy move to 59bis rue Pigalle. Achille studies the piano with Madame Mauté.

1872 Jules-Alexandre emigrates to England and settles at Chorlton, Manchester, teaching music privately and French at the Central High School, Manchester. Achille enters the Paris Conservatoire, 22 October, in the classes of Marmontel and Lavignac.

1873 Manuel employed as assistant book-keeper at the Compagnie de Fives-Lille, Paris, 15 January. Birth of Eugène-Octave Debussy (brother) in Paris.

1874 Achille wins third medal for *solfège*. Plays the Second Concerto of Chopin at a Conservatoire concert.

1875 Wins second medal for *solfège* and first certificate of merit for performance of the Second Ballade of Chopin.

1876 Public appearance as pianist at Chauny, January. First compositions: Songs on poems of Alfred de Musset (*Ballade à la lune* and *Madrid, Princesse des Espagnes*), Théodore de Banville (*Nuit d'étoiles*), Paul Bourget (*Beau soir*); piano, violin, and 'cello pieces (all *c.* 1876–80). Wins first medal for *solfège*.

1877 Second piano prize. Enters the harmony class of Emile Durand, 24 November. Marriage of Jules-Alexandre to Mary Ann Saddington at Chorlton, 27 December.

Death of Eugène-Octave Debussy in Paris.
c. 1878 Song *Fleur des blés* (A. Girod) written, published 1891.

1879 Engaged as pianist in the service of Marguerite Wilson-Pelouze at the Château de Chenonceaux, July. Enters class of accompaniment and practical harmony of Auguste Bazille, October.

1880 First prize in practical harmony, July. Engaged by Nadezhda von Meck as pianist, July, and accompanies her to Interlaken, Arcachon (Villa Marguerite), and Fiesole (Villa Oppenheim),

July–October. Composes *Danse bohémienne* in Italy submitted to Tchaikovsky, September, and a piano trio. Transcribes dances from Tchaikovsky's *Swan Lake*, October. Enters composition class of Ernest Guiraud, 24 December.

Writes the songs *Mandoline* (Verlaine), *La Belle au bois dormant* (Vincent d'Hyspa), *Voici que le printemps* (Paul Bourget), *Aimons-nous* (Banville), *L'Archet* (C. Cros), *Fleur des eaux* (Maurice Bouchor), *La Fille aux cheveux de lin* (Leconte de Lisle), *Caprice*, *Séguidille* (J. L. Vauthier), *Eclogue* (Leconte de Lisle) for soprano and tenor (all *c.* 1880–3). Composes *Symphonie en si* (? January).

1881 First visit of Achille to Moscow as pianist to Nadezhda von Meck, July–October. Visit to Gourievo, September.

Accompanist at the singing class of Madame Moreau-Sainti. Meets Blanche Vasnier to whom his early songs are dedicated.
    c. 1881 Composes *Zéphyr* (Banville), *Daniel*, cantata. Plays at the Cabaret the Chat Noir.

1882 At a public concert with Madame Vasnier and the violinist Thieberg, Paris, 12 May, he appears for the first time as a composer, accompanying his song *Les Roses*, and the pieces for violin and piano *Nocturne* and *Scherzo*. Fails to pass preliminary examination, May, for the Prix de Rome with a fugue on a theme of Gounod and a choral work *Printemps* (Comte de Ségur) published as *Salut, Printemps* (1928). *Flots, palmes, sables* (Armand Renaud) written 2 June. *Intermezzo* based on poem of Heine for orchestra composed 21 June. Second certificate for counterpoint and fugue, July. Second journey with Madame von Meck (Pleshcheyvo, Moscow, and Vienna), August–November. First version of *En Sourdine* (Verlaine) composed, Vienna, 16 September.

Rondeau (A. de Musset) dedicated to Alexander von Meck. Composes *Triomphe de Bacchus*. Accompanist to the choral society La Concordia. Death of Madame Roustan (*née* Clémentine De Bussy) at Suresnes.
    c. 1882 *L'Aimable printemps* for vocal quartet. Songs on poems of Banville (*Pierrot*) and Verlaine (*Clair de lune*,

first version, and *Pantomime*). Project for *Florise* on play of Banville. Music for *Hymnis* and *Diane au bois* (plays of Banville).

1883 *Coquetterie posthume* (Th. Gautier) written 31 March. *Silence ineffable* (P. Bourget) written September. *Paysage sentimental* (P. Bourget) written November.

Invocation (Lamartine) written for male chorus and orchestra. Wins Second Prix de Rome with *Le Gladiateur*, cantata.

1884 *Apparition* (Mallarmé) written 8 February; *Regret* (Bourget) and *Romance d'Ariel* (Bourget) written February. Fugue on theme of Massenet and *Printemps* (Jules Barbier), choral work, both written for preliminary examination for the Prix de Rome. Wins first Prix de Rome with *L'Enfant prodigue* (Edouard Guinand), 27 June.

Commission offered but not accepted for three-act ballet.

1885 Leaves for Villa Medici, Rome, 27 January. Secret flight to Paris, April, returning to Rome, 25 April. Begins work on *Zuleima*, May, temporarily abandoned in June. Returns to *Diane au bois*, June; holidays in Paris, July; stays at the house of Count Primoli at Fiumicino, near Rome, August. Plans to leave Rome definitely, September, but is dissuaded by Vasnier; hears Liszt, November, who recommends him to hear works of Palestrina and Orlando di Lasso in Rome.

Work begun on *Salammbô*. Plans further series of songs on poems of Paul Bourget with whom he corresponds. Portrait painted by Marcel Baschet.

1886 Second flight to Paris, February or March. *Zuleima* completed June (?), condemned by the Académie, December.

Reads Moréas, Verlaine, Baudelaire, Shelley, and Shakespeare. Accepts offer to write music for Maurice Vaucaire's adaptation of *As You Like It*. Studies *Tristan*. Visit to Orvieto.

1887 *Printemps* composed, February, criticized at the Académie for its 'vague impressionism', December. Returns finally to Paris, February, living with his parents, 27 rue de Berlin. Manuel Debussy dismissed from the Compagnie de Fives-Lille,

12 April. Probably hears *Lohengrin*, 3 May. *La Mort des Amants* (Baudelaire) written December.

Reads Gabriel Sarrazin's *Les Poètes modernes de l'Angleterre* and begins *La Damoiselle élue*. Forms friendship with Etienne Dupin.

1888 *Le Balcon* (Baudelaire) written January. Visit to Bayreuth, summer, where he hears *Parsifal* and *Meistersinger*. Friendship with Robert Godet.

Publishes *Ariettes, Paysages Belges et Aquarelles*, six songs on poems of Verlaine (*C'est l'extase, Il pleure dans mon coeur, L'Ombre des arbres, Chevaux de bois, Green, Spleen*) re-issued in 1903 as *Ariettes oubliées*. *Deux Arabesques* written.

1889 Becomes member of the Société Nationale, 8 January. *Harmonie du soir* written, January. Songs on poems of Verlaine sung at the Société Nationale, 2 February. *Petite Suite* for piano duet (*En bateau, Cortège, Menuet* and *Ballet*) played by Debussy and Jacques Durand, 1 March, and later published. *Le Jet d'eau* (Baudelaire) written, 2 March. Visit to Bayreuth, summer, where he hears *Parsifal, Meistersinger*, and *Tristan*. Hears the Javanese gamelan and visits the Annamite Theatre at the World Exhibition in Paris, summer. Contracts pneumonia, December.

La Damoiselle élue completed. *Fantaisie* for piano and orchestra begun. Outlines new conception of harmony in conversation with Ernest Guiraud. Reads Maeterlinck's *La Princesse Maleine*. Begins a symphony on Poe's *Fall of the House of Usher*. Writes music for a scene of Villiers de l'Isle Adam's *Axel*.

   c. 1889   Liaison with Gabrielle Dupont.

1890 Breaks with the Académie following his refusal to write an Overture. Forbids performance of the *Fantaisie*, April, which is engraved by Choudens but not published. Begins the opera *Rodrigue et Chimène* on libretto of Catulle Mendès, dedicated to Gabrielle Dupont, April (?). Plans unsuccessfully to go to England, October.

Cinq Poèmes de Baudelaire on poems from *Les Fleurs du Mal* (*Le Balcon, Harmonie du Soir, Le Jet d'eau, Recueillement, La Mort des Amants*) published. *Ballade Slave* for piano published, re-published as *Ballade*, 1903. *Tarantelle styrienne* for piano published, re-published as *Danse* (1903) and orchestrated under this title by Ravel (1923). Piano pieces *Rêverie, Valse Romantique,* and *Nocturne* published. Writes *Suite bergamasque* for piano (*Préludes, Menuet, Clair de lune, Passepied*), published 1905.

1891   Following an emotional crisis, plans again to go to London, February. Attends benefit performance for Gauguin and Verlaine at the Théâtre du Vaudeville, of works by Verlaine, Charles Morice, and Catulle Mendès, 21 May. Sees Maeterlinck's *L'Intruse*, preceded by recitations of poems of Poe, June.

Requests permission from Maeterlinck to set *La Princesse Maleine. Marche des anciens comtes de Ross* for piano duet published; re-published 1903 as *Marche écossaise* and later orchestrated. Writes the songs *Deux Romances* on poems of Paul Bourget (*Romance* and *Les Cloches*); *Trois Mélodies* on poems inspired by English scenes by Verlaine (*La Mer est plus belle, Le Son du cor s'afflige, L'Echelonnement des haies*); *Dans le jardin* on poem of Paul Gravolet from the collection *Les Frissons,* and *Les Angélus* (G. le Roy); *Mazurka* for piano. Becomes acquainted with the music of Moussorgsky and the painting of Turner through Jules de Brayer. Friendship with Gabriel Mourey and Erik Satie (with the latter possibly before). Score announced of *L'Embarquement pour ailleurs* (Gabriel Mourey). Project for *Les Noces de Sathan* in co-operation with Jules Bois. First Exhibition of the Nabis, 47 rue le Péletier.

1892   Abandons *Rodrigue et Chimène*, January. *Trois Scènes au crépuscule* based on poems of Henri de Régnier (later the *Nocturnes*) near completion, September. Plans visit to the United States, September, at the instigation of Prince Poniatowski. Two poems of Debussy (from the *Proses lyriques*) published in the *Entretiens politiques et littéraires,* December.

Fêtes Galantes (Paul Verlaine), first series, written (*En sour-dine*, second version, *Fantoches*, *Clair de lune*, second version). Begins *Prélude, Interludes et Paraphrase finale pour l'après-midi d'un faune*. Introduces Poniatowski to Mallarmé. Friendship with Ernest Chausson and Henri Lerolle. Exhibition of the paintings of Maurice Denis at Debussy's birthplace, Saint-Germain-en-Laye. Moves to an attic, 42 rue de Londres with Gabrielle Dupont.

1893   Meets Oscar Wilde at the home of Georges Louis, February. *La Damoiselle élue* performed Société Nationale, 7 April. Gives first performance with Raoul Pugno of extracts, arranged for two pianos, of *Rheingold* at the Opéra, 6 May. Hears *Die Walküre* at the Opéra, May. Hears Maeterlinck's *Pelléas et Mélisande* at the Théâtre des Bouffes-Parisiens produced by Lugné-Poe, 17 May. Finishes String Quartet. Visit to Maeterlinck at Ghent with Pierre Louÿs and compo-sition of *Pelléas* begun, September. Quartet performed by the Ysaÿe Quartet, 29 December, at the Société Nationale.

Proses lyriques (*De Rêve*, *De Grève*, *De Fleurs*, and *De Soir*) completed. Meets Pierre Louÿs at the Auberge du Clou. Moves with Gaby to 10 rue Gustave-Doré. Receives financial support from Prince Poniatowski.

1894   Plays an arrangement for piano duet of Rimsky-Korsakov's *Capriccio Espagnol* at the Société Nationale, 20 January. Accompanies Thérèse Roger in *De Fleurs* and *De Soir*, Société Nationale, 17 February. Receives 1,000 francs for piano performance of the first act of *Parsifal* at a society gathering at the home of Henri Lerolle, February. First concert of Debussy's works conducted by Ysaÿe, and given at an exhibition of Impressionist paintings and the Art Nouveau at the Libre Esthétique, Brussels, 1 March. *Prélude à l'Après-midi d'un faune* completed, September; performed 22 December at the Société Nationale conducted by Gustave Doret, and attended by Mallarmé and Pierre Louÿs.

Writes four *Images* for piano (including the *Sarabande* and *Jardins sous la pluie* later incorporated in *Pour le Piano* and *Estampes*). Plans *Amphion* with Paul Valéry. Receives grant

of 500 francs per month from the publisher Georges Hartmann. Engagement to Thérèse Roger broken off (? March).
Marriage of Emmanuel Debussy. First exhibition of the
paintings and pastels of Odilon Redon at Durand Ruel.

    c. 1894 Arrangement for two pianos of Schumann's
Am Springbrunnen (*A la fontaine*); of Schumann's studies
(*Six Etudes en forme de canon*); of a waltz of J. Raff
(*Humoresque en forme de valse*); and of Saint-Saëns's
Second Symphony.

1895 Manuel Debussy reappointed as book-keeper with the Compagnie de Fives-Lille, 1 January. First version of *Pelléas*
finished, spring. *Nocturnes* in second form (for violin and
orchestra) near completion, September. Plans stage work on
Balzac's *La Grande Bretèche*, September. Opposes performances of extracts of *Pelléas* in Brussels, October, and in
London, November. Unsuccessful project for performance
of *Pelléas* at the Théâtre de l'Oeuvre, December.

Projects a stage work, *Cendrelune*, with Pierre Louÿs. Meets
the clowns Footitt and Chocolat at Reynold's bar in the rue
Royale.

1896 Works on ballet on subject of *Daphnis and Chloe*, the scenario
by Pierre Louÿs derived from Oscar Wilde, January–May.
Plays in first performance of Guillaume Lekeu's Quartet,
Société Nationale, 1 February. Publication of *Sarabande* in *Le
Grand Journal*, 17 February, as one of the *Images*. Work begun
on *La Saulaie* (Rossetti's *Willow-wood*), May; near completion, October.

Play, *Les Frères en Art*, begun in co-operation with René
Peter.

1897 Performance planned of *La Saulaie*, 24 January, postponed to
February but finally does not take place. Attends dinner given
to Mallarmé to celebrate publication of his *Divagations*,
2 February. Debussy's orchestration of Satie's *Deux Gymnopédies* performed Société Nationale, 20 February. Works on
score of pantomime on scenario by the wife of Forain,
February. Attempt at suicide by Gabrielle Dupont, February.
Trois Chansons de Bilitis written, spring and summer.

Final version of *Nocturnes* for orchestra begun. Second version of *Pelléas* accepted by the Opéra-Comique.

1898 Impressed by Ravel's *Habanera* at the Société Nationale, 5 March, Debussy asks Ravel to lend him the score. Haunted by thoughts of suicide, March–April. Publication of Camille Mauclair's *Le Soleil des Morts*, in which Debussy is portrayed, 15 February–1 May, in *La Nouvelle Revue*, and later in book form. Prosecution to repay debts, June.

Writes *Berceuse* for René Peter's *Tragédie de la Mort*. Contemplates setting *Aphrodite* by Pierre Louÿs. Performance suggested of *Pelléas* at the home of Robert de Montesquiou. Conducts an amateur choir at the home of Lucien Fontaine and writes two pieces for *a cappella* choir on texts of Charles d'Orléans incorporated in the *Trois Chansons de Charles d'Orléans* of 1908. End of relationship with Gaby.

1899 Marriage of Pierre Louÿs, 24 June. Attends funeral of Chausson, June. Marries Rosalie Texier, 19 October. Nocturnes for orchestra completed, December.

1900 *Trois Chansons de Bilitis* sung by Blanche Marot, 17 March. Death of Georges Hartmann, spring, is followed by demands to repay debts which Debussy cannot meet. Described as 'the Verlaine of Music' after performance of *Chansons de Bilitis*, Quartet, and *Damoiselle élue*, August. *Nuages* and *Fêtes* (from the *Nocturnes*) conducted by Camille Chevillard, 9 December.

Works on play *L'Herbe tendre* with René Peter.

1901 Performance of incidental music for mimed presentation of *Les Chansons de Bilitis* (later arranged as the *Epigraphes antiques* for piano duet) organized by *Le Journal*, 7 February. Becomes music critic for *La Revue Blanche*, creating as his *alter ego* the character of Monsieur Croche based on Valéry's *Monsieur Teste*, April. *Lindaraja* for piano duet written, April. *Pelléas* announced for performance at the Opéra-Comique, spring. First performance of *Nocturnes*, complete, 27 October. Publication of *Sarabande* in *L'Illustration*, 9 November.

1902 First pèrformance of *Pour le Piano*, 11 January, by Ricardo Viñes (the first of five performances of Debussy's

piano works entrusted to Viñes between 1902 and 1905).
Hartmann's heirs sell all published and unpublished works
of Debussy in their possession to the publisher Fromont,
March. Prosecution to repay debts, April. Dress rehearsal of
Pelléas et Mélisande, Opéra-Comique, 27 April, and first
performance, 30 April.

Plans stage work on *The Devil in the Belfry* (Poe).

BIBLIOGRAPHY

Apart from the work of Léon Vallas, *Claude Debussy et son Temps* (second edition, 1958), discussed in the Introduction, no serious attempt has been made to deal with the life and work of Debussy on an adequate scale. The most interesting aesthetic studies are by Vladimir Jankélévitch, *Debussy et le Mystère* (Cahiers de Philosophie, Neuchâtel, 1949; second edition, 1962), and the two specialized studies by André Schaeffner, 'Debussy et ses rapports avec la musique russe' in *Musique russe*, edited by P. Souvtchinsky, vol. 1, 1953, and *Segalen et Debussy*, 1962. The best technical analysis of Debussy's methods is by Constantin Brailoiu, 'Pentatonism in Debussy's Music' in *Studia Memoriae Belae Bartok Sacra*, Budapest, 1956. Other analyses that may be recommended are *Etude sur l'Harmonie moderne* by René Lenormand, 1912, and *Die assoziative Harmonik in den Klavier-Werken Debussys* by A. Jakobik, Berlin, 1940.

Important new biographical material is contained in Marcel Dietschy's *La Passion de Claude Debussy*, Neuchâtel, 1962. A good general bibliography, up to the time of its publication, appeared in *Claude Debussy* by Werner Danckert, Berlin, 1950. Debussy's published correspondence is listed in Appendix H.

General musical studies of the period are by L. Rohozinski, editor, *Cinquante Ans de Musique française (1874–1925)*, 2 vols., 1925; Julien Tiersot, *Un Demi-siècle de Musique française, 1870–1917*, 1918; and Martin Cooper, *French Music from the Death of Berlioz to the Death of Fauré*, London, 1951.

Literary studies include: Guy Michaud, *Message poétique du symbolisme*, 4 vols., 1947; André Billy, *L'Epoque 1900*, 1951; André Germain, *Les Fous de 1900*, 1954; Michel Décaudin, *La Crise des Valeurs symbolistes*, Toulouse, 1960; Edmund Wilson, *Axel's Castle*, London, 1931; Mario Praz, *The Romantic Agony*, second edition, London, 1951; and Roger Shattuck, *The Banquet Years*, London, 1959.

In the detailed bibliography that follows, publications used in consecutive chapters are not re-listed. From references in the text, however, the reader should have no trouble in readily identifying the sources. As elsewhere, all publications appeared in Paris unless otherwise stated.

CHAPTER 1

Debussy, C., *Lettres inédites à André Caplet*, 1957.

Dietschy, Marcel, 'The Family and Childhood of Debussy', translated by Edward Lockspeiser, in *The Musical Quarterly*, New York, July 1960.

Gregh, Fernand, *L'Age d'Or*, 1947.

Laloy, Louis, *Claude Debussy*, 1909.

Moreau, G., *Tonnerre pendant la Révolution*, 1890.

CHAPTER 2

Gauguin, Pola, *My Father Paul Gauguin*, translated by A. G. Chater, London, 1937.

Huyghe, René, *Le Carnet de Paul Gauguin*, 1952.

Lepelletier, E., *Histoire de la Commune*, 1908–14.

Lissagaray, Prosper, *Histoire de la Commune*, edited by A. Dunois, 1929.

Malingue, Maurice, *Gauguin*, 1948.

Pina, Ludovic Rodo, and Venturi, Lionello, *Camille Pissarro*, 1939.

Porché, François, *Verlaine tel qu'il fut*, 1933.

Prunières, Henry, 'Autour de Debussy' in *La Revue Musicale* (incorporating notes and letters from Robert Godet and Léon Vallas), May–September 1934.

Starkie, Enid, 'Rimbaud in England' in *Adam*, no. 244, London, 1954.

Verlaine, Mathilde, *Mémoires de ma Vie*, edited by F. Porché, 1935.

Verlaine, Paul, *Oeuvres poétiques complètes*, edited by Y. G. le Dantec, 1938.

CHAPTER 3

Bellaigue, Camille, *Souvenirs de Musique et de Musiciens*, 1921.

Emmanuel, Maurice, *Pelléas et Mélisande*, 1926.

Hoérée, A., *Inédits sur Debussy*, 1942.

Pierné, Gabriel, 'Souvenirs d'Achille Debussy' in *La Revue Musicale*, May 1926.

Pierre, Constant, *Conservatoire de Musique: Documents historiques*, 1900.

Saint-Saëns, C., 'Correspondance entre Saint-Saëns et Maurice

Emmanuel à propos de Debussy' in *La Revue Musicale*, no. 206
(*Maurice Emmanuel*, special number), 1947.

Stevenson, Ronald, 'Maurice Emmanuel' in *Music and Letters*,
London, April 1959.

CHAPTER 4

Bonnières, Robert de, *Mémoires d'Aujourd'hui*, 1883.

Burnand, Robert, *La Vie quotidienne en France de 1870 à 1900*, 1947.

Le Curieux, December 1887.

Dansette, Adrien, *L'Affaire Wilson*, 1936.

—— *Histoire des Présidents de la République*, 1953.

Dupont, Léonce, *Tours et Bordeaux*, 1877.

Laloy, Louis, *La Musique Retrouvée*, 1928.

Lavignac, Albert, *Le Voyage à Bayreuth*, 1903.

La Revue Wagnérienne, 1885–7.

Sherard, Robert H., *Twenty Years in Paris*, London, 1905.

CHAPTER 5

Concerts de Marie Olénine d'Alheim, Moscow, 1912.

L'Illustration, October, 1896.

Kosakov, Georgy, 'Debussy w rodzinie Meck' in *Muzyka kwartalnik*,
Warsaw, January, 1960.

Lockspeiser, Edward, 'Debussy, Tchaikovsky et Mme von Meck'
in *La Revue Musicale*, November 1935.

—— 'Claude Debussy dans la Correspondance de Tchaikovsky et
de Mme von Meck' in *La Revue Musicale*, October, 1937.

Louÿs, Pierre, *Poèmes*, edited by Y. G. le Dantec, vol. I, 1945.

Meck, Nicholas von, 'Achille-Claude Debussy' in *Debussy* by
E. Lockspeiser, 1951.

Meck, Sonia von, *Memoirs* (manuscript) in the Tchaikovsky Museum
at Klin (U.S.S.R.).

Moussorgsky en France (1896–1908), Moscow, n.d.

Schaeffner, André, 'Debussy et ses Rapports avec la Musique Russe'
in *Musique Russe*, vol. I, edited by Pierre Souvtchinsky, 1953.

Tchaikovsky, P. I., *Peripiska s N.F. von Meck*, vols. II and III,
Moscow, 1935–6.

Tchaikovsky, P. I., *Peripiska s P.I. Jurgensonom*, edited by V. A. Zhdanov, vol. II (1884–93), Moscow, 1952.

—— *Diaries*, translated by Vladimir Lakond, New York, 1945.

Le Temps, October, 1896.

CHAPTER 6

Curtiss, Mina, *Bizet and His World*, New York, 1958.

Dukas, Paul, *Ecrits sur la Musique*, 1948.

Emmanuel, Maurice, *Pelléas et Mélisande*, 1926.

Vallas, Léon, 'Les Travaux d'Ecole de Debussy' in *Comœdia*, 7 November 1927, and *Excelsior*, 21 March 1928.

—— 'Achille Debussy jugé par ses Professeurs au Conservatoire' in *La Revue de Musicologie*, July 1952.

CHAPTER 7

Albrecht, Otto E., *Census of American Music Manuscripts*, Philadelphia, 1953.

Banville, Théodore de, *Contes pour les Femmes*, 1881.

Bonheur, Raymond, 'Souvenirs et Impressions d'un Compagnon de Jeunesse' in *La Revue Musicale*, May 1925.

Bourget, Paul, *Les Aveux*, 1882.

—— *Etudes et Portraits: Portraits d'Ecrivains et Notes d'esthétique*, 1918.

Brussel, Robert, 'Claude Debussy et Paul Dukas' in *La Revue Musicale*, May 1926.

Catalogue de la Collection Walter Straram: Manuscrits de Claude Debussy, Rambouillet, 29 October 1961.

Gide, André, *Francis Jammes et André Gide, Correspondance (1893–1938)*. Edited by Robert Mallet, 1948.

Haraucourt, Edmond, *Mémoires des Jours et des Gens*, 1946.

Lockspeiser, Edward, 'Debussy's unpublished songs' in *Radio Times*, London, 23 September 1938.

Souffrin-Le Breton, Eileen, 'Debussy Lecteur de Banville' in *Revue de Musicologie*, December 1960.

—— 'Théodore de Banville et la Musique' in *French Studies*, Oxford, July 1955.

Vasnier, Marguerite, 'Debussy à dix-huit Ans' in *La Revue Musicale*, May 1926.

CHAPTER 8

Ambrière, F., 'La Vie romaine de Claude Debussy' in *La Revue Musicale*, January 1934.

Gregh, Fernand, *L'Age d'Airain*, 1951.

Peyre, Henri, *Shelley et la France*, 1935.

Prunières, Henry, 'A la Villa Médicis' in *La Revue Musicale*, May 1926.

Rebois, H., *Les Grands Prix de Rome de Musique*, 1932. (Contains memoirs relating to Liszt by Paul Vidal and Gabriel Pierné.)

Szabolcsi, Bence, *The Twilight of Ferenc Liszt*, Budapest, 1959.

Vallery-Radot, P., 'Souvenirs de Claude Debussy' in *La Revue des deux Mondes*, 15 May 1938.

Watteau, Antoine, Catalogue of works by Watteau in the collection of Count Giuseppe Primoli, Milan, 1934.

CHAPTER 9

Beaufils, M., *Wagner et le Wagnérisme*, 1946.

Cocteau, Jean, *Paris-Album*, translated by Margaret Crossland, London, 1956.

Cœuroy, André, 'Sur le Roman wagnérien français' in *Appels d'Orphée*, 1928.

Crane, Walter, *An Artist's Reminiscences*, London, 1907.

Daireaux, Max, *Villiers de l'Isle Adam*, 1936.

Debussy, C., *M. Croche Antidilettante*, 1921.

Jaeckel, C., *Richard Wagner in der französischen Litteratur*, 2 vols., Breslau, 1931–2.

Lalou, R., *Histoire de la littérature française contemporaine*, 1924.

Lavignac, Albert, *Le Voyage artistique à Bayreuth*, 5th ed., 1903.

Lockspeiser, Edward, 'Mahler in France' in *Monthly Musical Record*, March–April 1960.

Mann, Thomas, 'Sufferings and Greatness of Richard Wagner' in *Essays of Three Decades*, translated by H. T. Lowe-Porter (London, 1947).

La Revue Wagnérienne, edited by E. Dujardin, 1885–7.

Saint-Auban, Emile de, *Un Pèlerinage à Bayreuth*, 1892.

Samazeuilh, Gustave, 'Sur deux ouvrages inédits de Chausson et de Debussy' in *Musiciens de mon Temps*, 1947.

Schuh, Willi, *Renoir und Wagner*, Zurich, 1959.

Stoullig, E., and Noël, E., *Annales du Théâtre et de la Musique*, 1885–90.

Stravinsky, Igor, and Craft, Robert, *Conversations with Stravinsky*, London, 1959.

Vallas, Léon, *Les Idées de Claude Debussy, Musicien français*, 1927.

Villiers de l'Isle Adam, Count, *Axel*, translated by H. P. R. Finberg, preface by W. B. Yeats, London, 1925.

Wilson, Edmund, *Axel's Castle*, London, 1931.

Woolley, G., *Wagner et le Symbolisme français*, 1934.

Wyzewa, Isabelle de, *La Revue Wagnérienne. Essai sur l'interprétation esthétique de Wagner en France*, 1934.

CHAPTER 10

Debussy, Claude, *Lettres à deux Amis* (i.e. Robert Godet and G. Jean-Aubry), 1942.

—— Letters to Gabriel Mourey (1891–1915). Description in Catalogue Nicolas Rauch, Geneva, no. 20, 24, November 1958.

Godet, Robert, *Le Mal d'Aimer: Etats d'âme*, 1888.

—— 'En Marge de la Marge' in *La Revue Musicale*, May 1926.

Mourey, Gabriel, *Passé le Détroit*, 1895.

—— 'Tristan et Isolde' in *La Revue Wagnérienne*, 15 January 1887.

Schwartz, W. L., 'Imaginative Interpretation of the Far East' in *Revue de Littérature comparée*, vol. 40, 1927.

Valéry, Paul, *Lettres à Quelques-uns*, 1952.

CHAPTER 11

Brailoiu, Constantin, 'Pentatonism in Debussy's music' in *Studia Memoriae Belae Bartok Sacra*, Budapest, 1959.

Colette, *Mes Apprentissages*, 1936.

Denis, Maurice, *Théories, 1890–1910: Du symbolisme et de Gauguin vers un nouvel ordre classique*, 1912.

Fuller, Loïe, Manuscript letters. Description in Catalogue Nicolas Rauch, Geneva, no. 20, 1958.

Gauthier, André, *Debussy: Documents Iconographiques*, Geneva, 1952.

Gautier, Judith, *Les Musiques bizarres à l'Exposition de 1900*, 1900.

Gervais, Françoise, *La Notion d'Arabesque chez Debussy*, 1958.

Godet, Robert, 'En Marge de la Marge' in *La Revue Musicale*, May 1926.

Humbert, Agnès, *Les Nabis et leur Epoque*, Geneva, 1954.

Kunst, Jakob, *Music in Java*, translated by Emile van Loo, 2 vols., The Hague, 1949.

Levinson, André, *La Danse au Théâtre*, 1924.

McPhee, Colin, 'The Five-Tone Gamelan Music of Bali' in *The Musical Quarterly*, New York, April 1949.

Madsen, Stephan Tschudi, *Sources of Art Nouveau*, Oslo, 1956.

Poniatowski, Prince André, *D'un Siècle à l'Autre*, 1948.

Proust, Marcel, *Correspondance générale*, edited by Robert Proust and Paul Brach, vol. 4, 1933.

Sarrazin, Gabriel, *Les Poètes modernes de l'Angleterre*, 1885.

Schaeffner, André, 'Debussy et ses Rapports avec la Musique russe' in *Musique Russe*, vol. 1, edited by P. Souvtchinsky, 1953.

Selz, Peter, and Constantine, Mildred, editors, *Art Nouveau*, New York, 1959.

Tiersot, Julien, *Musiques pittoresques: Promenades musicales à l'Exposition de 1889*, 1889.

CHAPTER 12

Barricelli, J. P., and Weinstein, Leo, *Chausson*, University of Oklahoma Press, 1955.

Berton, Henry, *Henri de Régnier: Le Poète et le Romancier*, 1910.

Chausson, Ernest, 'Correspondance inédite de C. Debussy et E. Chausson' in *La Revue Musicale*, December 1925.

Debussy, Claude, *F.E.A. (Frères en Art)*, unpublished.

Denis, Maurice, *Henri Lerolle et ses Amis*, 1932.

Gourmont, Rémy de, *Promenades Littéraires*, 1919.

Guichard, Léon, *Jules Laforgue et ses Poésies*, 1950.

Laforgue, Jules, *Oeuvres complètes*, 1903.

Maus, Madeleine, 'Octave Maus et la Vie musicale belge, 1875–1914' in *Mémoires de l'Académie Royale de Belgique. Classe des Beaux-Arts*, vol. 6, series 2, Brussels, 1950.

Maus, Octave, *Trente Ans de Lutte pour l'art. 1884–1914*, Brussels, 1926.

Oulmont, Charles, *Musique de l'Amour*, 1935.

Painter, George D., *Marcel Proust*, vol. 1, London, 1959.

Peter, René, *Debussy*, revised edition, 1944.
Proust, Marcel, *Lettres à Reynaldo Hahn*, edited by P. Kolb, 1956.
Quintin, José, *Ysaÿe*, 1938.
Régnier, Henri de, *Poèmes anciens et romanesques*, 1890.
Souffrin-Le Breton, E., 'Swinburne et sa Légende en France' in *La Revue de Littérature comparée*, July–September 1951.
Vallas, Léon, 'Debussy, Poète' in *Les Nouvelles Littéraires*, 15 April 1933.
—— 'Claude Debussy aurait 85 Ans' in *Le Figaro Littéraire*, 23 August 1947.

CHAPTER 13

Adhémer, Jean, editor, *L'Oeuvre graphique de Toulouse-Lautrec*, Catalogue of an Exhibition at the Bibliothèque Nationale, 1951.
Banville, Théodore de, *Odes funambulesques*, 1857.
Bianquis, Geneviève, *Faust à travers quatre siècles*, 1935.
Büsser, Henri, *De Pelléas aux Indes Galantes*, 1955.
Colette, 'Le Journal de Colette' in *Le Matin*, 17 November 1923.
Coolus, Romain, 'Théorie de Footitt sur le Rapt' in *Le Rire*, 26 January 1895.
Debussy, C., *Lettres à deux Amis*, 1942.
Delay, Jean, *La Jeunesse d'André Gide*, 2 vols., 1956–7.
Donnay, Maurice, *Autour du Chat Noir*, 1926.
Doret, Gustave, *Temps et Contretemps*, Fribourg, 1942.
Frankenstein, Alfred, 'Edward La Vine' in *San Francisco Chronicle*, 11 March 1945.
Godet, Robert, 'En Marge de la Marge' in *La Revue Musicale*, May 1926.
Goudeau, Emile, *Dix Ans de Bohème*, 1888.
Haraucourt, Edmond, *Mémoires des Jours et des Gens*, 1946.
Lassaigne, Jacques, *Toulouse-Lautrec*, London, 1939.
Lemaître, Jules, *Les Gaîtés du Chat Noir*, 1894.
Myers, Rollo H., *Erik Satie*, London, 1948.
Perruchot, Henri, *Toulouse-Lautrec*, translated by H. Hare, London, 1960.
Peyre, Henri, *Shelley et la France*, 1935.
Rollinat, Maurice, *Les Névroses*, 1883.
Shattuck, Roger, *The Banquet Years*, London, 1959.

Tchaikovsky, P. I., *Diaries*, translated by Vladimir Lakond, New York, 1945.

Willette, Adolphe, *Feu Pierrot*, 1919.

CHAPTER 14

Austin, L. J., 'Mallarmé on Music and Letters' in *Bulletin of the John Rylands Library*, Manchester, September 1959.

Bernard, Suzanne, *Mallarmé et la Musique*, 1959.

Chassé, Charles, *Les Clefs de Mallarmé*, 1954.

Fowlie, Wallace, *Mallarmé*, London, 1953.

Hayman, David, *Joyce et Mallarmé*, 1956.

Mallarmé, Stéphane, *Oeuvres complètes*, edited by Henri Mondor and G. Jean-Aubry, Tours, 1956.

—— *Correspondance* (1862–71), vol. 1, edited by H. Mondor and J. P. Richard, 1959.

Mauron, Charles, *Introduction à la Psychanalyse de Mallarmé*, Neuchâtel, 1950.

—— *Mallarmé l'Obscur*, 1941.

Mondor, Henri, *Vie de Mallarmé*, 1946.

—— *Histoire d'un Faune*, 1948.

—— 'Mallarmé et Debussy' in *Les Cahiers de Marottes et Violons d'Ingres*, September–October 1954.

—— *Autres Précisions sur Mallarmé*, 1962.

Souffrin-Le Breton, E., 'Une Amitié de Poètes: Théodore de Banville et Stéphane Mallarmé' in *Le Goéland*, Paramé, June 1943.

Teissier, Léon, *Aubanel, Mallarmé et le Faune*, Montpellier, 1945.

Wais, Kurt, *Mallarmé*, Munich, 1952.

CHAPTER 15

Borgeaud, Henri, editor, *Correspondance de Claude Debussy et Pierre Louÿs*, 1945.

Cardinne-Petit, R., *Pierre Louÿs inconnu*, 1948.

Gide, André, *If it die (Si le grain ne meurt)*, translated by D. Bussy, London, 1951.

Gregh, Fernand, *L'Age d'Airain*, 1951.

Iseler, Paul, *Les débuts d'André Gide vus par Pierre Louÿs*, 1937.

Lebeau, Narcisse, 'Souvenirs sur Debussy confiés à Marius Richard' in *La Liberté*, 11 and 13 December 1931.

Louÿs, Pierre, *Journal intime*, 1929.

—— 'Lettres à André Gide' in *La Nouvelle Revue Française*, November 1929.

—— *Poèmes*, edited by Y. G. le Dantec, vol. 1, 1945.

Martin-Mamy, E., *Païens d'Aujourd'hui*, 1908.

—— *Les Nouveaux Païens*, 1914.

Poniatowski, Prince André, *D'un Siècle à l'Autre*, 1948.

Tinan, Jean de, *Document sur l'Impuissance d'aimer*, 1920.

Le Tombeau de Pierre Louÿs (containing chapters on Debussy and Louÿs by Paul Valéry and Jacques-Emile Blanche), 1925.

CHAPTER 16

Gide, André, *Journal (1889–1939)*, 1939.

Hart-Davis, Rupert, editor, *The Letters of Oscar Wilde*, London, 1962.

Louÿs, Pierre, *Broutilles inédites*, edited by G. C. Serrière, 1938.

Montgomery Hyde, H., Some unpublished recollections by Stuart Merrill [i.e. on Oscar Wilde in Paris] in *Adam*, no. 241, London, 1954.

Saix, Guillot de, 'Contes et Propos d'Oscar Wilde' in *Les Oeuvres Libres*, 15 September 1949.

—— 'Oscar Wilde et Pierre Louÿs' in *Vendémiaire*, 18 August 1937.

Seligman, V., *Puccini among Friends*, London, 1938.

Souffrin-Le Breton, E., 'La Rencontre de Wilde et de Mallarmé' in *Revue de Littérature comparée*, October–December 1959.

CHAPTER 17

Delarue-Mardrus, Lucie, *Mes Mémoires*, 1938.

Garden, Mary and Biancolli, Louis, *Mary Garden's Story*, London, 1952.

Godet, Robert, *Lettres à deux Amis*, 1942.

Pellerin, Henri, 'Claude Debussy et le Pays d'Auge' in *Le Pays d'Auge*, Lisieux, May–June 1957.

Peter, René, *Claude Debussy*, 1944.

Vallery-Radot, Pasteur, *Tel était Claude Debussy*, 1958.

CHAPTER 18

Ackere, J. van, *Pelléas et Mélisande*, 1952.

Debussy, Claude, 'Lettres Inédites à Ernest Chausson', *La Revue Musicale*, 1 December 1925.

Denis, Maurice, *Henri Lerolle et ses Amis*, 1932.

Emmanuel, Maurice, *Pelléas et Mélisande*, 1926.

Estrade-Guerra, Oswald d', *Les Manuscrits de Pelléas et Mélisande*, 1957.

Golea, Antoine, *Pelléas et Mélisande: Analyse poétique et musicale*, 1952.

Guilleminault, Gilbert, editor, *La Belle Epoque, Le Roman vrai de la IIIᵉ République*, 1957.

Halls, W. D., *Maurice Maeterlinck: Study of his Life and Thought*, London, 1960.

—— 'Some Aspects of the Relationship between Maeterlinck and Anglo-American Literature' in *Annales de la Fondation M. Maeterlinck*, vol. I, Brussels, 1956.

—— 'Les Débuts du Théâtre nouveau chez Maurice Maeterlinck', *Annales de la Fondation M. Maeterlinck*, vol. III, Brussels, 1957.

La Jeunesse, Ernest, *Les Nuits, les Ennuis et les Ames de nos plus notoires Contemporains*, 1896.

Lemonnier, Léon, *Edgar Poe et les Poètes français*, 1932.

Lockspeiser, E., *Debussy et Edgar Poe*, 1962.

Lorrain, Jean, *Pelléastres*, 1910.

Stoullig, E., *Les Annales du Théâtre et de la Musique*, 1893.

Thompson, Oscar, *Debussy: Man and Artist*, New York, 1940.

INDEXES

INDEX OF WORKS

There is no collected edition of Debussy's works, and although several studies of Debussy contain detailed lists of his works there has so far been nothing approaching a definitive catalogue. The catalogue published as an appendix to the first edition of Léon Vallas's *Claude Debussy et son temps*, giving details of publications and the whereabouts of manuscripts, formed an excellent foundation and any future catalogue must take Vallas's well-founded research in this field into account. Many unpublished works, however, not all of them complete, have since come to light and require to be assessed. It is also desirable to trace the origins of the titles of Debussy's works, as well as the changes of their title, since they nearly always had a direct musical significance to which the composer attached much importance.

The following lists set out the works mentioned in the present volume. The following volume is planned to contain a *catalogue raisonné* of all Debussy's works drawing upon research in both literary and musical fields.

PUBLISHED WORKS

UNPUBLISHED WORKS AND SKETCHES

PROJECTS

HASSELMANS, Mme, 162n.
HAWKINS, Louis Welden, 140
HÉBERT, Ernest, 74, 84
HEINE, Heinrich, 66, 74, 237
HÉRÉDIA, José-Maria de, 55, 151, 157n., 177; daughter of, 162
HÉROLD, Ferdinand, 217–18
HILLEMACHER, Paul and Lucien, 47n.
HINDEMITH, Paul, *Hérodiade* of, 158n.
HOCQUET, Vital, 168
HOLMÈS, Augusta, 37, 157n., 210
HUEFFER, Francis, 209–10
HUGO, Victor, 165n., 213
HUYSMANS, Joris Karl, 109, 143, 151n.; *A Rebours* of, 118, 119n.
Hydropathes-Hirsutes, Club des, 143

IBSEN, Hendrik, 190, 195
IMENEZ, José-Manuel, 35
Impressionists, 119, 120n., 124, 129, 241
INDY, Vincent d', at Bayreuth, 37, 92, 95n.; and Tchaikovsky, 51–2; Colette describes, 138; mentioned, 43, 99, 124, 224n., 233
INGHELBRECHT, D. E., 44
ISSY, battle of, 18, 236

JAMMES, Francis, 63–4
JARRY, Alfred, 233
JAVANESE MUSIC, 113–15, 239
JEAN-AUBRY, G., letters to, 11, 156, 232
JEANNIN, Paul, 57
JOYCE, James, *Finnegans Wake* of, 158n.

KEATS, John, 140–1, 143n.
King Lear, 110, 133n.
KOECHLIN, Charles, 124
KORSAKOV, Georgy, 44n.
KOUSSEVITSKY, Serge, 43n., 233
KRYSINSKA, Marie, 65n., 129n., 144
KUFFERATH, Maurice, 120n.

LA JEUNESSE, Ernest, 145n., 151n.
LA VINE, Edward, 137
LAFORGUE, Jules, 130, 170
Lakmé, 208
LALO, Pierre, 62; letter to, 50n.
LALOY, Louis, biography of, 16n., 17, 51n., 70; letter to, 39
LAMOUREUX, Charles, 90, 95n., 101
LAVALLÉE, Pierre, 121n.
LAVIGNAC, Albert, 31-2, 93–4, 145, 236
LAVISSE, Ernest, 133
Lawn-Tennis (Mourey), 110
LEBLANC, Georgette, 188, 201, 224
LECONTE DE LISLE, C. M. R., setting of songs of, 65n., 237
LÉGION D'HONNEUR, 10, 39
LEKEU, Guillaume, Quartet of, 242
LEPELLETIER, Edmond, 19
LÉPINE, Jean, 9
LEROLLE, Henri, 63, 123–4, 185, 241; letters to, 192–3
LEROLLE-CHAUSSON, Mme Etiennette, 126, 185
LESSEPS, Ferdinand de, 38n.
Librairie de l'Art Indépendant, 120-1, 177
LIBRE ESTHÉTIQUE, Brussels, 119, 128-9, 241
LISZT, Franz, 60-1, 82–3, 238; music of, 204
Lohengrin, 76, 90-1, 164, 239
LOMBARDI, V. Emm. C., 156n.
LONDON, Mourey describes, 109-10; Debussy in, 137, 182; Maeterlinck's *Pelléas* performed in, 190n., 195n.; Ternant on Debussy in, 209
LONG, Marguerite, 100
LORIN, Georges, 144
LORRAIN, Jean, 119n., 133, 140n.
LOUIS, Georges, 54n., 55n., 166, 177, 192n., 241
LOUŸS, Louise (*née* de Hérédia), 162, 181